The New Conservatives
A Critique from the Left

The New Conservatives
A Critique from the Left

Edited by
Lewis A. Coser and Irving Howe

Quadrangle/The New York Times Book Co.

Acknowledgments

"Does IQ Matter?," by David K. Cohen is reprinted from *Commentary* (April 1972), by permission; copyright © 1972 by the American Jewish Committee. This is a slightly revised version (1973).

"Theories of Industrial Society: Reflections on the Recrudescence of Historicism and the Future of Futurology," by John H. Goldthorpe is reprinted by permission from the *European Journal of Sociology*, XII (1971), pp. 263-288.

"The Politics of Pat Moynihan," by Gus Tyler is reprinted, by permission, from *The New Leader*, April 2, 1973, copyright © 1973 by the American Labor Conference on International Affairs, Inc.

Contents

The New Conservatives
A Critique from the Left

Introduction

Genuinely conservative thought—with its emphasis on degree and hierarchy, authority, hereditary status, deference, and the sanctity of tradition—has never had much of an impact in America. Our prevailing climate of opinion, as Louis Hartz and others have shown, has always been liberal. The relatively fluid class structure, the absence of a feudal tradition, and the prevalence of an acquisitive individualism—all inimical to the twin restraints of custom and deliberate control—have seen to it that Americans have been unreceptive to and even suspicious of the appeals of traditional conservative thought. Most of the time, what has passed for conservatism in this country has turned out to be, as in the ideas of Senator Goldwater and his speechwriters, a slightly adulterated version of Manchesterian laissez-faire liberalism.

The recurrent appeal of Edmund Burke's thought for certain American intellectuals would seem at first glance to contradict this assertion; but in fact it only strengthens it. American Burkeans have cared little, by and large, about his exultation of the aristocratic sense of honor and his obsessive interest in the maintenance of rank and hierarchy; they were hardly concerned with anchoring legitimacy in the aura of preindustrial society. They were drawn instead to Burke's rejection of a politics based on abstract ideals and to his stress on prudence and practicality as the basis of both morality and politics. It is this prudent approach, this stress on what a modern commentator has called Burke's distaste for speculative argument (M. Morton Auer-

3

bach in the *International Encyclopedia of the Social Sciences*), that had endeared him to certain American ideologues. "If we insist," writes Auerbach while interpreting Burke, "on imposing the simple perfection of a logical ideal on an imperfect, complex reality, we shall only succeed in destroying both the amount of good that already exists and the limited improvements that are feasible." Burkean conservatism in American dress, it turns out, has not really been a coherent doctrine but rather an injunction to go slow and not upset the applecart. The conservative stance has been used against those who dared to engage in a politics guided by general ideas and utopian desires. In the hands of American Burkeans, a lack of political and social imagination, by a curious alchemy, is transformed into a positive virtue.

Hanna Pitkin's masterful dissection of Michael Oakeshott, the renowned British exponent of the politics of prudence and restraint, brilliantly illuminates his failure to deal adequately with our current predicaments. She shows why, in the last analysis, this modern brand of Burkean conservatism, with its nostalgia for a world we have ineluctably lost, is unable to come to grips with the strains, the conflicts, and the perplexities of postindustrial society.

Most of the essays in this volume are addressed to the current vogue of American neoconservatism. These new conservatives do not give the impression of having reflected in a sustained and systematic manner on political philosophy. They express a mood and a fashion rather than a deeply felt political stance. They seem to be sustained by a desire to seize the shifting *Zeitgeist* by its tail, and they batten on the mood of disillusionment that has seized the country after the hopes of the early 1960s. They wish to bring about a counterrevolution of declining expectations. While most radicals or liberals are aware of "the limits of social policy" and deplore the resistance of social reality to the infusion of novel ideas that transcend the givenness of the given, these authors positively rejoice in such limits. They conclude, in S.M. Miller's words, that "nothing is wrong with America that a lowering of our objectives won't solve."

These neoconservative writers bring to mind an encounter with an old-time Chinese gentleman many years ago. When discussing the failures of the Chinese prerevolutionary regime, I happened to remark upon its unconscionably high infant mortality rate. "The thing has been exaggerated," he said, "after all, *I* survived."

The most salient feature of the current vogue of neoconservatism is its infuriating complacency. A spirit of "I'm all right, Jack" permeates the writings of our new Panglossians. Most of these men belonged to the Left camp not so very long ago. They are former liberals who got cold feet in the late 1960s. At an earlier time they were young men eagerly making their way onto the intellectual scene, sometimes even writing about it, and acutely sensitive to the shortcoming of the social and political order. They have now made it, and having made it they are concerned with the maintenance of an order that has been good to them. But gratitude, though an estimable private virtue, too often degenerates into smugness when extended to public institutions.

Irving Kristol, the prototype of the group, printed a short while ago an essay "About Equality" in *Commentary*. To him, the idea of equality is not, as most people might have thought, a perennial aspiration that has stirred the imagination of countless men and women through the ages and has been one of the great energizing ideas of the whole tradition of Western thought. It is an idea that turns out to be the self-interested ideology of "a mass of several millions of 'intellectuals' who are looking at their society in a highly critical way. . . ." because they "are engaged in a class struggle with the business community for status and power."

Kristol has been converted to the kind of reductionism that used to flourish in gatherings of the Chamber of Commerce of Sinclair Lewis's Zenith. When men proclaim generous ideas and ideals, all you have to ask is, "What's in it for them?" You will soon discover that behind all their fine rhetoric there is nothing but envy and greed. "Professors," we learn, "are genuinely indignant at the expense accounts which business executives have and they do not". . . . "They suffer, it seems, from martini envy. The top executives of our large corporations . . . cannot drink a martini on the expense account without becoming the target of a 'populist' politician." This, we learn, "is what the controversy 'about equality' is really about. We have an intelligentsia that so despises the ethos of bourgeois society, and that is so guilt-ridden by being implicated in the life of this society, that it is inclined to find even collective suicide preferable to the status quo."

Irving Kristol certainly does not suffer from guilt. As he calmly surveys the social scene he might notice that there are some large "functional differences" between the clients of Neiman-Marcus and those of the food stamp office around the block, but what do such mere material differences count in his exalted scale of values? "The idea of progress in the modern era," he writes, "has always signified that the quality of life would inevitably be improved by material enrichment. To doubt this is to doubt the political metaphysics of modernity and to start the long trek back to premodern philosophy. . . . It seems to me that this trip is quite necessary."

In the meantime, the richest 10 percent of the American population receives 29 percent of all personal income and own 56 percent of the national wealth, while the poorest 10 percent receives 1 percent of the income and is in debt. Maybe it's all because I suffer from guilt, but I cannot help thinking that this is a scandalous state of affairs. And this leads me to believe that Irving Kristol is a bit disingenuous when he concludes that, "It is the death of God, not the emergence of any new social or economic trends, that haunts bourgeois society." Bertolt Brecht no doubt was much less of a subtle moralist than Kristol, yet I think that he was a little closer to the truth when he wrote, "*Erst kommt das Fressen und dann die Moral.*"

Picking up a theme first enunciated by "atheists for Niebuhr" in the 1950s, the new conservatives make much of the recalcitrance of intractable social realities and sinful men to the deliberate planning of human affairs. They stress what Max Weber called the unanticipated consequences of human action. Man proposes and God disposes. Frail earthlings cannot foresee the consequences of what they are doing so that well-intended actions may lead to horrifying results. But instead of concluding that there is a need for improving methods of forecasting and predicting, the conservatives counsel instead that it might be best not to act at all. Better not to go into the water since even good swimmers sometimes drown. When you are not sure about consequences, the prudent course if to do nothing whatever.

"The fundamental problem of the central cities," writes Edward Banfield, "is of such a nature that it cannot be 'solved' or even much relieved by government action on any level." So long as the city contains a sizable lower class consisting of individuals "living from moment to moment . . . whose behavior is governed by impulse," any deliberate effort at reviving the urban centers is bound not only to fail but to backfire. There remains only the hope that "social problems sometimes disappear in the normal course of events."

Looking at reports on the society page, one gets the distinct impression that living from moment to moment and behavior governed by impulse seem fairly common in the upper reaches of the social scale; but no matter. Banfield had already become notorious by his explanation of the riots of the 1960s in terms of ghetto-dwellers' desire for "fun and profit." Will it offend the academic proprieties if I say that a man who can write in this way somehow lacks an elemental sense of common humanity?

Nathan Glazer lately has come along with another version of the doctrine that doing nothing, or as little as possible, is the essence of social wisdom. Writing on "The Limits of Social Policy" in *Commentary,* he has discovered that "every piece of social policy substitutes for some traditional arrangement . . . [and is] a new arrangement in which public authorities take over. . . . in doing so, social policy weakens the position of . . . traditional agents and further encourages needy people to depend on the government, rather than on the traditional structures." Glazer concludes that "the breakdown of traditional modes of behavior is the chief cause of our social problems." This last statement is as true as it is trite. If the peasants had never seen Paree, if the blacks had only stayed on the plantation, we wouldn't suffer from our current problems. As to the rest, Glazer inverts the causal sequence: it isn't that family, neighborhood, and ethnic associations broke down because public authorities took over, but rather that public authorities took over—and God knows they didn't take over enough—because these traditional institutions had decayed in the wilderness of the modern city.

I cannot forgo a brief mention of one of the ludicrous extremes to which Glazer is driven in his effort "to prevent further erosion of the traditional restraints that still play the largest role in maintaining a civil society." Extolling the part played by tradition in health and medical care, he writes: "Ultimately we are not kept healthy . . . by new scientific knowledge or more effective cures or even better organized medical care. . . . We are kept healthy by having access to traditional means of support in distress and illness, through the family, the neighborhood, the informal social organization." Life expectancies in, say, the Middle Ages, when tradition was surely not wanting, was such that people of his age or mine were unlikely to still be around.

I hope I have said enough to whet the reader's appetite for the essays that follow, in which the themes I have here only adumbrated are explored in detail. These introductory remarks are merely to indicate that, while neoconservatism need not be taken too seriously as a new departure in political philosophy, it should be taken very seriously indeed as a sign of the regressive drift of social thought in these barren times.

Our neoconservatives pride themselves on their practicality and pragmatism. Not for them the flights of the utopian imagination; but practical men always fall victim to their own practice. Any wish to solve present-day problems that is not guided by general conceptions of a transcendent ideal future must in the end succumb to the blind forces of the factual. The practical men are right when they assert that the utopian imagination attempts the impossible and that politics is the art of the possible. But they forget that the key question is precisely: what *is* possible? Max Weber, himself sufficiently free of illusions yet deeply steeped in historical understanding, answered: "Certainly all political experience confirms the truth that man would not have attained the possible unless time and again he had reached out for the impossible."

—Lewis A. Coser

Joseph Epstein

The New Conservatives: Intellectuals in Retreat

Ten years ago, who could have predicted the rise of a new conservatism in American life? Yet such a conservatism has arisen, and what among other things is new about it is that, unlike previous incarnations of conservatism in America, it speaks neither in the gruff voice of established privilege nor in the hollow one of aristocratic pretension. No, the novelty of this new conservatism resides in the fact that it appears to be a conservatism arrived at upon disinterested grounds—a conservatism more purely intellectual, and hence more formidable, than any in recent decades. The names associated with it are reputable, belonging mostly to men of solid achievement in the social sciences or intellectual journalism, many of them having themselves once been figures of impeccable liberal or radical standing. Could this be the serious conservatism America has so long lacked?

Over the past century in America, conservatism has had an ample popular and a scant intellectual following. In American intellectual life, in fact, it was not so very long ago that conservatism seemed a dead issue. In the early 1950s, Peter Viereck, echoing Edmund Wilson's plea to intellectuals of two decades earlier to "take communism away from the communists," im-

9

plored them now to "take conservatism away from the conservatives." But if any American intellectuals of earnest conservative propensities were out there, they either were not listening or felt it a mistake to heed Viereck's call. Conservatism by and large remained with the conservatives, which meant with those who had a vested interest in existing economic and political privilege and those who were temperamentally opposed to change.

As a political program, an intellectual response to events, or a body of thought having something pertinent to say about contemporary society, the stock of conservatism ran low among intellectuals. The only intellectuals who could be said to participate in it were those who believed in the principles of the market economy (F.A. von Hayek and Milton Friedman), or who believed Senator Joseph McCarthy on balance a good thing for the country (William F. Buckley, Jr., and the editors of *National Review*), or who began with a libertarian hatred of Communism that in time turned into a strong distaste for the liberal-left generally (Sidney Hook and others whose primary political preoccupation was with the Cold War). Taken together, these men could doubtless find as much to disagree as to agree about; but even assuming a rough consensus among them, as a group they were very far from able to confer any sort of serious standing upon conservatism as an intellectual force in American life.

It took the New Left, both in its political and cultural aspects, to do that. As recently as the middle 1960s, it could still be said with some confidence that conservatism counted for little in intellectual circles. It took the political madnesses committed in the name of the left to make conservatism not merely intellectually respectable but to many intellectuals deeply appealing—no small task in the United States, where the overwhelming political intellectual tradition has been clearly liberal-left. It took a Tom Hayden, an Eldridge Cleaver, an Abby Hoffman, it took Weathermen and Panthers and an evening at the apartment of the Leonard Bernsteins to reveal the unmistakable premonition that, should these various people have their way, society as we know it, in all its imperfections but also in all its glories, would be replaced by a desert inhabited by the nihilistic and the bored rich.

Yet could one be against the congeries of personalities, organizations, and trends that went by the name of "the Movement" without having to think of oneself, or for that matter actually being, conservative? One could indeed, and many liberal-left intellectuals opposed the Movement from its earliest days for its totalitarian cast—for its disregard of basic democratic forms, its casual accommodation of violence within its own ranks, its feverish hatred of America, and its heavy antinomian strain—without themselves abandoning their own traditional yet still valid left politics. Other intellectuals drew a different moral from the experience of the 1960s, seeing the decade not as a serious and sad deviation from liberal-left politics but as their logical outcome. Many of these men, turning away from the liberal-left, were to be in the forefront of a new conservatism that was to loom large in the politics of the 1970s.

II

We see that, if M. Dumont had died in 1799, he would have died, to use the new cant word, a decided "Conservative."

—LORD MACAULAY

Macaulay called conservative "the new cant word" in an essay on Mirabeau in 1832, and no doubt many people who have had the word applied to them since have felt much the same about it. "Conservative" was still a fairly new word in Macaulay's day, having come into usage only after the French Revolution—the first modern political event sufficiently grand in sweep and unnerving in impact to turn people's minds to thoughts of "conserving" their traditions, their property, and not least their heads. But the word has remained in use ever since, picking up and dropping off nuances over the years, its meaning changing all the while, sometimes subtly and sometimes not so subtly.

Like liberalism, conservatism has never been either a very compact or an altogether coherent body of doctrine. Again like liberalism, it has traditionally been part of a controversy, one side of a long argument over the true nature of the historical process—over the question, that is, in what direction and at what pace change ought to take place in society. As such, conservatism has appeared in different guises over the decades: as the extoller of tradition and older values, as the philosophy of economic freedom, as the defender of order and the status quo, and as the label affixed to a political mood or temperament. Again as with liberalism, there is nothing immutable about conservatism, and truths that in one generation were thought to be liberal or radical can turn up a generation or two later under the banner of conservatism. To cite an example that has by now become a cliché in the history of political philosophy, nineteenth-century liberalism is in its broadest lineaments very nearly congruent with twentieth-century laissez-faire conservatism.

Because one of conservatism's best-known guises has been as a rationalization for whatever happens to be the existing distribution of power, it has never been in very good odor with American intellectuals. American intellectuals as a class, at any rate since the Civil War, have tended to be quite distant from centers of power. And the intellectual's ideological heritage as it has accumulated over the years has tended to be anticonservative at its base. As described by Edward Shils, a sagacious student of intellectuals and no friend to the ideological caste of mind, the best of this heritage includes: "the demand for moral equality, the distrust of authority and of the institutions which it conducts for its own continuance, the insistence on justice, and the call to a heroic existence, even the belief in the earthly paradise and the realm of freedom. . . ." Where intellectuals in America have in any significant fashion served power, as during the presidential terms of Franklin Roosevelt, it has been under liberal auspices; or, as during the presidential terms of Kennedy and Johnson, under the facade of liberal auspices.

Until now, at least the facade had to be preserved. No longer, apparently. Evidence of this is not difficult to find. In November 1969, in one of his many attacks on what he called the outrageous bias of the news media, [then] Vice-President Agnew quoted from the work of a number of intellectuals in defense of his own position. In some intellectual quarters there was a certain embarrassment about this. *Commentary,* for example, where one of the pieces from which the Vice-President quoted had originally appeared, saw fit to print a letter by its editor disassociating the magazine from Mr. Agnew and his line on the media. Three years later, some of these same intellectuals, and a good many others besides, purchased an ad in *The New York Times* to announce their intention to vote for Nixon and Agnew and to encourage fellow citizens to do the same. The point is less relevant to electoral politics than to what it has to say about a major shift in the political mood of some influential intellectuals. Coming out for Richard Nixon, a figure who more than any other in American public life had been the target of unreserved contempt on the part of the intellectual community, was a starkly symbolic act demonstrating how totally disenchanted these men had become with the politics of the liberal-left.

III

> How does a radical—a mild radical, it is true, but still someone who felt closer to radical than to liberal writers and politicians in the late 1950's—end up by early 1970 a conservative, a mild conservative, but still closer to those who now call themselves conservative than to those who call themselves liberals?
> —NATHAN GLAZER, "On Being Deradicalized"

Once one gets down to naming the names of those who might fairly be described as "new conservatives," one quickly discovers how various a lot these men are, as well as how very different they are from those whom till now one had been accustomed to think of as American conservatives. Many of the new conservatives disavow the label.

Nathan Glazer, who readily enough admits to some conservative inclinations, argued in the pages of *Commentary* for George McGovern for president—surely an unusual gesture even for a "mild" conservative. Irving Kristol, one of the two coeditors of the *Public Interest,* is perhaps the quintessential new conservative in that many of the ideas, feelings and tendencies most characteristic of new conservative thought find their boldest expression in his writing. Yet Kristol, in the Preface to *On the Democratic Idea in America,* a collection of his recent essays, remarks: "It is fairly clear, I would hope, that I am not comfortable with what passes for either liberalism or conservatism in the United States today." Daniel Bell, the other coeditor of the *Public Interest,* is less easily described. Although the journal he has helped edit has in effect become the house organ for new conservative thought, Bell did not sign *The New York Times* ad endorsing Richard Nixon for president, nor has he written much in a directly polemical way that would prove him to have altogether dropped his liberal-left stance.

Norman Podhoretz qualifies as a new conservative largely by default. As editor of *Commentary* and an exceptionally talented journalist, Podhoretz has run much material with a strong new conservative flavor, providing many of the new conservative writers, who normally appear in the *Public Interest,* a home away from home. In his personal monthly column, Podhoretz has spoken without equivocation against quotas, the mentality behind the zero population growth movement, the New Left, the New Politics, and that group of moneyed, morally smug, and well-schooled Americans David Bazelon once described as the New Class. No single one of these positions would necessarily qualify Norman Podhoretz as a conservative, new or old; in fact, a democratic radical could in good faith hold to any of them. Yet by adopting these positions in combination with the single-minded concentration of his editorial firepower on the (very real) excesses of New Left rhetoric and countercultural idiocy, to the near-total exclusion of the (equally very real) excesses of the Nixon-Agnew administration, not to speak of abrasions and abuses still dealt out to great numbers of people in America, Podhoretz has in effect allowed his liberal-left credentials to lapse. While he may well think his own current political position to be "centrist," no other intellectual, save perhaps Irving Kristol, has done more to bring the new conservatism into prominence.

Norman Podhoretz, Irving Kristol, Nathan Glazer—is the new conservatism in the main restricted to New York intellectuals, yet another phenomenon bred in the cafeterias at City College and nurtured on Morningside Heights? Not at all. Although the strands of origin and influence are not so easily separated, it is clear that the new conservatism is very much a national matter. Some of its staunchest academic adherents —Edward Banfield, for example, or James Q. Wilson—were trained as social scientists at the University of Chicago. Daniel Patrick Moynihan, currently U.S. ambassador to India, and doubtless the best-known of the new conservatives, came by his views at least in part in the rough-and-tumble of urban Irish politics. Robert Nisbet, who is scarcely a newcomer to conservatism but has long brought a deep intelligence and high principles to his political writing, acquired his political orientation at the great university that was Berkeley in the 1930s. Others frequently mentioned among the new conservatives, with varying accuracy, are James Coleman, Morris Janowitz, Seymour Martin Lipset, and Harry Johnson. But the main point is that the new conservatism is neither parochial in outlook nor powerless in the world. In government, in the academy, in journalism—in short, in all those modern institutions out of which influence can be radiated with the greatest intensity—the new conservatism is extremely well-placed.

IV

My brother Evgeni Yakovlevich used to say that the decisive part in the subjugation of the intelligentsia was played not by terror and bribery (though, God knows, there was enough of both), but by the word "Revolution," which none of them could bear to give up.
                              —NADEZHDA MANDELSTAM,
                              Hope Against Hope

Before attending to what the new conservatives are saying, to the quality of their thought, and to their likely impact on American politics in the years immediately ahead, let us first look to what they have thus far accomplished.

First, although they were not alone in this, the new conservatives helped push back "the mob." Edmund Burke once described the mob as the linkage of "obnoxious wealth to restless and desperate poverty," but in the America of the last half of the '60s much more than these elements was linked. Involved were great hordes of the disaffected middle class, comprised in unequal parts of students, middle-aged men and women terrified of being left behind by youth, and psychosexual adventurers like

Dotson Rader who in the passage below about Andy Warhol conveys how the "swinging" radicalism of the '60s allowed those who engaged in it to play out their separate little fantasies:

> Certainly in the Velvet Underground and the Exploding Plastic Inevitable, in the disaster paintings, in his films beatifying manhood through violence through the cult of leather, with his bike boys and hustlers and impotent studs worn through and phasing out on scag and the pretenses of the butch, in that vision he [Warhol] joined with much of what rumbled in the consciousness of the New Left, much of what was true for the Weatherman and the Panther and, for a time, true for me.

Then there were those older radical intellectuals who should have known better but, when it came to the crunch, didn't: Dwight Macdonald, like some sad Sabbatian, thinking that the revolutionary messiah had come to Columbia University (of all places!) and consequently cheering on the students in their mischief; [the late] Philip Rahv, playing at being Plekhanov; and Paul Goodman, toward the end of his days regretting many of the forces loose among the American young that he had himself helped unleash.

Many of the same events that brought out the pathetic worst in several intellectuals traditionally aligned with the liberal-left caused the conversion of others so aligned to the new conservatism. Nathan Glazer notes that he came to believe that "the radical thinking of the late 1960s was almost completely misguided, based on an amazing ignorance of the lineaments of modern society and an almost equally amazing arrogance." Norman Podhoretz, as editor of *Commentary,* tirelessly tracked down and clubbed away at each fresh outcropping of "swinging" radicalism. Marcuse, the *New York Review of Books,* the Panthers, the Population Controllers, the Radical Educational Theorists, one by one *Commentary* went after each, and many others beside, in a thankless,[1] though often successful, demolition job. It was almost as if the magazine had taken its cue from the final sentence in Nathan Glazer's essay "On Being Deradicalized," which read:

I, for one, indeed, have by now come to feel that this radicalism [that of the late '60s] is so beset with error and confusion that our main task, if we are ever to mount a successful assault on our problems, must be to argue with it and to strip it ultimately of the pretension that it understands the causes of our ills and how to set them right.

If the new conservatism stood up to the New Left onslaught upon rationality, it had also, in the course of doing so, shown how thin American thought on the left had become. When one looked closely, it became apparent that what passed for the American left had grown mentally stale, dumb in fact. The New Left had no program to speak of, nor did it appear much interested in putting together a coherent critique of American life. It was organized around a number of soft, exceedingly vague issues, calling less for thoughtful than for emotional responses. Do you feel opposed to the Establishment? Are you on the side of Youth? How badly do you despise Oppression, a state known equally to blacks, Chicanos, students, housewives, and account executives deprived of fulfillment? Where, finally, do you stand in regard to the Revolution? Establishment, Youth, Oppression, Revolution—these were the buzz words of the late '60s, sounded over and over again without much in the way of thought behind them. "The enemy," Orwell once wrote, "is the gramophone mind, whether or not one agrees with the record that is being played at the moment."

The new conservatives were soon to put a new record on, a much more interesting and skillful one, and it wouldn't be long before people began to dance to it.

V

We engage in political activity so that we may, as societies of men, deal with the world as it is. This is not a slight endeavor; the world as it is, as experience teaches us, is not easy to deal with
                    —HENRY FAIRLIE, "Camelot Revisited"

In response to theories of conspiracy in places high and low (the

Ramparts-syndrome), the new conservatives answered with the soothing voice of social science; to cries about the wretched of the earth, with cool displays of statistics; and to hysterical shouts of "Fascist Amerika," with historical perspective. The New Left of the late '60s spoke out on behalf of the world as it ought to be, as radicals had traditionally done, but they went down to defeat by the new conservatives because they were woefully ignorant about the world as it is.

The world as it is versus the world as it ought to be—this, when the issue hasn't simply been one of naked power between two men or factions, is what the conflict between right and left in politics has always been about. In looking across the invisible line that divides men politically, left and right each sees the other as not merely mistaken in its views but deficient in precisely those virtues that it especially prides itself upon. The left, which sees itself as on the side of decency, looks upon the right as heartless. The right, seeing itself as richly endowed with a firm grasp on reality, looks upon the left as naive.

Realism, or so its adherents would claim, is the long suit of the new conservatism. In his very tough-minded book on cities, *The Unheavenly City*, Edward Banfield notes that he will doubtless be taken to be an "ill-tempered and mean-spirited fellow." He adds: "But facts are facts, however unpleasant, and they have to be faced unblinkingly by anyone who really wants to improve matters in the cities." In the essay on his "Deradicalization," Nathan Glazer remarks on the influence a year spent working at the Housing and Home Finance Administration had on the maturation of his political views: "It was a big country," he learned, "and it contained more kinds of people than were dreamed of on the shores of the Hudson." In describing his own political position—about which more directly—Irving Kristol writes that it "is not an obviously secure position, but neither is it, I would insist, a completely unrealistic one." Facts are facts, it's a big country, let's be realistic—such is the dominant tone of the new conservatism.

The other great note sounded by the new conservatives is "complexity." In a recent issue of the *Public Interest* Daniel Patrick Moynihan writes:

Political society wants things simple. Political scientists know them to be complex. . . . One could argue that, in part, the leftist impulse is so conspicuous among the educated and well-to-do precisely because they are exposed to more information, and are accordingly forced to choose between living with the strains of complexity or lapsing into simplism.

This is hitting the note of complexity more sonorously than usual, yet the note itself recurs throughout new conservative thought. "In a world of infinite complexity," Nathan Glazer writes, "some things had emerged and survived. . . ." Among the new conservatives, the world is not only too much with us, but, given its complexity, damn near indecipherable.

The world is also heavy with irony. This quality is especially underscored in the work of Daniel Patrick Moynihan, who is in some respects the most attractive of the new conservative writers. Moynihan is, first, really a writer, as opposed to someone who merely writes; and, unlike others of the new conservatives, he brings long and varied experience of government to his writing—some 13 years of it, by his own count, over the past two decades. As a prose writer, Moynihan has a decided craving for elegance, and along with it a strong taste for generalization, and the two combined render him especially delighted at the discovery of irony in contemporary events. Thus, in *The Politics of a Guaranteed Income,* his recently published account of the development and ultimate defeat of the Family Assistance Plan, Moynihan early on writes: "There was irony as well as tragedy in the history that followed." As so often in new conservative writing, the tragedy could be laid at the door of liberal foolishness, the irony that the liberal-left had once again acted against its own avowed best interests.

In this particular instance, whether the liberal-left's defeat of Richard Nixon's plan for a guaranteed income was a case of looking a gift horse in the mouth or instead a more prudent examination of the teeth of merchandise offered by an old horse trader of dubious reputation depends upon the credence one invests in Moynihan's portrait of Nixon as a tory radical. ("Tory men and liberal policies," Moynihan quotes Nixon remarking, "are what have changed the world.") But a more compact example of Moynihan's method—and, by extension, of the new conservatism's—is to be found in an essay entitled "The Schism in Black America."

The schism has to do with the fact that, as Moynihan reads and understands the census data, things for blacks are going in two directions simultaneously. *"Some things are getting better, others worse."* Briefly, things are getting very much better for young black husband-wife families, which are everywhere beginning to close, and in some statistical situations have closed, the gap in income between themselves and white families of equal education. "This improvement did not 'just' happen *to* blacks," Moynihan writes. "It was made to happen *by* black persons working hard for things they want." In the other direction, the number of those who were down slipped further. "In gross terms, the number of blacks below the poverty line declined 49.4 percent between 1959 and 1968 for families with male heads; but it increased 23.6 percent for those with female heads." But Moynihan's real point in this essay has less to do with these particular trends than it does with his belief that *"considerable energy is devoted to denying either trend."*

The liberal-left, nearly as much as poverty itself, soon becomes the villain of the piece. Why, Moynihan asks, does progress toward equality, such as the above-mentioned success of black husband-wife families, go ignored? "Social change," he notes, "is not easily achieved. When it successfully occurs, we ought to know about it, and permit it to cheer us up." Moynihan adds: "Nothing I have written in this article provides *any* grounds for complacency," and he elaborates in terms no one on the liberal-left need disagree with (except for their incompleteness):

> Lower-class behavior in our cities is shaking them apart. Upper-class lying—that the men in jail are political prisoners, that the fatherless child is happier, that the welfare system is a conspiracy to keep the proletariat passive—is destroying standards of discourse. The language of politics grows more corrupt. . . . We approach a fantasized condition.

Yet it is open to question whether we all don't have a stake, not in denying progress where it has legitimately been made, but in not featuring it. Where genuine progress is made, it ought duly to be noted, both because, as Moynihan suggests, it may improve our morale and because it may serve as a guide to setting future social policy. But as for celebrating it in any large-scale way, this scarcely seems what is called for. With millions of people in America still living quite wretchedly, and the conditions of others worsening, it still seems best that, in the main, we accord what progress is made "benign neglect," to coin a phrase. As Bayard Rustin once noted, writing about Moynihan in another connection: "To point out improvements where they have been made but not to couple this with an urgent call for more action is to provide an excuse for complacency and criminal inaction."

Rustin would go—indeed has gone—further. Having noted that some years back, at a national board meeting of Americans for Democratic Action held after the riots in Newark and Detroit, Moynihan "urged that liberals form a coalition with conservatives in the interests of social order," Rustin, tying this in with Moynihan's "benign neglect" memo to President Nixon, went on to remark: "From this point of view Moynihan's role in the Nixon administration becomes tragically clear. As liberal cover for a conservative administration, he is not advancing liberalism so much as helping to entrench conservatism."

Which brings up the interesting point about the political context of the rise to prominence of the new conservatives. This context has of course been the first and second administration of Richard Nixon, which in many respects makes the position of the new conservatives anomalous. On the one hand, the new conservative intellectuals have been among the ablest chroniclers of the excesses of the New Left, especially (and deservedly) in its countercultural and antidemocratic aspects, while they have also been the first group of intellectuals to question liberal assumptions in America from a point of view that is at once sophisticated and not to the left of liberalism. Yet it is not exactly as if all they are saying isn't entirely welcome to the Nixon administration. This situation has had consequences that reverberate well beyond the confines of debate among intellectuals.

Consider Moynihan's own position. As former assistant to the president for Urban Affairs and executive secretary of the

Nixon administration's Urban Affairs Council, Moynihan, by his own account, was in the forefront of the fight to achieve a guaranteed income for the poor through a negative income tax. In the course of that fight, he came out strongly against those "service" programs—community action, manpower retraining, etc.—which, as he has said, he "had not the least confidence in." Between a guaranteed income and more service programs—or, in the parlance of government social science, between an "income strategy" and a "service strategy"—Moynihan clearly much preferred and argued forcibly on behalf of the former. Yet, as everyone now knows, the battle for the guaranteed income was defeated in the Senate. Curiously enough, the week after the final installment of Moynihan's account of that defeat in the *New Yorker,* when the Nixon budget was announced, the amplest cuts were precisely in those service programs for the poor and elderly that Moynihan had so disdained in favor of the guaranteed income. In the final reckoning, then, on the question of how best to deal with poverty in America, the Nixon administration would be offering *neither* an income *nor* a service strategy; not Benign but more nearly Total Neglect was apparently to be its answer. Now United States ambassador to India, Daniel Patrick Moynihan, a man who appreciates a heavy irony, might wish to brood over this one of a hot and sleepless night in New Delhi.

VI

> By reading this book one discovers what Spiro Agnew would sound like if he had gone to CCNY in the Thirties.
>
> —YOSAL ROGAT, *New York Review of Books*

The book in question is Irving Kristol's *On the Democratic Idea in America,* and reading it one discovers nothing of the kind. Instead, one discovers a keen polemical mind of the sort that belongs to an intellectual maverick as well as to a man who lives to argue and does it well. Irving Kristol's mind, in short, is neatly calculated to encourage precisely the exaggerated response it can usually be relied upon to receive. A Kristol essay, command-

ing in tone, supremely confident about subjects that are elsewhere held to be still in the flux of controversy, assuming always
that anyone who thinks differently is perverse or inept, is
scarcely designed to incite reasoned discussion.

Other intellectuals show one or another aspect of the new
conservatism in high relief; in Irving Kristol the full and finished
edifice is on display. He is at once the new conservatism's leading
journalist-publicist and its prime exemplar. As he seems to have
no intellectual doubts, neither does he deal in political equivoca-
tions. Kristol avows his own political instincts to be conservative,
and, characteristically, remarks that he has come "to believe that
an adult's 'normal' political instincts should be" conservative.
What is characteristic is the disparagement; anyone who has
reached a certain age and has not yet become conservative politically must either be at best "immature," or at worst "abnormal."

Unlike others of the new conservatives, many of whom came
to their views as a result of the devastations of the '60s, Kristol's
conservatism is not altogether new. As an editor of *Commentary*
(under Elliott Cohen), a founding editor of *Encounter,* and an
editor of the *Reporter,* Kristol has over the years tended to be
viewed as a liberal when in fact he has long been something of a
closet Tory.[2] Roughly a decade ago, for example, Kristol was
jabbing holes in the reports of widespread poverty in America by
insisting that no matter how rich our nation, one-fifth of it would
always be poor (or poorer than the other four-fifths), that poverty was after all a comparative thing (compared with the poor,
say, of Asia, the American poor lived in splendor), and (though
this was never said, it was implied in the foregoing) so why
bother!

That Kristol could write so in a preponderantly liberal climate
was a tribute to the sharpness of his prose. Everyone had heard
ideas of this kind before, but it was rather a novelty to see them
cast in such fine prose. There is something in the grand English
amateur tradition about Kristol's prose. (If City College can be
said to have put the blacking on his education, then London,
during his years as coeditor of *Encounter,* must have supplied the
polish.) His prose, certainly, has a very high shine—so high, in
fact, that it is likely to blind a hurried reader to the fact that
Irving Kristol often wouldn't have a subject to write about if it

weren't for what he construes to be the cowardice, stupidity, and general intellectual confusion so rampant on the liberal-left.

Although a slim volume, the eight essays in Kristol's book comprise a thoroughgoing attack on the liberal-left ethos. Sometimes Kristol is directly on target in his attack, when, as in his essay "Urban Civilization and Its Discontents," he writes:

> The moral code for all civilizations must, at one time or another, be prepared to face the ultimate subversive question: "Why not?" Our civilization is now facing that very question in the form of the drug problem, and, apparently, it can only respond with tedious, and in the end ineffectual, medical reports.

But just as often he misses the target. He can, for example, write disparagingly of the "highly apocalyptic notions of the present" in one essay, then turn round to sound the apocalyptic note himself: "Today," he wrote in *Fortune* in 1968, "one does have cause to believe that we are approaching one of those historical watersheds that separate worlds in time." He can be a poor prophet, as when, in an essay entitled "American Intellectuals and Foreign Policy," he predicts the transformation of the American two-party system to make room "for a mass party of the ideological left, as in most European countries—except that its grass roots will be on the campus rather than in the factory." But a contradiction here or there, a mistaken prophesy, a patch of factual thinness—these, while they exist in Kristol's essays, are less important than the assumptions under which he writes in the first place.

Kristol's conservatism derives from a deep distrust of "the ideology of liberal democracy, in its twentieth-century version," which he was born and grew up in "as into a civil religion." Alongside this distrust has grown a deep suspicion of liberal-left activism. "I have observed over the years," Kristol writes, "that the unanticipated consequences of social action are always more important, and usually less agreeable, than the intended consequences." Finally, Kristol holds that many of our institutions "have become so debased as to need substantial reformation, not only to survive but to merit survival." All this being so, he sees his own position being on the side of the "enterprise of conservative reform."

"Conservative reform" sounds eminently respectworthy, except that when Kristol comes to address himself to particular areas he is generally all conservative criticism with the reform side absent. On the question of what ought to be the role of intellectuals in foreign policy, his answer, despite many an interesting observation along the way, is that intellectuals, having no real responsibility, ought probably to stay the hell out. On the issue of inequality, after taking his readers down a fascinating detour having to do with power struggles between intellectuals and the business community, he concludes that the issue is in reality a cover for a deep and unappeasable anguish at the loss of religion. On the question "Is the American Worker Alienated?" the answer Kristol supplies is, Not Really, only the sociologists who study him are. On the problems of our public schools, it turns out that many of these problems don't really exist, being the product of minds in the grip of social hypochondria, feverishly thinking up new crises, and that in fact, by and large, the system is working and that "since it is our system . . . perhaps we ought to be less ill-tempered about it than we usually are."

Read separately, when they are not dominated by fits of bad temper, Irving Kristol's essays can give off a whiff of political philosophy and of subtlety; read together, they come to acquire an odor curiously akin to Couéism. Every day, and in every way, in Kristol's version, American society is becoming better and better.

VII

One often advises rulers, statesmen, and peoples to learn from the experiences of history. But what experience and history teach is that peoples and governments have never yet learned from history, let alone acted according to its lessons.

excellent!

—G.W.F. HEGEL, *Reason in History*

To what extent is the Couéism found in Kristol, which takes the form of denying any strenuous flaws in American life, built into the new conservatism? Irving Kristol notes that he considers himself part of the tradition of conservative reform. Norman Podhoretz insists that his own deradicalization has nothing to do with any "sudden lapse into indifference over the remediable ills which afflict the world." Yet reading Irving Kristol, or *Commentary*, or Irving Kristol in *Commentary*, the reigning impression one gets is that what is mainly wrong with America today is a number of bad ideas, a handful of intellectuals acting in bad faith, and some confusions about the glories of our national life—all coming from or inspired by the liberal-left intelligentsia—and that once these are eliminated the country can get on with the business of gradual reform (and, as it often seems, the more gradual the better).

Yet, one wonders, who is the enemy that continues to draw the new conservatives' fire? Where once he was substantial, surely now he is no more than a wraith. The New Left is not merely any longer not New, it is by now moribund if not deceased. The Democratic party, done in by its own divisiveness, is in shambles. Whereas the radical politics of the '30s could in some rough sense be said to have ended in the New Deal—a qualified but still real victory for the American liberal-left—those of the '60s ended in two presidential terms for Richard Nixon. Whereas James Q. Wilson once wrote that "empathy (though not outright approval) governed the liberal response to urban riots and campus disorder," surely if once true, this is true no longer, urban riots and campus disorders having come to an end and liberal empathy for them having long since been snuffed out. The heat is off, and a large number of those on the liberal-left as well as new conservatives seem frankly relieved.

The heat in question is, of course, that for social change. The election of Richard Nixon meant a real lowering of the thermostat in this connection, and perhaps the chief function of the new conservatism, though one suspects they are not about to own up to it, is to keep it down. There is much talk in the *Public Interest*, and from new conservatives generally, about "the limits of social policy." Yet it is one thing to say that on certain brutally tough social problems we don't as yet have any convincing solutions; quite another to say, as those who talk about the limits of social policy imply, that none exist or are likely to be found.

Already, anyone who cares to look closely can perceive a sad dialectic at work among the new conservatives. Opposing itself to the strongly antidemocratic New Left, it appears to be setting itself up as the false antithesis to a false thesis. Where the '60s radicalism was anti-American, committed to a dreary view of the country in all its aspects and prone to see the nation as generally headed toward hell in a handwagon, the new conservatism is pro-American, committed to a cheery view of the nation's current estate and prone to see the good society as having very nearly arrived. Thus, Irving Kristol doubts that the average American feels more powerless today than in the past; Norman Podhoretz, quoting a Gallup Poll on his behalf, sees no "social meanness" in America; and Daniel Patrick Moynihan remarks that one of the great secrets of American politics is that while ideologically Americans are conservative, in practice they are liberal. What we have here, raised to an intellectual power, is the spirit of Rotarianism.

Viewed thus far in its brief history, the new conservatism strongly resembles another abrupt shift in political orientation among American intellectuals—namely, that undertaken by the group of intellectuals who came to be known as the Cold Warriors. Observe some parallels. Both the Cold Warriors and the new conservatives initially pitted themselves against very real enemies—for the former, Stalinism at home and abroad; for the latter, the antidemocratic New Left. Both the Cold Warriors and the new conservatives took up positions that in some respects were not only correct but required courage to hold, in that they went against the grain of the majority of their intellectual peers. Both groups were essentially victorious; and both contributed significantly to the defeat of their avowed enemies by disqualifying them intellectually.

At the same time, the efforts of both the Cold Warriors and of the new conservatives were warmly encouraged by the administrations in power—as the CIA sponsored a number of the intellectual activities of the Cold Warriors, so are the new conservatives said to be widely read and appreciated within the Nixon administration. In each case the explanation was scarcely subtle: intellectuals were doing the bidding of their government. Not, it should be added, directly or by formal contract or secret pact, but because the interior logic of their situations had driven them into near (if not complete) accord with the government's own purposes—in the case of the Cold Warriors, the shared unanimity was on the implacable opposition of East and West; in that of the new conservatism, the shared unanimity is on the dangers of undertaking precipitate social action (the "limits of social policy"). The respective positions of the Cold Warriors and of the new conservatives locked each into an exceedingly optimistic view of their own society: the former had their "free world," the latter their America without "social meanness." The overall effect seemed to be the same. With both the Cold Warriors and the new conservatives one saw men with good minds and initially fine intentions fall victim to an emotional investment in a single idea—anti-Stalinism for the Cold Warriors, antiradicalism for the new conservatives—an investment that grew so deep as to blur out all else in the world, not least the most obvious injustices all around them. The tragic flaw for both the Cold Warriors and for the new conservatives, then, has been monomania.

Again as with the Cold Warriors, so now with the new conservatives—once astride the stallion of intellectual monomania, it is not so easy to dismount. Apparently one must ride out one's obsessions beyond the fringes of reality. This the new conservatism is currently doing. It continues to flog away at its old enemy, the liberal-left, even as that enemy falls into greater political disarray. On matters of social policy, it cautions that the nation go slow—"today's solution," Irving Kristol warns, "is tomorrow's dilemma"—even as the Nixon administration makes certain it goes nowhere. It claims to believe in the improvability of man's lot, yet ignores his more flagrant social problems, arguing that these problems do not exist (Norman Podhoretz on Pollution), that they have been grossly inflated (Daniel Patrick Moynihan on the plight of blacks in America), or that they are not really problems at all (Irving Kristol on the redistribution of income).

Vested interest, it appears, is not a notion restricted to property alone. The new conservatism has evidently acquired such an interest in its own ideas and, though it began as an anti-ideological force, has itself become ideologized. The bitter sadness is that, with its strong intellectual sophistication, it may well end up a more genuine obstacle to the alleviation of social pain than the obtuse and retrograde conservatism of the privileged that preceded it.

Michael Harrington

The Welfare State and Its Neoconservative Critics

The failures of the welfare state in the sixties have served as stimulus for, and rationale of, the rise of neoconservative thought in the seventies.

The neoconservative ideologues base themselves on what they regard as the data of the sixties, but they do not take into theoretical account how the limitations of the period permeate their evidence and skew their conclusions. They universalize about social policy, equality, the professionalization of reform, and so on, when actually they are talking about what was done, and not done, in a specific political and social context. As a result, they lack a sense of what might be done under other circumstances—and of the degree to which "circumstances" themselves are aspects of a structure of power created by struggle, not destiny.

I will challenge this approach on three different levels. First, I differ as to at least some of the facts. The neoconservatives tend to exaggerate the amount of social innovation attempted in the sixties, mistaking promises for operational plans and ignoring the hidden agenda established by the priorities of power. So

29

what they offer as *Realpolitik* is actually rooted in a certain naiveté. Second, their interpretations of the data, even when the latter are accurate, abstract from the unique historical setting —the late capitalist welfare state—which largely determines how the data function. Third, their methodological errors have political significance leading them to counsel a national policy of timidity, which is the cause of, not the solution to, most of the problems they pose.

I will take three men as representative of this neoconservative trend: Nathan Glazer, Daniel Patrick Moynihan, Daniel Bell. There are obvious ambiguities in my choice of examples. Two of them, Glazer and Moynihan, have sometimes spoken favorably of conservatism, but Bell, as far as I know, has not. Two of them, Bell and Glazer, were public supporters of McGovern in 1972; Moynihan was silent on his vote saying that a Democrat who had been in a Republican administration should stay out of the campaign. All of them—and particularly Glazer—advocate various liberal reforms, and Bell may still consider himself a man of the Left. Yet whatever their personal predilections, their ideas have a consistency and import which in the recent period have been conservative. I honor them when they contradict their own premises, but unfortunately they do not accompany their essays to explain to the reader their velleities to the contrary. I discuss them, then, as a social-intellectual phenomenon, not as individuals.[1]

In thus criticizing these pessimistic thinkers, I do not suggest that there are "easy answers" to the issues of the seventies. There are, as the neoconservatives insist at every turn, unintended consequences which sometimes overwhelm the best-intentioned plans. Of course! But this constant harping on the complexity of social policy has itself become a new oversimplification. Therefore this essay will conclude on what by now may seem a subtle and obscure truth: that there *are* some solutions to some of our problems.

I

To begin with, there is the neoconservative version of what actually happened in the sixties.

The government did too much. In *The Politics of a Guaranteed Income,* Moynihan offers a statement of this theme:

> A further argument which in retrospect may be adduced on behalf of the new conservatism is that diffusing social responsibility for social outcomes tends to retard the rise of social distrust when the promised or presumed outcome does not occur. The modern welfare state was getting into activities no one understood very well. It had not reached the point of picking every man a wife, but it was getting close enough to other such imponderables to find itself increasingly held to account for failures in areas where no government could reasonably promise success.
>
> The conservative argument had heft. This became even more evident in the course of the 1960s as the Federal government undertook an unprecedented range of social initiatives designed to put an end to racial and ethnic discrimination, to poverty, and even also to unequal levels of achievement among groups variously defined by race, class, religion, national origin, and sex, primarily through the strategy of providing new, or "enriched," social services.

Moynihan, as will be seen shortly, turns out to be a most persuasive witness against his own case. Yet the theme of "too much government intervention," which he states here so straightforwardly, is crucial to the neoconservative approach. In vulgarized version it also appears in George Wallace's racist Populism with its attack on the "pointy headed bureaucrats" in Washington; in Richard Nixon's reactionary charge that the sixties liberals (among whom some would count Moynihan himself) "threw money" at problems; and even in the agitation of some advocates of "community control" on the Left. Here, however, I am concerned with its sophisticated variant.

The difficulty with this interpretation of the sixties is that the central event it describes—a pervasive government intrusion into the private sphere—*never took place.*

Moynihan lists three areas in his indictment of liberal ultrareformism: ending racial and ethnic discrimination, abolishing poverty, and promoting equal achievement by means of enriched social services. If, however, one examines the record, his case simply does not hold up. The Civil Rights Acts of 1964 and 1965 hardly deal with "imponderables." In legislation that was long overdue, the Congress provided some minimal guarantees of basic rights in public accommodations and voting. Southern racists regarded that as intolerable interference with the states' right to be Jim Crow. Moynihan and the rest of the neoconservatives did not, happily, share that assessment; they favored these laws. Moreover, the 1964 and 1965 measures must certainly be regarded as successful examples of government action: the "promised or presumed outcome" *did* occur.

Then there is the supposedly excessive federal involvement in the war on poverty and the related attempt to end "unequal levels of achievement among groups . . . through the strategy of providing new, or 'enriched' social services." This last point does not attack "affirmative action" programs or inveigh against quotas (a neoconservative criticism which will be taken up in due course). Rather, it opposes the "service strategy" in aiding the poor, as a means of obtaining equality of result. As a Nixon counselor, Moynihan made this a major argument in persuading the President to adopt the "incomes strategy" of the Family Assistance Plan (FAP). Right now, however, the question is relatively simple: did the government in fact innovate extensively to end racism, poverty, and inequality in the sixties?

In the same book in which he charges overreaching federal involvement, Moynihan answers this question brilliantly. He writes,

> The social reforms of mid-decade had been oversold, and, with the coming of the war, underfinanced to the degree that seeming failure could be ascribed almost to intent. There was indeed considerable social change going on, and much of it in the direction most desired by those who were discontented, but it was progress clearly linked to the economic boom brought on by the war, which made it difficult to take much satisfaction in it.[2]

The government's own figures corroborate Moynihan's judgment that the reforms of the sixties were "oversold and

underfinanced." Between 1955 and 1965, the Brookings Institution study of the 1973 Budget shows, there was practically
no change in federal civilian expenditures as a percentage of
GNP. Then, between 1965 and 1970, that percentage almost
doubled. But when one looks at where this quantum leap occurred, it does not support the thesis of widespread federal innovation in social policy.

Between 1960 and 1970, there was a $44.3 billion rise in the
funds for Social Security and Medicare ($33.9 billion and $10.4
billion respectively). This was three times the increased expendi-
ture of public assistance (welfare, Medicaid, food stamps, housing subsidies, student aid.) Social Security is neither innovative
nor intrusive for—as Nathan Glazer pointed out in the May 1973
Commentary—"the program's objectives are clear and simple, and
thus it is easy to evaluate." Medicare can be criticized—primarily
on the grounds that it is an utterly inadequate installment on
national health insurance—but its difficulties certainly do not
derive from too much federal experimentation with the "imponderables" of social policy.

In the Budget of the United States government for 1974,
these patterns of expenditures are projected up to 1975. In the
1955-75 period, that Budget tells us, the "human resources"
percentage of the Budget will have increased from 21.1 percent
to 64.8 percent, or from $14.5 billion to $134.9 billion. But of
that total, more than 70 percent, or over $93 billion, is accounted
for by Medicare, Medicaid, Social Security, veterans' benefits,
and aid to the blind, aged, and handicapped. By contrast, the
Office of Economic Opportunity, a quintessential Great Society
agency, received less than $10 billion in the nine years between
its creation under Johnson and its dismemberment under
Nixon, with a peak appropriation for a single year of $1.9 billion
in 1969. And even that figure overstates the federal largesse in
this area, since by 1969 a significant portion of OEO funds were
going, directly or indirectly, to private business paid to hire
hard-core unemployed—whom they probably would often have
hired anyway.

Thus, Edward Banfield, a conservative conservative who
sometimes fellow-travels with the neoconservatives, is quite
wrong when he says that "it was not for lack of money that the

Great Society programs failed. Some of the principal efforts —Model Cities, for example—had more of it than they could spend." In fact, as Nathan Glazer has remarked, in the "most original area" of Great Society innovation—such neighborhood-controlled programs as Model Cities and Community Action —there was "not very much" money. In 1972 (the 1974 Federal Budget tells us) Model Cities spent all of $500 million, and it is quite clear that one of the reasons this program did not live up to its expectations was, and is, "lack of money."

II

Why then, if the funds for innovating programs were so scant, is there such a resonance to Moynihan's charge? Why has Nixon made such political mileage out of just such allegations?

First of all, the frantic style of the Johnson administration convinced people that the government was intervening in every area of life. Moynihan, for instance, notes that the New Towns in Towns Program, which was to use surplus federal land to build homes for the poor, was given a major White House send-off in 1967—and by 1971 had only 300 units of housing under construction.

Second, there were two specific areas in which important constituencies felt that the federal government was indeed moving in on them. The antisegregation laws—and court opinions—attacked deeply entrenched customs and were viewed as unwarranted interference by many Southern racists. When Nixon talked of Washington doing "too much," the Dixiecrats, to whom the Southern strategy was designed to appeal, did not have to consult the Budget or the Brookings Institution to know what he meant.

The question of school segregation and busing, however, went beyond the issues of public accommodations and voting rights. For one thing, this problem was posed in the *de facto* segregated districts of the North as well as in the *de jure* systems of the South. For another, it involved, as difficult cases almost always do, a conflict of rights rather than a right versus a wrong, as in the case of discriminatory voting and accommodation statutes. If minority demands for quality education through integration were, and should have been, the dominant consideration, still, ethnic and class concerns for the integrity of neighborhoods were not simply a mask for racism, they derived from an authentic emotion.

Moreover, the sweeping orders sometimes handed down in these cases came from the courts, i.e., from the least representative, most insulated of democratic institutions. The reason for that unfortunate—but to my mind, necessary—reality runs counter to neoconservative theory. If the executive and legislative branches, with their attendant planners and technocrats, had intervened vigorously on this count, the courts would not have acted. It was precisely the default of federal action, not its ubiquity, which turned the judiciary into an agency for the redress of long-overdue grievances.

Also, had there been a serious housing program in the sixties, with new cities and towns and new towns in towns, it could have furnished the basis for neighborhood and city-wide integration. But because the urban struggle became more and more of a battle between have-nots among the minorities and the poor and have-littles from the white working class, with the prize coming to be scarce resources such as schools and housing, the courts were called in as arbiters. Here, as in so many recent events, it was the lack of a radical program, the absence of innovation, that was crucial, not, as the neoconservatives have it, our prodigality.

So the evidence does not back up the first count of the neoconservative indictment of the welfare state in the sixties: that it did too much.

In a way, the second count is a refinement of the first. It asserts that

The government was too egalitarian in its policies.   Thus, Nathan Glazer writes of "the revolution of equality": "Perhaps only a Tocqueville saw its awesome potency. For it not only expresses a demand for equality in political rights and in political power; it also represents a demand for equality in economic power, in social status, in authority in every sphere." Leaving for later the issue of the democratization of authority, what Glazer is doing is calling into question the traditional socialist demand for economic and social democracy. That is, of course, his civil liberty, but it puts him on the side of the status quo.

Second, there is no question that some movements in the

sixties stood for the kind of radical, egalitarian redistribution of wealth and power that Glazer distrusts. But if one is not to be mesmerized by rhetoric it must be quickly added that *the egalitarians lost.* There is no factual basis whatever for the assertion that there was a massive trend toward equality in the sixties, particularly in income and status. Perhaps the most ambitious attempt to argue the contrary is to be found in Daniel Bell's *Public Interest* article, "Meritocracy and Equality" (Fall 1972); I will make a fairly close reading of some of its assertions since they are a perfect illustration of the way the sixties are read by neoconservatism.

Bell writes, " . . . the university, which once merely reflected the status system of the society, has now become the arbiter of class position. As the gate-keeper, it has gained a quasi-monopoly in determining the future stratification of society." And,

> Any institution which gains a quasi-monopoly over the fate of individuals is likely, in a free society, to be subject to quick attack. Thus, the Populist revolt which Michael Young foresaw several decades hence has already begun at the very outset of the post-industrial society.
>
> One sees this today in the derogation of the IQ and the denunciation of theories espousing a genetic basis of intelligence; in the demand for "open admissions" to universities; in the pressure for increased numbers of blacks, women and specific minority groups such as Puerto Ricans and Chicanos on the faculties of universities, by quotas if necessary; and in the attack on "credentials" and even schooling itself as the determinant of a man's position in society.

Is it true that the university "has now become the quasi-arbiter of class position"? That it has a "quasi-monopoly over the fate of individuals"? That "schooling itself" has ever been the "determinant of a man's position in society"?

That is most questionable sociology. As Daniel Patrick Moynihan and Frederick Mosteller summarize the Coleman Report (the Equal Educational Opportunity Report): " . . .

studies do *not* find adult social achievement well predicted by academic achievement" and "family background, measured in social class terms—primarily education of parents, but including many other considerations such as the presence of an encyclopedia in the house—is apparently a major determinant of educational achievement." This latter assertion, it should be noted, inverts Bell's cause and effect, making educational achievement a function of class position rather than the other way round. Christopher Jencks's study of inequality (which Bell cites in his essay) came to an even more pointed conclusion as to the lack of relationship between scholarly and economic success. And David K. Cohen reported in the April 1972 *Commentary* that high school seniors in the bottom fifth both economically and in terms of IQ had a 10 percent chance of going to college—while seniors who were in the top income fifth and the bottom IQ fifth had a 40 percent chance.

These figures hardly confirm the thesis that we are on the verge of Michael Young's meritocracy where IQ is the decisive determinant of class position. Rather they back up Cohen's statement that "nowhere can we find any empirical support for the idea that brains are becoming increasingly more important to status in America." So Bell's basic assertion of a trend is, to put it mildly, quite debatable. Equality of opportunity, Bell writes (and there is more than a hint of nostalgia in his tone),

> derives from a fundamental principle of classical liberalism that the individual—and not the family, the community or the state—is the basic unit of society, and that the purpose of social arrangements is to allow the individual the freedom to fullfill his own purposes—by his labor to gain property, by exchange to satisfy wants, by upward mobility to achieve a place commensurate with his talents.

Counterposed to this approach is the current idea of equality of result: "Today we have come to the end of classic liberalism. It is not individual satisfaction which is the measure of social good, but redress for the disadvantaged as a prior claim on the social conscience and on social policies." This theory of equality of opportunity is, Bell says, a socialist ethic.

It should be said in passing that classical liberalism was, in some part, a swindle. If it helped liberate men from feudal relationships of personal dependence, the "individual" of whom it spoke was mostly the bourgeois, the affluent, the privileged individual. For him, the system worked; for the majority it did not, and one reason classical liberalism has faded is that people came to see its limitations.

But is it indeed true that "today . . . it is not individual satisfaction which is the measure of social good, but redress for the disadvantaged as a prior claim on the social conscience and social policies"? In part, Bell is here talking about theories, like John Rawls's writings on equality; but in part, he is making assertions about current practice. Witness his remark, "The Kennedy and Johnson Administrations had made equality the central theme of social policy." Is that true?

Again, the sixties sometimes talked as if moved by egalitarian passions. Ironically, Moynihan himself might plausibly claim some credit—or, would he now himself bear some blame?—for introducing the idea of equality of result into the mainstream of political debate. In Moynihan's report on the Negro family in 1965 he wrote of a new period beginning after the victories over juridical segregation. Now, Moynihan said,

> the expectations of the Negro Americans will go beyond civil rights. Being American, they will now expect that in the near future equal opportunity for them as a group will produce roughly equal results, as compared with other groups. This is not going to happen. Nor will it happen for generations to come unless a new and special effort is made.

In Lyndon Johnson's Howard University speech, inspired and partly composed by Moynihan, the President said, "We seek not just freedom but opportunity, not just legal equality but human ability, not just equality as a right and a theory but equality as a fact and a result."

As a statement of moral obligation toward people who have suffered discrimination for centuries, this argument seems quite compelling. As a political tactic, I have the same criticisms

Moynihan eventually formulated: that programs to deal with the special needs of blacks and other minorities must also be designed so as to raise the living standards of others, the white working class in particular. Real full employment, for example, betters the bargaining position of all workers, but it aids the relative position of the most vulnerable more than that of any other group.

But if the sixties sometimes spoke—and rightly so—of national obligations to the victims of discrimination who are not dreamed of in the philosophy of classical liberalism, it did not act radically on that premise. Whatever one might think of the philosophic questions,[3] the welfare state in the last decade was anything but egalitarian. Big business was encouraged, and sometimes paid, to become an "equal opportunity employer." Colleges dramatically increased the number of minority students. The best placed blacks made significant gains, i.e., the young educated Negroes with stable marriages were able to take advantage of the new opportunities.

This progress was not negligible. Yet neither does it justify Bell's sweeping generalization: "A sticky fact of Western society over the past 200 years has been the steady decrease in income disparity among persons—not by distribution policies and judgments about fairness, but by technology, which had cheapened the cost of products and made more things available to more people." This presumed trend is then made the basis of what Bell calls the "Tocqueville effect," an explanation of the ingratitude of the new Populists who recently benefited from the progress toward equality.

For according to Tocqueville, Bell says, democratic institutions and equality "develop sentiments of envy in the human heart." So, paradoxically, it is our more and more egalitarian reality, in Bell's view, which is the cause of "excessive" egalitarianism.

A few general words about Bell's "sticky fact" are needed before turning to specifics in the sixties. The extent to which there has been a *relative* change in income shares over the past 200 years in the West is difficult to document and certainly open to debate. There has, of course, been an absolute increase in the standard of living of the masses, but that is something else again and not relevant to Bell's assertion's about "disparities." Second, to the degree that some relative progress may have been achieved, it was the result not only of technology but also of a furious social conflict—a class war—over the distribution of the fruits of technology.

However, once one reduces the focus from two centuries to two decades—that is, to the period in which Bell perceives his "Tocqueville effect"—we can be somewhat more precise about the figures (but only somewhat; the dirty little secret of the rich in a democracy is the extent of their wealth). All the evidence shows that there has been no change in basic income distribution since at least 1947 (there are those who argue that there were some changes between 1929 and 1947 because of the Depression and the War—two rather unfortunate instruments of social policy—but even that proposition has been criticized by serious analysts).

Lewis Mandell of the University of Michigan Survey Research Center has computed that the top 5 percent of the wealth-holders in America own 40 percent of the wealth, and that the top 20 percent possess three times as much as the 80 percent below them. A 1972 *Business Week* summary of recent research pointed out that the bottom 50 percent of the income recipients received 23 percent of total personal income in 1969 and represented only 3 percent of net worth. And James D. Smith of Penn State has concluded that the rich get richer because they start from a higher base. In stock ownership, as Letitia Upton and Nancy Lyons have documented, the disparities are severe: the top 1 percent of the wealth holders own 62 percent of all publicly held corporate stock; the top 5 percent have 86 percent, the top 20 percent have 97 percent. So much for our stockholder democracy.

These tendencies, it must be remembered, were reinforced, not reversed, by the Kennedy-Johnson administrations of the sixties (and, of course, by the Nixon administration). Because John Kennedy had such a narrow presidential margin and a shaky position in Congress, he moved to stimulate the economy through investment credits, accelerated depreciation and tax cuts, all of which notoriously benefited the rich more than anyone else. During the sixties, as the AFL-CIO has documented on many occasions, unit labor costs were stable for the first half of the decade while profits soared (and also the much more significant figure of corporate cash flow, profit, plus depreciation allowances and internal financing). During the second half of the decade, workers were forced to strike simply to keep pace with the cost of living and some of them suffered a decline in real purchasing power. The UAW's bitter battle with GM in 1970, for instance, was in considerable measure necessary because the union had to catch up with inflation, running furiously just to stay in place.

Indeed, the staff studies and hearings of the Joint Economic Committee in 1972 showed that the Internal Revenue Code alone contains a welfare system, primarily for the rich, worth $77 billion a year (it takes the form of deductions for capital gains, mansions, etc.). The government—under Kennedy and Johnson as well as Nixon—used its power to favor corporate investment in machines even at times of high unemployment. Lyndon Johnson refused to fund the public-service jobs advocated by the Automation Commission of 1966 and the Civil Disorders Commission of 1968. Instead, he paid private business a bonus for hiring hard-core unemployed workers.

Even those increases in Social Security which formed the bulk of new government expenditures in the sixties contributed somewhat to this antiegalitarian trend. For as the Social Security tax, one of the most regressive in the nation, was increased, so was the burden on working people. (The Social Security tax does not vary according to family size, responsibilities, etc; and it is only charged against the first $12,500 of income, which makes it a bargain for those with over $12,500 a year and regressive compared even to the federal income tax.)

So the notion that our troubles are caused by the egalitarianism of the welfare state in the sixties, as suggested by both Glazer and Bell, is not true. Instead of talking of a "Tocqueville effect," perhaps it is necessary to speak of the "Sisyphus effect": the anger felt by people when they intuit that, despite the fact that they have more money to spend, they have not advanced their relative position in a society which regards that as the supreme good.

* * *

III

The neoconservative error in this regard constitutes the faulty basis for yet another proposition: since the Kennedy-Johnson years were excessively idealistic and egalitarian but still promoted discontent, this shows that

The consequences of government intervention are, more often than not, unintended and usually negative.   This proposition is central to the new conservatism and it will be examined in some detail.

The philosophy behind this theory goes back at least to Edmund Burke and his assertion of an organic development of society as an argument against state interference with the providence of the natural order of things. Perhaps the best known contemporary writer in this intellectual tradition is Michael Oakeshott. In his *Politics of a Guaranteed Income,* Moynihan cites Oakeshott in the course of analyzing the dispute over the Family Assistance Plan, saying that he "has defined the conservative temperament in terms which showed with great distinctiveness, and not a little advantage, in the debate. . . ."In Oakeshott's view, innovation involves "certain loss and possible gain" and is best when it resembles the process of growth. Oakeshott concludes that "as the conservative understands it, modifications of the rules should always reflect, and never impose, a change in the activities and beliefs of those who are subject to them." (On this calculus, much cited by the Dixiecrats at the time, the Civil Rights Acts of 1964 and 1965 were clearly unwise.)

The now-famous "notch" is invoked by the American neoconservatives as an instance of Oakeshott's wisdom. The "notch" defines that point at which working, or increasing income, or even escaping from poverty becomes irrational because government policy turns a marginal increment into a substantial loss. Under the provisions of Aid for the Families of Dependent Children (Unemployed)—AFDC(U)—states were given the right to provide AFDC benefits even though there was an able-bodied, though unemployed, man in the house. However, if the man worked more than 30 or 35 hours, he and his family would lose all assistance. Similarly, in states with decent Medicaid programs, a person who raises his income by five dollars but thereby fails the means test for Medicaid, forfeits much more than five dollars in medical benefits. There is, consequently, a positive incentive to stay under the "notch," i.e., to remain, or at least appear to remain, poor.

These cases do meet Oakeshott's criteria for unintended consequences, since they are the result of good, reformist intentions. The AFDC(U) legislation was a victory for those liberals who were aghast because the requirement that no man could be in the house literally drove fathers to leave their families (or to pretend that they had done so). And Medicaid was, of course, a sleeper provision of the Medicare law which permitted the most advanced states—notably New York, Massachusetts, and California—to provide a partial installment of socialized medicine. Yet both of these efforts, laudable as their intent was, tended to provide inducements to poverty.

There can be no doubt that this "notch" effect took place. But does this prove, as Oakeshott, Moynihan, and the neoconservatives assume, that such mishaps are inherent in the very process of reform and therefore are an argument for caution with regard to innovation? That would be true only if other factors did not contribute to the "notch" effect—which is precisely the case. The "notch" was the creation of timid governmental action, not of sweeping programs.

First of all, it must be emphasized that both AFDC(U) and Medicaid were palliatives, not radical departures. AFDC(U) recognized that the government's full-employment policy was unable to provide work for a significant number of able and willing family heads. It was extremely limited in its application, required the states to act—and spend money—and therefore only operated in a significant fashion in a few areas. Had there been genuine full employment—through the mechanism of a federal guaranteed right to work—AFDC(U) would have been unnecessary. The "notch" in this case was therefore the result of an inadequate response to a problem that should not have been allowed to exist in the first place.

Similarly with Medicaid. The reason the "notch" arises in this area is that National Health Insurance, first vigorously advocated by Harry Truman in 1949, was rejected and the nation decided, after wasting more than a decade in indecision, on a second best: some medical care for the elderly; a states-right Medicaid provision that was practically smuggled into the law. It is a notorious fact that Medicare and Medicaid have, along with their undeniable accomplishments, bid up the cost of medical care for those under 65 and not poor. This provides an enormous incentive for someone to keep his income below the Medicaid cut-off line. But if there were National Health Insurance—had we passed Truman's 1949 proposal or were we to pass the Kennedy-Griffith bill now before the Congress—the "notch" would simply disappear. So it is not the result of the immemorial frailties of the human condition, but of our own conscious, perverse, and reversible political decisions.

In saying these things, I do not want to suggest for a moment that reform is a seamless, utterly predictable affair. Of course it isn't. Admitting that is one thing; overgeneralizing from it, as the neoconservatives have done, is another thing.

There is, however, one area where the complexities do more nearly accord to the neoconservative account of them: education. The Coleman Report—the Equal Education Opportunity Survey and Report—is prime evidence in this regard. As Moynihan tells it, everyone assumed prior to the Report that an increase in educational inputs—money for schools, teachers, books, equipment, etc.—would result in better outputs: academic achievement. Therefore, it was said, particularly after the 1954 Supreme Court decision against segregation in public education, that the disparity in intellectual performance between the poor and the non-poor, or the minorities and the majority, was to be explained by the lack of school inputs in poor neighborhoods. And this was the rationale of the various federal education programs of the sixties: they were to close the academic gap by channeling new resources to those who had suffered discrimination and neglect.

Some of these propositions were indeed shared by almost all liberals and radicals. To the extent that the Coleman Report disproved them—and the Report itself, it must be understood, is still the subject of debate—it did indeed expose an area of well-meaning ignorance. The Report did show that the objective disparities between black and white educational inputs were not as great as had been imagined by many; and that the academic outputs which could be won by money were lower than most had thought.

But Moynihan and company exaggerate the degree to which the assumptions subverted by Coleman had been shared by the Left. The belief that schools could—apart from changes in class position, the labor market, housing, etc.—transform life at the bottom of the society is not a radical thesis. Indeed, it does not even represent the best of liberalism. Coleman's findings, that family background measured in social-class terms is a more important determinant of educational achievement than school buildings or chemistry labs, confirms a traditional socialist analysis.

Second, thinking in terms of input and output assumes that education can, and should be, described as a production function appropriate in a factory: X dollars invested yields Y increases in reading scores. That equation, however, utterly fails to take into account some of the most crucial variables. The schools do not simply develop cognitive skills; they are also a basic socializing institution for a democratic society. If such a formulation strikes one as sentimental, a nonquantifiable claim, then it can be translated into economic projections. For there are serious experts who believe that it is not so much what a child learns in school, but the school experience taken as a whole, which is crucial for increasing intellectual productivity.

Third, part of our inability to deal with education relates to unprecedented changes that have taken place. Just before World War II, about a third of American youth went to high school. Now that figure is around three quarters of the available population. A generation ago, grade schools functioned to provide minimal literacy, and high schools were the preserve of the more fortunate and motivated students. Now there is a massive group in the high schools such as never existed before and one of the reasons that "Johnny" is not doing better is that this is the first time he has been asked to go beyond that basic literacy. We have most certainly failed to respond adequately to this challenge but our difficulties stem from a new and worthy problem.

Still, I would distinguish between two areas of unintended consequences in the recent history of the welfare state. First, there are the cases where our deficiencies are the result of timid,

pinch-penny programs, which create unnecessary "notches."
Second, there are areas—education, and drug addiction, for
instance—in which our ignorance plays a role and our good
intentions may sometimes be counterproductive. But the first
category is a refutation of the Oakeshott analysis, and the second
by no means confirms it. Nevertheless, the neoconservatives
build upon this faulty base and argue against a "service strategy"
that is seen as an unwarranted intervention in the domain of
social complexity. They have persuaded the Nixon policy-
makers on this count, providing them with a rationale for dis-
mantling a number of Great Society programs—though they
failed to win Nixon to a serious fight for the alternative of an
income strategy.

IV

The critique of the service strategy was basic to Nathan Glazer's
enormously influential article, "The Limits of Social Policy"
(*Commentary*, September 1971). Glazer wrote: "In its efforts to
deal with the breakdown of these traditional structures [family,
ethnic group, church, neighborhood], however, social policy
tends to encourage their further weakening." Services become
professionalized; our lack of knowledge creates new problems
rather than solutions. So, Glazer concluded, one of the things to
recommend the Nixon Family Assistance Plan (FAP) is that it is
not a service strategy. And in a later article Glazer praised
another program based on an "income strategy": "Thus we
know enough generally about Social Security to act (although
there are plenty of complexities in that program, too). The same
amount of money is sent out from a central point to everyone in
the same status. The program's objectives are clear and simple,
and thus it is easy to evaluate."

Moynihan carried the attack against the service strategy into
the White House itself in 1969 and 1970, persuading—if only
briefly—Richard Nixon to advocate a guaranteed annual income (which the President constantly asserted was not a guaranteed annual income). "The service strategy," Moynihan wrote in
his retrospect on the battle for FAP, " has been quintessentially
that of political liberalism in the middle third of the twentieth

century. And yet the actual *effect* of service programs such as education is probably to reallocate resources *up* the social scale, taxing, as it were, factory workers to pay schoolteachers." An income strategy, Moynihan said, did not involve the intrusions and confrontations of a service strategy. And, he added in a somewhat radical mood, "The concept of an 'income strategy' entailed many risks—it could only in the end mean *income redistribution. . . .*"

This analysis contains both an interpretation of the recent history of the welfare state and policy conclusions to be derived from it. Moreover, it is typical of a strand of thought that is to be found in almost all of neoconservative writing. So it deserves rather careful attention.

First, it is *not* true that the service strategy has been "quintessentially that of political liberalism in the middle third of the twentieth century"—nor even in the decade of the sixties. There were probably some social workers who believed in such an approach, but they were relatively few in number and certainly not the arbiters of liberalism. The traditional New Deal liberals of the labor-liberal coalition always made full employment their demand, as Moynihan must remember from his days at the Department of Labor. A. Philip Randolph's Freedom Budget, which was endorsed by John Kenneth Galbraith as well as by a good number of international union presidents, put this issue at the very heart of government policy.

It is true that in the original infighting over the Economic Opportunity Act, the Department of Health, Education, and Welfare (through Wilbur Cohen) and the Council of Economic Advisers (through Walter Heller) battled the Secretary of Labor (Willard Wirtz) and his associate (Moynihan) on this question. Cohen, Heller, and their allies wanted to make the war on poverty into a community action program; Moynihan and Wirtz were for a job emphasis. But even then, the community action proponents never isolated that idea from the whole range of macroeconomic measures in which the government was engaging. Heller, as the chief architect of what was then called the "New Economics," could have hardly thought that services were "quintessential."

I do not cite this history merely to demonstrate that

Moynihan's memory is faulty. It relates to establishing the broader context of all the welfare state debates of the sixties. The Kennedy-Johnson manpower policies did reduce joblessness from the Eisenhower levels down to less than 4 percent, and that was probably the most effective single accomplishment in the "war" on poverty. But in 1966 and 1968 when, as I have already noted, presidential commissions recommended a ranging federal program of funding public-service employment, Lyndon Johnson turned down that liberal proposal and took the conservative ("trickle-down") line of encouraging private hiring by subsidizing it. In this case, the realistic politicians were wrong, the liberal intellectuals right.

It is precisely Moynihan's amnesia on this count which flaws his analysis of the Family Assistance Plan. In explaining why the Nixon proposals set the minimum so low (in the neighborhood of $2,500 for a family), Moynihan says that this was necessary because the working poor were being included in the program. Since they were to be given the right to keep a portion of the earnings (in contrast to the 100 percent tax on such income in most welfare systems), a $2,500 base for the dependent (nonworking) poor thus meant some support to the working poor up to $5,000 of income. If, therefore, the minimum were set at $6,500, as urged by Senator Eugene McCarthy and the National Welfare Rights Organization, that would have required supplementing the income of everyone with less than $13,000, i.e., of the majority of the people. So, Moynihan concludes, it was essential to peg the minimum low if there was any hope of passing the plan.

In other words, the undeniable needs of the working poor, who would gain from FAP, were counterposed to the undeniable needs of the dependent poor in states with relatively high benefits. The latter would not get any increases at all—they might even lose in the shuffle. But this was true only because of an enormous and intolerable fact which Moynihan ignores: that there were unconscionably high levels of unemployment and underemployment creating that scandalous category of the "working poor." If the Nixon administration, in which Moynihan served, had not systematically increased unemployment as part of a strategy for price stability in 1969 and 1970, the problem would have been much less difficult. If the liberal proposals for full employment had been adopted in the sixties, it would not have existed at all.

Second, there is Moynihan's assertion that the service strategy reallocates resources "*up* the social scale." That depends, not on the nature of the service strategy, but on the tax system. If, for example, one were to finance community action programs in the next period out of those $20 billion in loophole savings that would be realized if the reforms advocated by George McGovern and George Meany were adopted, Moynihan's regressive effect would not take place. It is true that in the sixties the burden of paying for social services—and for the war in Vietnam—fell discriminatorily upon working people. That, however, was a function of the antiegalitarianism of federal wealth and income policy, which has already been documented in the discussion of Daniel Bell's view on equality.

Similarly, Moynihan's assertion that FAP had to mean "*income redistribution*"—and it is interesting that, as a neoconservative, he counts this as a point in its favor—is, in and of itself, not true in the least. If FAP were accompanied by a tough tax-reform proposal, that might have been the case; and it was debated at a time when Nixon, as the Joint Economic Committee showed, was increasing the tax relief of the rich substantially. (He reduced taxes by about $20 billion a year.)

Third, Moynihan is somewhat ambiguous—and somewhat wrong—in another aspect of his critique of the service strategy. In the introduction he wrote (along with Frederick Mosteller) to the essays on the Coleman Report, which were produced by a Harvard seminar, he said,

> One of the patterns of the 1960s was that of middle-class persons, in large measure professionals, conceiving a great range of social programs, supported by tax monies, which undertook to assist the poor through a process of employing middle-class persons. Reform was becoming professionalized.

In this formulation, Moynihan seems to be giving sophisticated utterance to a popular myth: that welfare programs are a cheat designed by social workers. In the process, he overstates the class bias of the service strategy. Nathan Glazer is much closer to the truth when he writes,

> . . . we hired great numbers of social workers and consultants, increasing their income. Many of these—few at the beginning, more later—came from minority groups; we were providing the jobs through these programs for the barely college trained that other programs were producing; and from the same communities.

In the case of teachers, whom Moynihan has attacked on this count, my own guess is that a very large number of them are the children of working-class families.

But then Moynihan himself is ambiguous in his critique. In the same essay in which he deprecated the middle-class beneficiaries who allegedly profiteer from poverty programs, he also wrote, "Increasingly the most relevant findings concerning the state of society are the work of elites and must simply be taken—or respected—by the public at large, at times even by the professional public involved, on . . . faith." Social reality, Moynihan argues in this mood, is often "counter-intuitive" and therefore the society must accept the data from the experts. So Moynihan is,—as is Bell, who is at least as anxious to defend the perquisites of expertise—of two minds about the professionals in charge of the service strategy.

In this, as in the entire critique of the service strategy, there is the imprecision of overgeneralizations. In a good many cases, the flaws which are said to be inherent in such programs turn out, on closer examination, to be the result of the limitations —usually the cheapness—of the welfare state itself. President Nixon did not, however, bother to make such discriminations. He allowed himself to be persuaded, or perhaps it would be more precise to say that he permitted his prejudices to be reinforced, by the blunderbuss blast against the service strategy. And after a brief infatuation with Family Assistance, he abandoned the income strategy, too.

* * *

V

The neoconservatives cannot, of course, be held responsible for a reactionary misreading of their views. But they should be aware of how their philosophy disposes itself to such a fate. This is particularly true of their largest, and most conservative, abstraction:

The preference for the unplanned, and even the irrational, as opposed to conscious government policy.   This is a fundamental conservative theme, the nostalgia for the vanished *Gemeinschaft,* the suspicion of the contemporary *Gesellschaft.* From Burke to Dostoevsky to Spengler it has been at the very center of conservative thought.

In the early pages of *Maximum Feasible Misunderstanding,* Moynihan indulges in some romantic medievalism which leans heavily upon Robert Nisbet. But then, Moynihan is partly a product of Catholic social thought, which has always idealized the period of the Church's dominance. In the writings of Chesterton, Belloc, Gill, and others, the Middle Ages were held up as a model. But it is Nathan Glazer, sharing Moynihan's outlook yet coming from a completely different (socialist) tradition, who provides the most interesting example of this mood.

"Social policy"—Glazer wrote in "The Limits of Social Policy"—"is an effort to deal with the breakdown of traditional ways of handling disasters." What the family, church, ethnic group, *Landsmanschaft,* etc. once did, the government now attempts to do. "In the effort to deal with the breakdown of these traditional structures, however, social policy tends to encourage their further weakening." Putting it that way is to confuse the effect for a cause and to overlook a revolution. The "traditional way of handling disasters" broke down, in good measure, because of unprececdented new problems and disasters. By focusing on the breakdown as the author of our woes, one holds out the hope that all can be well again if only it can be repaired; by stressing the cause of the breakdown, a revolutionary process that has been going on for some centuries, one knows that the revival of the old *Gemeinschaft* is impossible.

Glazer believes that Humpty Dumpty is going to be put together again: " . . . some important part of the solution to our social problems lies in the traditional practices and restraints." But when the economic and social conditions for those practices and restraints have been destroyed, how can they rise from the dead to solve our problems?

I suspect that Glazer's emphasis derives in part from a very real and understandable concern about the breakdown of "traditional practices and traditional restraints" in his own neighborhood: the university. So it is that the climactic charge in Glazer's indictment of the "revolution of equality" is that it seeks to create "equality in authority." And Daniel Bell defends the "authority represented in the superior competence of individuals" from the scorn of the New Populists.

In part, these neoconservative fears have substantial content. There has indeed been a decline of ethical standards accompanying the effective collapse of organized religion. The emancipation of the psyche from the restraints imposed upon it by the hierarchical authority of the past has not, as Marx and the socialist tradition hoped, led to the emergence of a new, humanist and rational code. For one thing, this cultural revolution has occurred, not within the context of a political and social revolution, but under the domination of conservative social structures. As a result, the revolution was marketed, vulgarized, co-opted. There are, then, reasons to be disturbed. But this upheaval has been going on for perhaps a century, and it is hardly the result of recent—Populist or New Left—trends in American life. Moreover, if there is any possibility that this cultural revolution can become a vehicle for social emancipation, what is required is a radical response, a reshaping of the social structures, and not, as in the neoconservative proposal, a retreat.

On a more prosaic level, Glazer deduces some very faulty policy from his attempt to revive *Gemeinschaft* past. He writes: "Ultimately, we are not kept healthy, I believe, by new scientific knowledge or more effective cures or even better-organized medical care services. We are kept healthy by certain patterns of life." That, I submit, is not true. England and Sweden are beset by the same cultural convulsions as the United States. Their churches, family structure, etc. are no more secure than ours. Yet their health is. The reason is simple enough: they have better-organized medical care than we do.

In some ways, this celebration of the organic as against the rational is the most unfortunate aspect of neoconservatism. It takes that fledgling ideology back toward conservatism pure and simple, to the notion that the hope of the future lies in the past.

VI

This critique of neoconservatism can now be generalized: the failures of the welfare state in recent years are the result of its conservatism, not of its excessive liberalism or, more preposterously, of its radicalism.

There has, of course, been a counterprogram implicit, and sometimes explicit, in my analysis of the neoconservatives. I propose to sketch it out in symbolic detail, i.e., not to offer a legislative shopping list, but to illustrate an emphasis, to exemplify an approach to a program rather than the program itself. In order to do that, I will first summarize the critique of the welfare state that is the point of departure for my strategy. There are the inherent limitations of this social formation itself, which are to be found in all of the advanced capitalist powers; and the special limitations of the most conservative and pinch-penny welfare state in the world, the United States of America.

Some General Propositions

1. _All welfare states are antiegalitarian and resist income redistribution._ Sophisticated businessmen, the decisive though not always dominant class of welfare-state society, have learned that a Keynesian government following corporate priorities is their friend, not their enemy. They have also accepted the establishment of social minimums of income, health care, etc. They came screaming to this wisdom because they were educated in it by militant labor, socialist, and liberal movements. And they did so with all the grace exhibited by the English industrialists who, as Marx said, accepted restrictions upon the working hours of factory labor for the same reason that they spread guano on their fields: because they did not want to exhaust a productive resource.

But even though the ruling class can thus be driven and cajoled into a modicum of decency, it refuses to allow the welfare state to change the *relative shares* of wealth. So it is that Richard Titmuss has documented the sharp limits of redistribution even under a Labour government in England and that the figures for the United States show that there has been no shift in the *portions* allotted to the different social classes in at least a generation. Even in Sweden, where a social democratic government has created one of the most imaginative and progressive welfare states in the world, there was tremendous resistance when Olaf Palme fought for a very modest redistribution several years ago. Significantly, the opposition came not from the blue-collar working class, which was willing to make concessions to better the lot of the worst-off in the society, but from the educated salariat.

The reason for this persistence of the maldistribution of wealth are not to be found, as Irving Kristol argued in his essay "About Equality," in a bell-shaped distribution of human talents which determines a bell-shaped distribution of rewards. For one thing, Kristol was simply, and shockingly, wrong on the facts: the distribution of rewards in America is not bell-shaped at all but skewed outrageously in favor of the rich. For another, as some of the data already cited indicate, the influence of class subverts, or at least vitiates, much of the effect of genetic endowment.

The persistence of maldistribution results from the concentration of "creative" wealth in the hands of a tiny minority. *The top 5 percent of income recipients who own 86 percent of all publicly held corporate stock receive greater increments of the governmentally planned and induced growth in national product than does any other group.* Precisely to the degree that state management of the economy is successful, Harold Wilson noted in 1960, there is "a law of increasing returns to the rich."

However, the powers-that-be do not trust simply in trends; they help them along. Welfare state governments constantly intervene on behalf of those whom the *Wall Street Journal* calls the "most productive" citizens, i.e., the possessors of wealth who often engage in no activity more strenuous than the clipping of coupons. David Lewis of the New Democratic party has documented the existence of "corporate welfare bums" in Canada who fatten themselves on the privileges that the government provides for them. Their similars can be found in every advanced capitalist nation. This reality, it must be emphasized, is not merely a concoction of conservatives when they take their turn at running the welfare state. It is sometimes encouraged by liberals as well. The Kennedy-Johnson tax cuts in the sixties gave enormous subsidies to the richest people and corporations in America. One result, as the AFL-CIO has stressed repeatedly, was a one-sided capital-goods boom initiated by government policy, which made significant contributions—along with the government's war in Vietnam—to the raging inflation at the decade's end.

These things do not happen because liberals in America, or social democrats in Europe, are insincere, sell-outs, or anything of the sort. Such explanations of social behavior almost always miss the mark. Much more profoundly, private wealth dominates the economy of the welfare state. Therefore, a government that seeks to maximize growth—and with it full employment, tax revenues to fund new social services, etc.—must keep corporations happy. If there is a strike of capital, as happened to Leon Blum in the France of the thirties and to Harold Wilson in the England of the sixties, the system will not work.

2. *The welfare state does not simply tend to distribute rewards according to the priorities of private wealth and power; it also plans production according to the same antisocial calculus.* The pre-World War I German socialists noted this trend under Bismarck. They called it "state socialism": the use of techniques such as nationalization, planning, and social services. During the heyday of French "indicative planning"—that conspiracy for economic growth between the state and the capitalists, as one critic called it—the companies were able to utilize what was, in effect, government-subsidized market research for their own ends; but the unions, even though seats were allocated to them in the planning bodies, did not have the resources to take advantage of the same information. In the process, the joint decisions of the state and the business community determine the shape, as well as the distribution, of the national product.

In the United States, as we have seen, the Kennedy-Johnson policies did not simply favor rich individuals. They also channeled private money into new investment at a time when there was still relatively high unemployment. Richard Nixon, who is straightforwardly reactionary in such matters, proposed to expand that contradiction with his "job development credit." In agriculture, federal subsidies have favored the big, corporate operation and helped to drive small farmers out of existence. In housing, policies determined in Washington—and corresponding to a calculus of private profitability rather than public need—encouraged suburbia with princely assistance while the central cities were allowed to rot. The very structure of the American economy, then, is becoming more and more the work of the hidden agenda that determines the priorities of federal policy and orients them toward the interests of big business.

This tendency, one can be assured, will assert itself in the current search for a solution to the energy crisis. The crisis itself is, of course, the result of government policies that were in the service of the 23 major petroleum producers. Quotas on imports, tax write-offs to domestic producers, and other federal actions led to a rapid consumption of continental reserves. Now Senator Henry Jackson has proposed a $20 billion research and development program, in which Washington is going to bail out the authors of our crisis. John Connally toured the Middle East as the unofficial representative of the President of the United States and the official lawyer for Texas (worldwide) oil interests. Connally then joined the Nixon staff, with special responsibilities for energy policy (the fact that he could not fit into the paranoid atmosphere of the post-Watergate White House does not alter the essential point).

If there are going to be billions spent on solar, geothermal, and tidal energy research, as now seems to be the case, and if the structure of our welfare state remains much as it is, then one can predict with certainty that the chief beneficiaries of the new, publicly developed technology will be the villains from the old, publicly subsidized technology. Washington, in short, socializes both production and distribution for private profit.

3. The welfare state is, by its very nature, a contradictory phenomenon.   This is a crucial point to grasp, for it provides the opening for positive political action and keeps the foregoing analysis from leading to a weary fatalism.

On the one hand, the welfare state represents the interests, and the achievements, of the Left. It is a means of imposing nonmarket considerations upon a capitalist economy, of making the society somewhat more humane. Therefore the great mass movements for reform in all of the advanced capitalist countries seek to control the welfare state and to impose their, the people's, priorities upon it. Moreover, in periods of crisis and change, real gains have been, and can be, made. The New Deal, the Labour government in England after 1945, the Swedish accomplishment achieved from the thirties to the present, the legislative acts of the Popular Front in France, all represent a significant advance for working men and women and their middle-class allies.

On the other hand, the welfare state exists within a capitalist economy and, particularly in "normal" periods, it is permeated by the values of that society. There is consequently a built-in tendency to erode the progress made by the mass movements in times of militancy. Even so, the contradictions of the welfare state offer a point of departure for change—above all, for structural change. But before turning to that question, a few notes on its American model.

The American welfare state is the most conservative variant. It is the most narrow and pinchpenny, since this country spends a smaller percentage of its GNP on social programs than any advanced nation, capitalist or Communist. There are, for example, the scandalous absence of national health insurance, the routine toleration of levels of unemployment which would topple a government in most European countries, the failure to do anything serious about the housing of the poor over the past generation.

Also, the American welfare state is antisocialist, while all other welfare states have been profoundly influenced by socialist thought and action. This means, as John Kenneth Galbraith recognizes, that the United States tends to regard government undertakings as part of the area of unfreedom and inefficiency, a conviction that often operates as a self-fulfilling prophecy. It has been a major obstacle to the passage of national health insurance, and it will surely be used by the oil companies as an excuse for profiteering on the energy crisis. In this context, the fight for socialist legitimacy in this country is crucial to the process of liberal reform. For our antisocialism is really directed against improvement in the welfare state, not, alas, against a serious socialist threat within America.

And finally, there is the federal nature of American politics. This has meant that so many of our programs—welfare, unemployment insurance, Medicaid, to name a few—have been subjected to states' rights vetoes. The states which adopt policies based upon a modicum of humanity are penalized; the most reactionary areas advertise their callousness as an inducement for investment.

So the very phenomenon of the welfare state, as well as its American exemplar, is based upon a conservative power structure. In their reading of the sixties, one crucial error the neoconservatives make is that they ignore the hidden agenda which follows from these interrelationships of power. By taking official declarations at face value, they conjure up an egalitarian, innovating, semiradical decade—which never existed. Moreover, even if it may sound a little arrogant, it should be remembered that this writer and DISSENT and others on the democratic Left were not taken in, that we predicted the intended consequences of the real American agenda.

VII

This analysis is not, however, simply a critique of the neoconservatives. It also obviously points the way to action. The strategy I propose would take advantage of every contradiction within the welfare state to win whatever gains are possible here and now. But it would also seek to transform structures, particularly the maldistribution of wealth and the use of governmental power to shape the national product according to private priorities. My ultimate aim is, *pace* Nathan Glazer, the democratization of economic power and the socialization of the private sector. For now, however, let me simply discuss a few important measures which are transitional in character, i.e., rooted in immediate and politically possible demands, yet capable of effecting some increments of change in the structure of power itself.

A guaranteed right to work. The failures of most manpower

programs in the sixties are not to be explained primarily by the difficulties of providing educational services, the unintended consequences of overly ambitious schemes, etc. They are, more than anything else, a function of the country's refusal to provide a decent job for every citizen. There are urgent needs for the human talents now being squandered in unemployment and underemployment, particularly in the nonprofit sector. The Emergency Employment Act of 1971 was much too narrow, underfinanced, temporary, etc. That is to say, it bore all the marks of President Nixon's effort to make it as inadequate as possible. Yet in some areas it did prove that Washington can act effectively to fund useful jobs. It now needs to be generalized, or rather turned into a fundamental principle of the society: that federally financed work will be provided, sometimes as a first resort and sometimes as a last resort, but always and automatically in the case of need, so that every employable worker has a job.

Such legislation would entail a certain danger of inflation by tightening up the labor market, a risk that is infinitely more acceptable than the reality of chronic joblessness since the passage of the Employment Act of 1946. In part, the inflationary effect will be offset by increased productivity—by the fact that unused human resources will be put to work producing valuable goods and services that people want, in housing, health, education, and the like. In part, an inflationary tendency must be recognized as an inherent, but manageable, problem in any full-employment economy (Joan Robinson says that Keynes himself understood this point a generation ago.) Therefore, on this count, as on many others, there must be an incomes policy.

Incomes policy is an area in which the pessimistic analysis of this essay has been, alas, confirmed every time. In England, for instance, it was first proposed by the left wing of the Labour party as a means of redistributing wealth. However, the imperatives of the capitalist economy—above all the argument that profit income is a source of further growth and therefore performs more important services than wage income, which is merely consumed—overwhelmed that excellent intention. So it is that the Labour Left and the Trade Union Congress are now bitter opponents of any kind of incomes policy. And in the United States, the unions have a similar suspicion of—but not such an implacable hostility toward—an incomes policy. There is no alternative to an incomes policy if there is to be full employment with inflation under control. That, however, means a much greater invasion of "management prerogatives" than has as yet been undertaken. Price and investment and profit and dividend decisions must become a matter of public debate and determination. The Internal Revenue Code must be transformed from an instrument of negative redistribution, placing greater burdens on the working people than on the rich, to a means of positive redistribution. In particular, and here I simply restate an excellent principle introduced in the 1972 campaign by George McGovern, there should be a positive and systematic bias against all forms of unearned income: capital gains, dividends, interest, etc.

Even such a program is too cautious, in danger of being subverted by private economic power. Take the common corporate practice of concealing profit income. Big business already spends millions in order to conceal billions and, with an effective incomes policy, it would be motivated to become even more wily and evasive. In the 1973 Report of the Council of Economic Advisers, for instance, one reads of how the profit percentages of nonfinancial corporate monies dropped from 22.1 percent in 1950 to a mere 10.6 percent in 1971. The Council was lending a helpful scholarly hand to the companies who want to plead poor mouth. However the same table indicates that "capital consumption allowances" went from 5.7 percent to 10.7 percent. In 1972, those capital consumption allowances were worth $67.7 billion—compared with after-tax profits of $52.6 billion. These enormous increases in capital consumption allowances reflect the various credits and depreciation gimmicks of the Kennedy, Johnson, and Nixon administrations. A good part of that $67.7 billion in 1972 represents hidden profits (when, for example, actual depreciation is not at all as rapid as the legal rate of accelerated depreciation, a point which Philip Stern, among others, has documented).

In short, the institutional prejudices of the tax system, of the legal system, and of the accounting profession lean toward the falsification of unearned income statistics and profit rates. So, in addition to changes in the tax code, there must be major transformations in the status of the corporation, all of them toward making it a more "transparent" and publicly accountable institution. Specifically, there should be both public and employee members on the board of directors of all major companies, with funds for expert assistance to aid them in representing the consumer and worker interest—and in systematically betraying management "secrets" as a matter of principle.

If there were a guaranteed right to work and an effective incomes policy, then there could be a realistic *Guaranteed Annual Income.* Almost all of the difficulties attendant upon Nixon's Family Assistance Plan would disappear if the context were thus dramatically altered. If the "working poor" were abolished as a category by the operation of a full-employment policy, then one could provide a decent minimum for the dependent poor who are not in the labor market. In doing this, one is not going to solve all the human problems which collect under the title of "welfare." The 300,000 black women and children added to the poverty figures in 1972, and the hundreds of thousands who had arrived there before them, are going to constitute a tragic, difficult challenge for some time to come. But at least we can put a federally established floor under misery.

Medical care is another area in which it is not the limitations of our social intelligence but the perversity of our politics that stops us from action. The Kennedy-Griffith bill is not, alas, socialized medicine; it does not establish a single medical system in America, collectively paid for, with access determined solely by medical need and a maximum of individual choice for doctor and patient. But it is a gigantic step forward, with the great merit of substituting group and preventive medicine for fee-for-service medicine. It has been criticized by the keepers of liberal moderation, the Brookings Institution, as being too radical, which I regard as a substantial point in its favor. (Those Brookings analyses of the Budget are certainly invaluable, but not, as some liberals and editorialists seem to think, holy writ. They are written from the viewpoint of decent and humane Kennedy-Johnson liberals, which means that they are infinitely superior to the proposals from the Nixon administration—but also inadequate.)

Housing is somewhat more problematic. The housing project is a genuine example of a liberal idea whose unintended consequences were more important than its good intentions. Moreover, we know from the experience of George Romney and the federal subsidy of rental and home ownership (the "234" and "235" programs) that the private market is not an answer, since it will, given the least opportunity, fleece both the public and the poor. We also know that the Joint Economic Committee has computed that the 1971 subsidies to private home ownership, disproportionately allocated to the wealthy and their mansions rather than the workers and their bungalows, were on the order of $12 billion.

New cities and new towns are possible. These have been built in Scandinavia, England, and, to cite the depressing American example, in Florida where Disney World utilizes some of the most innovating ideas in urban design for its profits. Why not do the same thing for social purposes throughout the United States?

In all of this I do not claim access to some secret solution to all of our ills. But I do think that the evidence demonstrates that there are areas—most particularly, full employment, income tax reform, incomes policy, guaranteed income, medicine, and more problematically housing—where this country can act. In my analysis, and in the conclusions based upon it, there is a common assumption I share with the neoconservatives: that social reality is counterintuitive. They take this to mean that the organic complexities of this reality are such as to frustrate any government impious enough to intrude upon them. I take it to mean that the reality of society is expressed neither in its formal declarations, even when they are liberal, nor in some organic providence, but in a system of power that is man-made. They therefore look for the causes of the recent failures of the welfare state in the fundamental limitations of the human condition. I see them as a result of a hidden agenda which follows the priorities of private wealth. They therefore think that the revolution of these times will moderate itself if only we aspire less; I am convinced that the revolution is going to take place, willy-nilly, and that the only hope we have is to take control of it.

In this conflict, there is a disagreement over the welfare state. They take it as a given and largely ignore its influence upon the failures they decry. I regard it as a transitional social phenomenon, perched midway between the laissez faire past and the collectivist future. It could serve as the first step toward a society of authoritarian and corporate collectivism in which the Richard Nixons of this world would use the techniques that the Left initiated for the purposes of the Right; it might be a bridge toward a society in which people will actually control the state that directs the economy.

Insofar as the abstract and unhistorical view of the welfare state propounded by the neoconservatives persuades us to timidity and acquiescence, it is not preparing the way for the miraculous resurrection of *Gemeinschaft*. It is, for all the decency and intelligence of its proponents, unwittingly doing the work of the reactionaries who will have unchallenged dominance over the collectivism of the twenty-first century, if once the people are persuaded that they are impotent.

Bernard Rosenberg and
Irving Howe

Are American Jews
Turning Toward
the Right?

The question persists. In both Jewish organizational and nonor-
ganizational circles—left, right, and center, secularist and
religious—there are tentative discussions, occasionally elated
but mostly troubled: Has the traditional American Jewish commitment to liberalism been weakened in recent years? Are the
Jews becoming more conservative as they grow more affluent?
Or is it those Jews who are *not* affluent that become more
conservative? And if such trends exist, what are we to make of
them?

There has always been a small number of conservative Jewish
intellectuals in America. A few write for the *National Review;* a
few others, at the Jewish Theological Seminary, have been trying
to work out a coherent conservative position. The influence of
such people is small in general, smaller still within the Jewish
world. Whatever conservatism there has been among American
Jews has generally been indigenous and nonideological, rooted

in sentiments of religious orthodoxy, and seldom requiring the ministrations of secular intellectuals. Similarly, there has been a Republican vote among American Jews, in the early years of this century a national majority, after the 1930s a decided minority. Whatever its social meaning, this vote has not seemed to require much intellectual justification.

The overwhelming thrust of Jewish thought and writing in America these past several decades has been liberal, notably more so than in the population at large; and whatever radicalism we have had in America has found disproportionate support among Jews.

Now, some people say, all this is changing. But the evidence anyone can muster for (or against) this impression is very tentative. If a major change is indeed taking place, then we are in the midst of it—never a good vantage point for historical perspective. There are some signs of a rightward turn among Jewish intellectuals, but how extensive this is and, more important, to what extent it reflects widely based changes among American Jews is a matter for speculation.

One sign is the recent evolution of *Commentary,* which under the editorship of Norman Podhoretz, and with the help of Milton Himmelfarb, has been conducting a fierce campaign not only against the New Left (or its shattered remnants) but also against some of the ideas traditionally associated with socialism, social democracy, and even liberalism. Irritable and overreaching as this campaign has been, its thrust has thus far seemed not so much toward a conservative ideology as against recent versions of what Podhoretz takes to be vulgarizations of liberalism. What we have been witnessing here is a collective tightening-up of exradical Jewish intellectuals who wish to keep the liberal community within the "centrist" camp of such politicians as Hubert Humphrey and Scoop Jackson; who are impatient with proposals for social changes that go much beyond the present limits of the welfare state; who have become skeptical about the possibility or desirability of governmental social action; and who are inclined to see connections between the left-liberal New Politics and the authoritarian excesses of the New Left. All this may be symptomatic of, or contribute to, a burgeoning Jewish conservatism but certainly does not yet comprise it. To what extent *Commentary* reflects growing sentiments within the Jewish community, or to what extent it runs counter to the dominant sentiments of that community, no one really seems to know.

The closest to a coherent effort at developing an ideology for a new Jewish conservatism is in the writings of Milton Himmelfarb—yet we are not quite certain that Himmelfarb himself would accept this designation, since one of the most curious aspects of his polemics is that, even while assaulting traditional liberal "fallacies," he fiercely "defends" American Jews against charges that they have become less liberal. He betrays a touching, sometimes delicious ambivalence on this matter: as if to say the liberals with their defense of quotas, their evasion of black anti-Semitism, their indifference to Jewish needs, are poison for the Jews, yet don't let me catch anyone suggesting that we aren't as good liberals as we used to be. Himmelfarb has recently brought his writings together in a book, *The Jews of Modernity,* which merits the attention of anyone interested in these matters.[1]

Still, it would be exaggerating to say that even he offers a sustained statement of Jewish conservatism. Perhaps all that "Jewish conservatism" consists of right now is a growing disillusionment with liberalism. Perhaps it will take another decade before a distinctive Jewish rationale for conservatism emerges. Meanwhile, it may not be presumptuous to offer a few summary points of the thrust toward a Jewish conservatism, as these can be gleaned from Himmelfarb's book, in *Commentary*'s pages, and elsewhere:

The notion that Jews are by centuries-long tradition a people of liberal inclination is a parochial error, the consequence of ignorance of Jewish history. Before the Enlightenment, Jewish attitudes toward politics were essentially static, detached, and conservative.

The argument that it is "good for the Jews" that they be on the side of social change is manifestly wrong or, at the least, much too simple. Anti-Semitism flourishes in most of the European Communist countries; it has been shown to be deeply entangled with radical ideologies; it took powerful hold of the New Left here and abroad. On the contrary: Jewish survival is closely dependent on social stability, order, and moderation.

The "universalist" outlook of modern, secular, and progressivist Jews is a moral and practical disaster. It disarms the Jews as an ethnic group that must adjust itself to, and sometimes enter combat against, other ethnic groups. It is an outlook quick to offer sympathy to all other groups—blacks, chicanos, Puerto Ricans, homosexuals, radical students—all except the Jews themselves, who are asked, in the name of their "traditions," to make unreasonable and masochistic "sacrifices."

Now, it would be mere polemical excess to deny that in this cluster of propositions one can find some nuggets of truth. The Communist countries have shown themselves to be hospitable to, and sometimes actively employing, anti-Semitism. "The Jewish tradition," as an alleged foundation of liberalism, is a delusion, since there are many and conflicting Jewish traditions, contemporary liberalism seems to have little genuine linkage with the "prophetic Judaism" it sometimes invokes, and most efforts to improvise such a linkage are mere frivolous conveniences. And there is good reason for dropping a certain kind of bleached universalism favored among "progressive" Jews in America. This much out of the way, let us now turn to an examination of some recent trends in American Jewish life that may prompt a drift toward conservatism.

II

That most American Jews are economically better off than heretofore in this century is a fact. Many of them have moved into the middle- and upper-middle class. The Jewish poor, "the Other Jews" whose visibility is even lower than that of "the Other America," are still with us, and estimates of their number steadily grow as they are rediscovered. The very rich, the Jewish millionaires, who were but a sliver before are no doubt a larger sliver now. But since World War II, there is no longer a proletarian majority even among immigrant Jews, and the bulk of the Jews in America is clearly middle class, with a large proportion of professionals and academics. Most likely, American Jews feel a little more secure and less "peculiar" than ever before.

With upward mobility and a high degree of cultural assimilation has come a remarkable redefinition: Jews who constitute a tiny numerical group are increasingly taken to be part of the majority. The very novelty of this transformation of status can unnerve those who are its beneficiaries, and sometimes serves to veil still-painful disabilities to which Jews are subject, e.g., subtle kinds of economic and social discrimination. With the vicissitudes of their long history, the Jews have been prepared for almost anything but to be taken as part of the dominant "majority." Perhaps this is a blessing prematurely bestowed.

At the same time—and surely, to one or another extent, because of their sense that they remain a group incompletely absorbed, one that never *can* be fully absorbed, into American society—the American Jews have persisted in their overwhelming commitment to political liberalism. When one comes to think of it, this is a remarkable fact. The Jews seem to be the only ethnic community in the United States in which significant numbers of people, though they rise rapidly in socioeconomic condition, do not change—or at least until recently have not changed—their political views. A consistent, often intense alignment with liberalism characterizes the politics of American Jews since at least World War I, even, it should be stressed, when that alignment seems to threaten the immediate interests of some or many Jews. It is hardly a secret that the number of Jews active in liberal, protest, radical, and civil libertarian movements is highly disproportionate. Traditional sentiments play a stronger role here than social class, at least so far.

On what has this commitment to liberalism been based? On at least two factors: the powerful tradition of secular Jewish socialism, very strong in the earlier decades of the century, now fading but still felt and remembered, and sometimes affecting younger people who do not know the historical forces that are working upon them; and the premise, shared by many Jews for perhaps two centuries, that Jewish survival and interests are best served by an open society promoting social justice. The whole question of the supposed new conservatism among American Jews boils down to whether these factors, and others linked to them, still continue to operate.

But before turning to that question, we should note another basic fact about the life of American Jews, indeed, Jews in most parts of the world during the post-Holocaust years: it is a life inherently "schizoid." At home, sharp improvements in condition, a leap forward socially, economically. Internationally, the greatest horror in human history, the extermination of six million Jews, with consequent feelings of guilt, fright, shame, and sentiments of apocalypse. How can these two elements of Jewish experience be reconciled? They cannot; and anyone who feels the slightest sense of Jewish identity must live with this doubleness as best he can. It is easy to sneer at affluent Jews who go to their expensive Community Center to hear lectures on the Holocaust; but it is cheap and foolish to sneer at them, for whatever may seem discordant in their behavior is also discordant in the behavior of everyone else. Nor should it be supposed that "ordinary Jews" who go about their daily life, running their business or working at their professions, have forgotten the Holocaust. Perhaps their children have, but *they* have not. What to do or say about the Holocaust they hardly know, any more than do the rest of us; but the stubborn if residual attachment they show to Jewish "identification," their readiness to contribute large amounts of money to an astonishing variety of Jewish causes and agencies shows that they still retain a stabbing awareness of what the nature of this century has been. They remain "sensitive"—and why should they not?—to the faintest intimations of attack, and they feel that their security is always shadowed by the recurrent possibility of attack.

III

Several motifs can be isolated in the drift, insofar as there is one, toward Jewish conservatism:

(1) THERE is a growing feeling—but still, as we have suggested, qualified by historical memory—that Jewish life in America is reasonably secure, or at least *as secure as Jewish life ever can be.* Hence, it may be supposed, there follows or will in time follow a gradual decline in the felt urgency of American Jews to transcend narrow class interests and respond to universalist moral appeals. By now the Jewish middle and upper middle classes are

no longer a step away from immigrant parents and grandparents; they are two or three steps away. Rightly or wrongly, many Jews seem inclined to feel more and more "at home" in the United States; the messianic strand of Jewish sensibility (despite a remarkable outbreak in the New Left) keeps dimming within the mainstream of Jewish institutional life; the idea of *galut*, or exile, comes to be abstract, ideological, merely literary; and thereby the conclusion may be cultivated that Jews should start enjoying the luxury of responding to political events more and more "like ordinary Americans," that is, in accord with their individual socioeconomic, or class, interests. At the time of the last presidential election, it was said that some of the Jews switching to Nixon who justified their stand—it had, be it noted, still to be *justified*—in the name of Israeli security were "really" alarmed by the possibility that McGovern, if elected, would raise their taxes. How can one test such a proposition? How can one know that appeals to Jewish interest are "merely" a veil for a drift into affluent conservatism? And, for that matter, why must one choose?—since it seems likely that both motives operated together, in an all but inextricable mixture of group solidarity and personal interest.

The trend we are discussing here is, at most, a long-range one, and before it could be established as a reality, there would have to be maintained in the coming few elections the moderate Jewish shift toward the Republicans, as well as evidence offered that this shift has been particularly strong among wealthy Jews. Those who stress the likelihood that such a trend is taking shape feel that the Jews will not long continue to be an ethnic group that responds more to moral-universalistic appeals than to perceptions of class or group interest. But at least one major complication should be noted: the disproportionate number of Jews concentrated in the professions, academic life, and the communications industries (influential in national life if not always within the Jewish community) tends to remain committed to liberal and universalistic values.[2] They don't, as a rule, see their "class interests" as being linked with the political Right; indeed, they like to think they are superior to considerations of "class interest." And they don't respond very much to appeals, whether authentic or spurious, for Jewish solidarity.

If, then, the drift toward becoming more "like the others" continues—and to an undeterminable extent, we believe there is such a drift—then the rise of an influential segment of Jewish professionals and academics may help retard it.

(2) TOGETHER WITH this drift toward becoming more "like the others," and surely to some extent for linked reasons, there has also taken place a slow but inexorable decline of the Jewish labor movement. The consequences for Jewish life in America, and also, by the way, for socialists in America, are enormous.

Once an inspiring force for radical and secularist sentiment, the Jewish unions have become more moderate, sometimes conservative, with the passage of the years. A good number of them remain Jewish only at the level of their top leadership: thin layers of social democratic veterans. Few, if any, of the Jewish unions still have a majority of Jewish members: it is estimated, for instance, that less than 20 percent of the Amalgamated Clothing Workers' membership remains Jewish. Within a decade or two, such unions as the ACW and the ILGWU will have to undergo extreme transformations in leadership and sociopolitical orientation. The Jewish working class is shrinking, aging, dying off, losing its élan. Some Jewish labor groups seem more responsive to injustices in the Soviet Union than injustices at home: on certain issues the American Jewish Committee, once the stronghold of conservative German Jews, now takes a more liberal position than the Jewish Labor Committee, which reflects the views of the leaders of the Jewish garment unions.

In short, the traditional Jewish social democracy is leaving the scene and, with it, the Yiddishist-secularist tradition. The loss will be, already is, enormous—for the Jewish world, for whatever remains of American socialism, perhaps for intellectual life. Young people who experience vague yearnings to discover a "Jewish identity" are now rarely inclined to turn toward Jewish socialism or Jewish unionism, both of which have lost a good part of their vitality; they turn elsewhere, to religious improvisations, communal experiments, quasi-Hasidic retreats, a renewed interest in East European Jewish life.

And because the Jewish social democracy keeps fading, both in numbers and intensity, there occurs within the Jewish community a growth in the relative strength of Jewish orthodoxy, for by contrast the religious minority (e.g., the Hasidim in Brooklyn) retains some coherence, some passion, some strength of conviction. Politically, this often leads toward a reinforcement of conservative tendencies within the Jewish world.

(3)   THE PREVIOUS TWO TRENDS operate over an extended period of time, and if they have recently been felt more keenly in Jewish life, it is partly because of an accumulation of their effects and partly because more immediate causes of the conservative drift tend to bring these effects into play. For the last six or seven years a body of sentiment has been growing among many American Jews, especially those living in large cities such as New York and Philadelphia, that if, within the relative security of American life, there is indeed a threat to Jewish well-being, it comes mainly from below. Or, to be blunt about it, this threat comes from urban blacks who in the schools, a few industries, and some unions are pressing to undo Jewish positions and accomplishments—pressing, especially, to undermine the merit system that has made possible Jewish positions and accomplishments.

The possibility of black anti-Semitism has startled American Jews. If they know their past at all, they know about peasants, workers, and the lower orders being stirred up to commit pogroms. Cossacks, peasants in their rural idiocy, workers without consciousness, a mass of ignoramuses: these the higher-ups could manipulate to make the Jews into a scapegoat. That a similar process of manipulation, rage, and befuddlement could occur among American blacks did not seem, until recently, a conceivable course.

The American Negroes have served as a kind of buffer for American Jews. So long as deep-seated native resentments and hatreds were taken out primarily on blacks, they were less likely to be taken out on Jews. If Jews have been the great obsession of Christianity, blacks have been the great obsession of America. And as long as this condition obtained, both organized and spontaneous haters in America concentrated on blacks, and only secondarily on Jews.

Had Jews felt themselves to be part of "the white majority" and had they followed a mere crude calculus of self-interest, they might have joined other whites in holding nonwhites down. A few Jews did, of course, but the majority set itself up as an ally of the blacks, at times just about the only stable ally they had. Jews whose collective imagery was filled with the time they were "slaves unto Pharaoh in Egypt" could sympathize with former slaves in the New World. Smarting under prejudice themselves, often committed to radical and universalist goals, feeling a kinship—if, sometimes, a rather abstract one—with oppressed blacks, the Jews shared in the fight for civil rights.

The civil rights movement, as it arose in the 1960s, had exceptionally variegated components. At its height, organized labor, Catholic and Protestant church leaders, idealistic youth, and a liberal Administration coalesced around the person of Martin Luther King and his principle of nonviolence. At this time the Negro-Jewish partnership was closest. Jews who had "made it" set out to help blacks who had not.

As Southern segregation crumbled, blacks poured into Northern ghettos where they soon ran up against a complex of thus far unsolved problems: the backlash of neighboring white ethnic groups, the social-cultural traumas of adjusting to urban life, the economic deprivations of ghetto life in the North; and, perhaps most of all, the shock of discovering that they remained, even after their recent victories, a group still discriminated against, still suffering internal disruption and pathology, still overwhelmed by a heritage of centuries of oppression.

King lived to hear himself hissed by his own comrades, derided as "de Lawd," put down as an Uncle Tom. Black power, black separatism, black nationalism were growing before his assassination, but that event dramatized the end of integration as a common goal of American blacks. Thereupon the Negro-Jewish alliance approached collapse. The "Black Revolution," stronger in subjective expressiveness than objective results, expelled whites from its ranks. Very often that meant Jews.

Brewton Berry, a sociologist who specializes in race relations, remarks that

> On the one hand, the Jews are a notoriously [sic] liberal group, harboring less anti-Negro feeling than gentiles. . . .

Negroes, for their part, have often expressed a great admiration for the Jews, and frankly envy them their success
in overcoming the obstacles which have been placed in their
path.

On the other hand, continues Berry,

Anti-Semitism among Negroes has recently become a matter of some concern. It has been especially virulent in the
cities of the North . . . Negroes have engaged in boycotts of
Jewish establishments, have disseminated anti-Semitic
propaganda, have published vicious sheets like *Dynamite*
and *Negro Youth*. . . . [—Brewton Berry, *Race and Ethnic
Relations*—(Boston: Houghton Mifflin, 1965) p. 355.]

How widespread this anti-Semitism has been in the black
community remains a question, indeed, a crucial question. No
one seems to know with any exactitude, though some recent
studies indicate it is less widespread among blacks than among
white gentiles. But it is beyond question that anti-Semitism has
appeared at least on the more "radical" fringes of some black
movements, among the Black Panthers and groups dedicated to
"Third World Solidarity." Even our Jerry Rubins and Abbie
Hoffmans, who professed their allegiance to El Fatah, have been
rejected as Zionists by the Panthers, though they, as Marie Syr-
kin has pointed out, earned that designation as little as did the
Polish Jewish Communists who were expelled from the party.
    Soon enough, a number of American Jews would begin to
emulate the blacks. If black is beautiful, Jewish would be exquis-
ite. The Pandora's box of ethnicity was opened wide, for good
and/or bad. Lower-class Jews found allies in portions of the
organizational Jewish intelligentsia, the rabbinate, and
chauvinist ideologues—all together to proclaim an ethnic consciousness that fell easily enough into a *ressentiment* conducive to
hostility or at least suspicion of other groups.
    It is crucial to note that many American Jews still *feel* like
losers, and being able to buy a private home, or send kids to
college, or move into a suburb isn't quickly going to remove that
feeling. Black antagonism—whether deep-rooted or, as seems

more probable, the verbal upchuck of an enraged fringe—is linked in their minds with global anti-Semitism and the enmity of Arabs toward Israel. Personal fright on the streets, poor public schools, a meritocracy in decline—all merge psychically with the precariousness of Israel and the mortification of Soviet Jewry. Who can easily separate in such reactions the warranted concern from the "paranoid" excess?

With such fears there go urgent and painful, but completely real, problems of social friction between adjacent black and Jewish communities, the latter almost always composed of older and poorer Jews less inclined to articulate liberalism and more concerned with group survival and personal safety.

Consider, for just a moment, the problem of crime. Jews, as well as other whites, tend by now to see it as linked to the problem of blacks. That much of the crime among black youth is related to the pathology of drugs—and also, perhaps, to the rage that followed upon the discovery that the revolution of rising expectations would not be followed by a revolution of rising gratifications; that most of the victims of black crimes are themselves black; that, in some distorted way, even the ability to release this rage in antisocial acts indicates a gradual psychic freeing of blacks from earlier postures of submissiveness (though at great cost to both their immediate possibilities and their inner morale); that pathologies in the black community constitute a price for historical injustices such as no other group in America has ever had to pay—all this is true, important, urgent.

But it provides no immediate answer—perhaps none can be had—to the aging or retired Jewish garment worker or small shopkeeper in Crown Heights or the Bronx who is terribly frightened of being mugged, and often with good reason. One result is the rise of such demagogic types as Jerry Birbach, the redneck who inflamed every sensitive Jewish nerve in the Forest Hills struggle of 1972. Another result is a visible and distressing decline of sympathetic feeling among Jews toward the blacks —in some instances it almost seems as if the outbreak of marginal anti-Semitism among blacks serves as an occasion, or pretext, for the withdrawal of social generosity.

The painfulness of this problem is almost beyond imagining. Can we be indifferent to the agonies of blacks in this moment of transition? Can we be indifferent to the fears of Jews side-swiped in the course of that transition? And can we suppose that even the most humane and judicious consideration of all the elements in this clash could possibly lead to a quick and easy solution? The one thing it seems crucial to say is that such problems cannot be solved by local measures, though they may be eased by them or aggravated (as they sometimes were by the Lindsay administration, in its occasional high-minded ineptitude). What brings blacks and poor Jews into conflict is a combination of social difficulties as these rub painfully against both groups: difficulties ranging from bitter competition over scarce housing to enraged confrontations in poor schools. And these social difficulties can be removed, or at least significantly diminished, only through the kinds of large-scale measures that presuppose federal action. Of that, we have no signs.

It therefore seems likely that those Jews still trapped in poor or semislum neighborhoods will react toward their fears by turning, especially in local elections, to figures like Abe Beame—not toward ideological conservatives but simply mediocre politicians who promise what they may not be able to deliver: a return to earlier conditions of festering calm.

(4) DISENCHANTMENT over Communist anti-Semitism both in Russia and the East European countries has, for a segment of the older, "progressive-minded" or fellow-traveling Jews, been traumatic. If this has not led directly to conservative ideas, it has certainly encouraged conservative moods. For many in the once-influential segment of Yiddish-speaking workers in or close to the Stalinist movement, the series of events that begins with the Moscow Trials, continues through the Hitler-Stalin pact, and ends with the harassment of Jews who wish to emigrate from the Soviet Union—this series of events has had a chilling impact comparable to the dismay and disorientation that beset East European Jews in the 18th century after the collapse of the false messianic movements of Sabbatai Zevi and Jacob Frank. Intensifying such responses has been the flirtation of a portion of the New Left with Arab terrorism: it takes no great powers of imagination to conjure up the feelings of Jews when they see Jewish students collecting funds for El Fatah! As for those Jews

who never were in or near the radical milieu, Soviet anti-Semitism often brings about a generalized revulsion against all forms of radicalism, even liberalism. The '60s were not a decade that encouraged the making of distinctions.

(5) AMERICAN JEWS, apart from minuscule fringe groups, feel a deep involvement with Israel: this holds true for conservatives and socialists, believers and secularists, assimilationists and Yiddishists. Israel, they feel, is the one glory salvaged from a century of horror. And even Jews critical of Israel on one or another count, as we are, strongly share this feeling—a feeling that the Yom Kippur War only made seem more urgent.

Yet the paradox that must be recognized is that insofar as Israel functions—must function—as a state dealing with other states, its impact upon American Jews is—perhaps must be —conservative. That the Israeli government is a Laborite government, and that its prime minister attends conferences of the Socialist International, does not significantly change things. What we are talking about is political necessity, at least necessity as the leaders of Israel make their calculations for survival: it has little or nothing to do with the sentiments of Golda Meir or anyone else.

The Israelis, concerned primarily with their survival—and who is to tell them they are wrong?—find it necessary, as a state, to take a "pragmatic" attitude toward international arrangements of power. They feel, in effect, that their survival depends on American help; they have received, thus far, significant help from the Nixon administration; they were ready to pay for this help with declarations supporting the American role in Vietnam, some merely *pro forma* but others arising out of a "tough-minded" *Weltanschauung* that some Israeli figures, both in and out of the government, have begun to adopt.

Some American Jews now ask not, "Is it good for the Jews?" but, "Is it good for Israel?" Such people worried about Nixon's abandonment of Taiwan, not because they admired Chiang Kai-shek but because they feared it might presage abandonment of Israel—perhaps as part of an overall retreat to "isolationism" or, what is more likely, an effort to strike a deal with the oil-producing Arab countries.

It is betraying no secrets to report that in 1972 intimations came from at least some Israeli officials: "Nixon is our friend and we want him to remain in office. Nothing matters more to us than military aid from the U.S. We ask you, as supporters of Israel, to subordinate any other concern." How many Jews, either within or, more important, apart from the declining Zionist movement, responded to such intimations we cannot say; indeed, we have the impression that some Jews acted in accord with this position *without needing to be told* that it was held by influential Israelis. (To complicate matters, there were Israelis who winked approval of Jewish intellectuals supporting McGovern: perhaps out of genuine sympathy, perhaps out of embarrassment, perhaps to hedge their bets.)

When the Israeli ambassador in Washington made his political preferences a little too clear, he was admonished to stop by important American Jewish leaders. They feared his actions might be taken as gratuitous interference in domestic affairs. They may also have thought those actions would be counter-productive: Golda Meir's *sotto voce* endorsement of Nixon (bestowed upon him in this surreal world together with those of Mao and Brezhnev) might hurt his chances of winning . . . or reinforce suspicions of "dual loyalty."

In this complex of circumstances, American Jews could hardly avoid being torn by fierce tensions. Although only a tiny fraction belongs to the Zionist movement, Jews are, mostly, Zionists in some loose way. Except for a small minority of zealots, most American Jews who reflect upon such matters are quite prepared to recognize the possibility that serious conflicts may arise between their concern for Israel (which, if more than quixotic, *must* take into account its *Realpolitik* calculations) and their interests as Jews in America and American citizens.[3] Indeed, some of the Zionist leaders themselves recognize the probability of an *inherent* clash between a state and the universalistic movement (Zionism) attached to yet distinct from it.

The obligation to defend Israel collides with an equal obligation to maintain a certain distance from Israeli policy, lest Jews, Zionist or not, look a little like those American Communists who never deviate from the Kremlin line. Zionism, to be sure, was never close to being monolithic; its fractiousness is reflected every day in the Knesset. Yet there remain the realities of state-craft, and these evidently clash with the Labor Zionist ideology.

Speaking of this situation, Judah Shapiro, a leader of Ameri-can Labor Zionism, has remarked that two major consequences follow for American Zionism from its close identification with the State of Israel:

1. pragmatism and consensus replaced ideology and polemic;

2. the instrumentality for raising funds also became the arbiter for the allocation of funds; philosophies and pro-grams became beneficiaries and pleaders; fund raisers and large contributors became governors and leaders. [—Judah Shapiro, "The Assignment Was the Future," *Jewish Frontier*, December, 1972.]

This is diplomatically put, but it makes the point. Within the American Jewish world, the full-time fund-raiser and the *nouveau riche* donor swing a lot of weight, maybe more than old Labor Zionist comrades who did not go to Israel. . . . There follows a certain depoliticization of organized Jewish life in America, a weakening not only of Zionism or Labor Zionism but of *all* movements and causes. (This process, be it noted in passing, is of considerable duration, going back to a decision by Ben Gurion to weaken the position of Zionists in the West vis à vis those who were running the state of Israel.) And insofar as this signals a banking of old fires, the atmosphere of American Jewish life becomes a little more amenable, if not to ideological conservatism then to moods, compromises, resignations that serve as well.

The problem is galling. Some of us who are warm supporters of Israel had to say in 1972: "We are going to vote for McGovern because we think it would be best for the United States if he defeated Nixon [there seems recently to have accumulated a certain amount of evidence for this view] and because we also think that a McGovern victory will not harm Israel." On the first of these propositions, Israelis might not care to argue; on the second, the skepticism some had about our judgment was not simply to be dismissed. Politics is hard.

IV

It is only natural, in trying to estimate a Jewish drift toward conservatism, to turn to election results; but these prove to be uncertain and contradictory in character, perhaps because elections cannot be assumed to be precise registers of political sentiment and perhaps because Jewish political attitudes have become uncertain and contradictory.

Since 1966 is alleged to have been a turning point, let us go back to that year. What happened in 1966, "experts" keep saying, is that 55 percent of New York's Jews voted in a referendum, initiated by the Policeman's Benevolent Association, against Mayor Lindsay's newly created Civilian Review Board. This conclusion is based on a competent study by three political scientists, David W. Abbot, Louis H. Gold, and Edward T. Rogowsky. It is *not,* however, a study of how New York Jews voted. It is a comparative study of how Brooklyn Jews and Catholics, excluding Puerto Ricans, voted. This report was effusively praised by Daniel P. Moynihan in a foreword in which he could not refrain from gloating over a major liberal setback.

To left-liberal or radical Jews, as to civil libertarians, reflection on that setback is bound to be depressing. Proponents of a civilian review board considered it a channel through which blacks and Puerto Ricans might register their complaints against police brutality:

> The opponents of civilian review were organized in a coalition—Independent Citizens Committee Against Review Boards—dominated by the PBA. Its other constituents were the Conservative Party, American Legion Posts, parents' and taxpayers' groups, the Brooklyn Bar Association and the John Birch Society. Support for the board came from an impressive number of civic, labor, civil rights, and religious groups, organized into the Federated Associations for Impartial Review (FAIR), directed largely by the New York Civil Liberties Union and volunteers. [—Abbot, Gold

& Rogowsky, *Police Politics and Race* (New York: American Jewish Committee, 1969), p. 7.]

Then 63 percent, or 1,313,161, voted against the Board and 765,468 for it. In the Brooklyn sample of 374 whites who were interviewed, the religious breakdown was as follows: Protestant, 70.6; Catholic, 83.1; Jewish, 55.1.

> Among Catholics, ethnic extraction, education, and occupation were weak indicators of CRB sentiment, whereas among Jews both education and occupation appeared to be equally potent. Highly educated Jewish professionals overwhelmingly supported CRB, while poorly educated lower-class Jewish workers strongly opposed it.

We have no reason to doubt the validity of these findings; they dovetail with other, softer data that have the look of reliability. Sam Yorty's victory over Tom Bradley in Los Angeles (reversed in 1973, with Jewish districts now giving strong support to Bradley) and Carl Stenvig's victory in Minneapolis in 1969 lend some credence to the idea of a conservative Jewish trend. So does the 1969 New York mayoral election where two right-wingers, Mario Procaccino and John Marchi, got three votes for every two given Lindsay. In 1971, tough and reactionary Frank Rizzo became mayor of Philadelphia. Here too we have a small-scale study, by Henry Cohen and Gary Sandrow, two investigators who did their best and admit it is inadequate:

> The available data are limited in scope and accuracy. First, in some parts of the city no predominantly Jewish division could be found. Second, the most recent Jewish population survey is over three years old, and was never meant to be definitive or rigorously accurate. And finally, the U.S. Census Bureau has not yet released the 1970 figures on income and age.

All of which throws some light on the pitfalls of such research. Nevertheless, the Philadelphia story, insofar as Cohen and Sandrow can reconstruct it, is the Los Angeles and New York story all over again. The Jewish vote split along class lines, with lower income groups going mainly for Rizzo and upper income groups for his liberal Republican opponent. The Jews did not elect Rizzo; whites *in toto* voted around two to one for him; whereas Jews divided about fifty-fifty between Rizzo and his opponent. Cohen and Sandrow conclude:

> Jewish voters did not rush to Rizzo as did more than two out of every three non-Jewish white voters in Philadelphia; they voted for and against him in approximately even numbers. But that was not good enough for those who expected Jews—*and Jews alone*—to remain unaffected by the law and order issue [Emphasis added]. [—Henry Cohen and Gary Sandrow, *Philadelphia Chooses a Mayor, 1971* (New York: American Jewish Committee), 1972, p. 9.]

On the other hand, Cohen and Sandrow quote a Jewish leader in the 63rd Ward who had rather different expectations. Confessing that, despite his efforts, 60 percent of the Jews in that ward voted against Rizzo, he remarked: "Thank God for the *goyim.* I'm thoroughly ashamed of our Jews."

How American Jews voted in the last presidential election and in the congressional races is still an unassembled jigsaw puzzle. The polls did consistently show that neither presidential candidate was personally appealing to the voters, only 55 percent of them bothering to vote at all. American Jews ordinarily vote in greater numbers than do other citizens, but there is reason to believe that in 1972 larger numbers of them stayed away from the polls than in earlier years. By the best estimates, however, Jews remained second only to blacks in their support of McGovern. By the same estimates there was a drop in the Jewish Democratic vote of about 15 to 17 percent between 1968 to 1972. Why? McGovern's alleged "isolationism" or his record on Israel; the signals from some Israelis; the appearance of a tiny but influential segment of very rich Jews in the Nixon camp; the defection of the labor movement from McGovern (though the Jewish garment unions, perhaps responding to their large black and Puerto Rican memberships, endorsed McGovern); the McGovern position on taxes; the kind of chic celebrities who supported McGovern and could be identified by middle- or lower-class Jews as the kind who had supported Lindsay; the appearance of a group of Jewish intellectuals, mostly exradical, who supported Nixon on the bizzare ground that he was the more "prudent" of the two candidates—take your pick. All probably counted as contributing factors, but what no one knows is the relative weights to assign to them. It does seem clear, however, that the slippage in the Jewish Democratic vote was centered in the poorer, less-educated, and more religious urban segments. So there is at least a mini-trend.

At this point it would be well to acknowledge some anomalies, perhaps confusions. If it is true that in the main the wealthier, better-educated Jews are those who vote liberal most heavily, what then happens to the view suggested earlier in this essay, that the process of settling into American affluence may gradually undermine the traditional Jewish commitment to liberalism? And for that matter, if it is the wealthier and better-educated Jews who vote liberal, then, since Jews are by and large becoming both more affluent and better-educated, it ought to follow that the Jews as a whole are also becoming more liberal.

Perhaps one difficulty in such entanglements has to do with the phrase "more liberal." Such a phrase has no single, precise meaning, only a cluster of imprecise and at times contradictory meanings. Perhaps, while the majority of Jews remains committed to liberalism, it is to a liberalism increasingly "moderate" and conservatized, the kind represented by Senator Jackson rather than by Senator McGovern. It may be that while the general commitment to liberalism persists, the intensity with which it is held or the readiness to expend energy and experience inconvenience in its behalf gradually declines. And it may also be that while the Jewish middle class together with Jewish professionals and academics still vote regularly for liberal candidates, a small but crucial fraction of these groups is breaking away and turning to the Right, perhaps as a portent of things to come. Impressionistically, all of these seem to us likelihoods and thereby possible ways of coping with the difficulties we have just noted.

V

Within the Jewish world narrowly conceived, that is, within the Jewish organizational world, the theme of a possible upsurge of conservatism is often debated with regard to two problems: quotas and "parochialism." Let us glance, much too briefly, at each of these.

No issue or phrase is more likely to stir fears and anxieties among self-aware Jews than quotas: it rouses memories of exclusion from European cities and schools; it rouses memories of how hard it was for Jewish boys in America to enter medical schools. The rejection of quotas as a means of *holding down* minorities and the espousal of the merit principle according to which individuals are judged by their competence or potential, regardless of race or color—this is correct in principle, and we reaffirm it without qualification. But the application of correct principles can sometimes be very difficult, and men of good will can differ as to how it should be done. The difficulty at the moment is that quotas and "affirmative action" programs take on a new context: an effort to *help* minority groups, sometimes in disregard of the merit principle and sometimes, it is alleged, in order to realize the merit principle. The issue merits a full-scale examination, not possible here; we have no fixed or pat formula; we recommend an excellent article by Leonard Fein in *Midstream*, March 1973. Meanwhile, a few observations:

• In discussing quotas and "affirmative action," we must avoid the rhetoric of either/or. Simply to denounce quotas and say no more, is to disregard the claims and sensibilities of black spokesmen and black colleagues.

• Simply to attack quotas is to disregard, as well, the urgent and often justified feelings of minority groups that the entrenched systems of seniority in factories, and of recruitment of students and faculties in universities, are often discriminatory in practice, even though veiled by the claims of merit. So the issue is not merit vs. antimerit, but in actuality complex weighings of many factors.

• Merit is indeed a major principle, but it is not the only one. Justice, equity, recompense, minority rights: these also count. And let us remember that in a highly competitive society, like ours, it is the people on top who are most inclined to find the principle of merit a social convenience, for they are persuaded, of course, that their dominance is a consequence of merit. Tragedy occurs when two sets of standards, merit on the one hand, equity on the other, come into conflict.

• There are many situations with regard to jobs, promotions, status, etc. in which merit may be close to irrelevant, since the distribution of goods takes place, properly enough, according to other criteria.

• We have every reason to stress the differences between "affirmative action," which on the face of it merely requires universities to make special efforts to increase the number of black or female faculty members, and quotas, which set a fixed number for such an increase. To be sure, "affirmative action" can easily slide into quota, and thereby become objectionable; but sympathetic and sophisticated faculty people will take the "affirmative action" idea at face value and not simply dismiss it on the ground that it is "really" a quota.

• To what extent has "affirmative action" seriously damaged Jewish (or non-Jewish white) faculty members? The evidence is spotty and inconclusive. Paradoxically enough, it seems likely that Jewish women have profited from "affirmative action," since they comprise a rather large proportion of those academic women who have suffered discrimination. Some of the evidence brought against "affirmative action" in *Commentary* consists of absurd literalisms put forward in its name, such as an announcement that a college is looking for a black scholar to teach Hebrew. These are either a result of stupidity or of a not-so-clever attempt to discredit the whole idea. Nevertheless, it seems likely that some younger Jewish scholars have been hurt, and others may continue to be hurt, by "affirmative action."

• It is said in some quarters that black insistence on quotas or "affirmative action," when it occurs, constitutes a tacit admission that blacks cannot now compete in the universities or elsewhere on the basis of merit, or at least that not many or enough of them can. Perhaps; but to insist upon this point is to speak to black colleagues in the name of some pure realm of merit, whereas they see a decidedly impure reality in which merit has been far from dominant. And if, indeed, black spokesmen are making an admission of particularly acute difficulties, then that should prompt particularly acute kinds of help.

• There is the further fact that a formal defense of equality of opportunity can perpetuate extreme inequalities of condition, if only because of the radically different points from which competing social and racial groups start out. A hierarchy of merit, real or alleged, can end up being almost as offensive as a hierarchy of caste or status.

• Yet there is very serious ground for being disturbed by the slippage—in some instances, much worse—of academic standards in the universities which, while not caused by "affirmative action," is to some indeterminable extent encouraged by it. There is reason to be disturbed as Jews, as academics, as citizens. Black students obviously merit special consideration and need special help; but systematically to expect less of them than of white students, systematically to install a double standard of judgment is surely not to do them a service. The same holds for black faculty members. The question, then, becomes whether it is possible to compensate for an appalling history of outrage by giving blacks greater opportunities, more of the "breaks" (and in a way that is what "affirmative action" means or should mean) while at the same time holding in general to the value of merit. It would be fatuous to suppose that this is always possible, and in a given instance, it may be necessary to make painful choices. The situation is one that requires a complicated balancing of values that are sometimes in conflict.

• Leonard Fein, in the above-mentioned article, describes an historical incident in which Histadrut, the labor federation of Israel, used a quota system—it would appear, then, that the Jewish position on this matter has not been so inflexible after all, or more to the point, that there has been no *single* Jewish position. Word now comes to us from Israel that the ruling Labor party has recently put into effect a variety of quotas for its electoral candidates—25 percent women, 20 percent under 35, 33 percent Jews from Moslem countries. Speaking in behalf of the quota for women, Golda Meir said:

> In a free egalitarian society, there should be no need for a legal defense of the woman's position. Her place should be achieved on merit only, irrespective of sex. But in view of the present reality, better be ashamed that we have to pass such rulings than not pass them. [Cited in *John Herling's Newsletter*, Sept. 4, 1973.]

That this version of the quota system is used in Israel does not, of course, necessarily make it right; but at the least it ought to subdue the righteousness and soften the rhetoric of those in America who have made opposition to quotas into a symbol of "Jewish self-respect."

THE INWARD TURN of at least a segment of the Jewish community, with the attendant slogan, "let's take care of our own," is paralleled by similar turns among both white and black ethnic groups; and except for apostles of abstract internationalism (Jews who often find it possible to praise the ethnicity of all groups but their own), few commentators would be foolish enough to celebrate or denounce such a turn without qualification. There is, among the Jews, the complex inward turn of a thinker like Ben Halpern and the simplistic inward turn of a demagogue like Meier Kahane. There are those who say that, while remaining faithful to the tradition of universalist justice, they feel it necessary to emphasize Jewish rights at a time when these are threatened at certain points and systematically scoffed at by young "progressivist" Jews; and there are those who say that all the talk about universalist justice is rubbish, and that the Jews have to fight for their own turf.

The trend toward particularism in the Jewish world has already encountered some powerful critics. Dr. Nahum Goldman, head of the World Jewish Congress,

> warned that Jews, having become prosperous and influential in the world, are in danger of forgetting their timeless Jewish ideals . . . the tendencies [he said] which are developing, especially within American Jewry, which would have the Jewish people limit its problems and activities for its own benefit and which renounces the universal character of our national and religious ideals, are an indication of the dangers. . . . [—Jewish Telegraphic Agency, July 6, 1973.]

What Dr. Goldman says comes from on high, and within Israeli politics he leans toward the center-right; it takes more courage to say the same thing in Forest Hills, Jerry Birbach country. Rabbi Ben Zion Bokser, who heads the Forest Hills Jewish Center, has called for a revival of the "messianic vision" and has attacked ethnic isolationism, citing a lovely apothegm from the Hasidic Rabbi Nahman of Bratzlav:

Each person suffers pain according to the condition of his soul and the level of his service to God. There is one who knows pain only because of his children, his parent, or his neighbor; another, of a higher state, suffers pain because of the whole city; but there is one of a very high state who suffers pain because of the troubles of the whole world. [—Ben Zion Boskser, "Jewish Universalism & Jewish Parochialism," *Congress Bi-Weekly,* Nov. 24, 1972.]

So the issues are joined: in symbolic shorthand, Bokser confronting Birbach, with a spectrum of uncertainty, confusion, and mixed feelings between them. That significant trends within American Jewish life bespeak a conservative turn seems indisputable. That these trends are as yet decisive, or even dominant, seems unlikely. Probably, we are witnessing a regrouping of forces and ideas within the Jewish world that will bring into existence a stronger conservative wing, which will in time enable the emergence of a conservative Jewish intelligentsia. If Milton Himmelfarb can be patient, he is likely to find a growing number of allies. Certainly, we are witnessing a regrouping of forces within the Jewish world, which will result in a conservatizing of its dominant liberalism.

YET THE LIBERAL-LEFT OUTLOOK remains strong among American Jews. (To provide another New York example: a majority of the voters for Herman Badillo in the 1973 Democratic primary was Jewish.) If those who adhere to the values and ideas of the liberal left show renewed energy, it may well be able to retain a powerful and perhaps dominant position in the Jewish community. There are factors in Jewish life—not merely sentiments and attachments—which encourage the liberal-left. Were the tradition of social activism to be abandoned or seriously weakened, one result would be a very severe identity crisis among nonreligious yet "Jewish" Jews. For the Orthodox, nothing is finally crucial except an unbreakable tie with God: that defines them as Jews. But for many others, from Conservative rabbis to socialist intellectuals, being Jewish, though it cannot be reduced to social idealism, unavoidably means a crucial component of social idealism. Remove that component, and the problem of Jewish distinctiveness for both individuals and institutions becomes critically acute. (It is fashionable, we know, in some advanced circles to look down on the "bourgeois liberalism" or "bleached substitutes for religion" by which many American Jews live, but thinking about how much more dismal American politics would be if those sentiments were removed is enough to make one a little less condescending.)

Moralizing is not enough. In their present moods, most American Jews are not likely to respond to it. What the coming years require are concrete social programs that will recreate links between Jews and their former allies in the liberal-labor alliance. Resisting cuts in the public financing of hospitals or school lunch programs or education is a moral good in its own right, but it is also a way of bringing together Jews, blacks, Puerto Ricans, white ethnics. If, as seems likely, there will be areas in which the interests of Jews and blacks clash, then at the very least we should avoid journalistic apocalypticism. Every effort should be made to contain such clashes, to keep them within appropriate limits. And for Jews, it might be appropriate to remember the crucial difference in America between our discomforts and their ordeals.

It is an inherently dubious notion that a measure of affluence—and that, after all, is the modest limit beyond which a great many American Jews have yet to move—necessarily signifies or requires a turn to conservatism. It assumes that middle-class people don't share many interests with poorer people, interests ranging from tax reform to national health insurance, from good schools to urban renewal. It is a view of things that accepts a crudely Marxized vision of society in behalf of a Nixonite politics.

Moralizing may not be enough, it may even jar many nerves; but finally the moral argument is crucial. Those deep impulses of value and care that have drawn many Jews toward the liberal-left, regardless of whether it seemed to be in their personal interest—those impulses remain. The Messiah still has not come: not to New York, not to Chicago, not to Washington, not to Florida. The world still cries out with its torments. Ours is a time (when has it not been?) for compassion and commitment.

Dennis H. Wrong

The Rhythm of
Democratic Politics

Democratic societies with universal suffrage and competing
political parties experience a cyclical alternation of periods
dominated by protest from the Left and retrenchment by the
Right. The notion that politics conform to such cyclical periodicity is scarcely a new one: it is implicit in the most commonplace
language of political journalism, which regularly uses such
metaphors as "swing of the pendulum," "rising and ebbing
tides," or "waxing and waning" forces, to describe events.

The conception of a Left/Right continuum along which parties, movements, regimes, and ideologies can be located has
often been justly criticized,[1] yet some such conception seems
indispensable and invariably creeps back in hidden guise when
the conventional categories are repudiated. I shall use "Left" to
refer to programmatic demands for planned or enacted social
change toward a more equal distribution of economic benefits,
social status, and power, or, in unpropitious times, to the defense
of an existing, achieved degree of equality against advocates of
increased inequality. The classic Left demand is to realize for all
men the French revolutionary slogan of "liberté, egalité, frater-
nité." Since the Left as an established and permanent political
tendency came into being at the time of the French Revolution,

90

the "Right" is best defined residually as resistance, on whatever grounds, to any further movement toward equality in the distribution of material satisfactions, status, and/or power, or as the demand for restoration of a (usually idealized) *status quo ante* in which greater inequality prevailed.

Obviously, these sparse definitions raise all sorts of problems if they are applied to the rich diversity of past and present political movements. Yet they embody the most common, minimal understanding of the Left/Right distinction. In emphasizing the broad *content* of political demands, they avoid the difficulties raised by classifying political groups as Left or Right according to their social base—whether they are supported by or direct their appeals to the victims or the beneficiaries of the existing distribution of rewards and privileges. Thus Peronism in the 1940s and 50s was not necessarily a leftist movement because its main following was among industrial workers; nor must New Left student movements of the '60s be considered "really" rightist because their members were disproportionately drawn from upper-middle-class backgrounds.

Nor need the actual structure of a party or regime determine its classification as Left or Right: parties of the Left may be led and controlled by tiny, self-perpetuating elites, while parties of the Right may be organized in a loose, decentralized, "populistic" manner. Communist dictatorships appeal, at least outside their borders, to supporters of the demands of the Left, although, since my primary concern is with the politics of democracies, the problem of how to classify nondemocratic regimes that claim legitimacy through an identification with the Left can be safely put aside.

Before the Enlightenment, a "Left" in the modern sense of a vision of a more egalitarian future society to be created by organized political effort did not exist. Nor was there an identifiable "Right": conservative ideologies and organizations emerged only in response to the challenge of the Left. Citing Hegel's famous "owl of Minerva" metaphor, Karl Mannheim defined conservatism as traditionalism become conscious of itself and wrote: "Goaded on by opposing theories, conservative mentality discovers its *idea* only *ex post facto.*"[2] Since most societies through most of history have been traditionalist, claiming their legitimacy from continuity with the past rather than from a vision of the future, classical conservatives, viewing the world *sub specie aeternitas*, have dismissed the outlook of the Left as the expression of Enlightenment naiveté over the perfectability of man, as presumptuous intervention in the workings of "providential forces" (Burke), or as an attempt, necessarily tyrannical in its outcome, to destroy "organically" evolved societies and rebuild them according to an imposed design.

The more subtle conservative thinkers, from Burke to Michael Oakeshott, have repudiated efforts to construct a conservative ideology, recognizing that the strength of conservatism lies in the emotional attachment of mortal men to the world as they have known it, in an only apparently irrational conviction that "what is, is right," which actually implies the unspoken major premise that it is right *because it is*. All men, including men of the Left, cannot help forming emotional attachments to what has the inestimable advantage and power of actually existing. Even prisoners have learned to love their bars, and most of us feel nostalgic about the places and people of our childhood no matter how unhappy it may have been. This is the existential root of conservatism—of the "eternal Right." Its strength has been habitually underestimated by the Left, even within the Left's own constituency of the deprived and oppressed; the naturalness of conservative emotions is too often facilely dismissed as indoctrination by the ruling class (these days as "brainwashing by the mass media"), or, more pretentiously, as "false consciousness," a term that carries a heavy burden of responsibility not merely for ideological delusions but for actual political crimes.

Contemporary technocrats, of course, are committed to the planned application of scientific knowledge. Their anti-ideological animus seems very remote from classical conservatism with its religious piety and preference for faith over reason, its aura of knights and ladies and agrarian life, and, for that matter, remote, too, from the free market of nineteenth-century liberal capitalism. But there is a curious continuity between a technocratic outlook favoring a "pragmatic" politics engaged in by the representatives of established organizations and the implicit pragmatism of such conservatives as Oakeshott, who fear rational abstractions and universal principles and affirm instead their trust in the implicit truths of "experience."

But there is an "eternal Left" too, as deeply rooted in the human condition as the eternal Right even if it only became a conscious political tendency after the Enlightenment. The vision of the Left derives from the Vichean insight that man makes his own history, or "socially constructs his reality," in today's fashionable sociological parlance. Once this insight enters general awareness, the social world is demystified, and classical conservative veneration of a fixed social order sanctified by the past loses meaning. Men feel "alienated" precisely because they know that theirs is a man-made world of arbitrary makeshift social arrangements which they can imagine quite otherwise. We have learned only too well that they may respond to this alienation with frenzied efforts to remystify the world, to press the genie back into the bottle, rather than by embracing the challenge to try to create the now possible free and egalitarian community envisioned by the Left.

Political democracy makes actual the eternal Left in time and history. By giving a voice to the voiceless, mobilizing the apathetic, and organizing the unorganized it introduces planned and directed social change as a principle of historical movement. The voice of the people need not be sanctified as the voice of God, but democracy requires that it at least be heard and taken into account. Democratic politics legitimizes demands for reform and, introduced into societies that remain highly unequal and create new inequalities in the course of their economic and technological growth, is therefore incurably ideological. The end of ideology would mean the end of the Left as a political force and the end of democracy itself—either by the restoration or creation of an authoritarian or totalitarian regime, or by the achievement of utopia.

The institutionalization of the Left in democratic politics initiates a long-term movement toward realization of the goals of the Left, a movement inherent in the workings of political democracy. However, all firmly established groups, including parties of the Left, become committed defensively to their own continued survival within a system that has permitted them to develop and even flourish. Michels called this the "iron law of oligarchy"; it has recently been described more accurately and renamed the "iron law of decadence" by Theodore Lowi. As organized groups become frozen in defense of their own internal structure, the stasis of Lowi's "interest-group pluralism" threatens; the spirit of the Left seeks to reactivate not only itself but the very power of majoritarian democracy through those nascent rather than fully organized groups we call "social movements."[3] But the resistance offered by the Right—as organized minority power, as inarticulate mass sentiment, as metaphysical reflection of the human condition—produces the oscillating pattern I have called the rhythm of democratic politics. How does this rhythm manifest itself and what is its source?

The periodicity of Left and Right in democratic political life is not necessarily equivalent to an alternation of parties in power, nor of governments actually pursuing more or less egalitarian or conservative policies. Political leaders, in office or out, frequently talk one way and act another, or follow inconsistent policies whatever their rhetoric. The achievements of politics are often symbolic ones—which is not to minimize their significance. The rhythm or cycle is rather one of *the kinds of issues* that dominate political debate, and often intellectual and cultural life as well. Nor is this rhythm the sole, or even always the major, substance of democratic politics. If the division between Left and Right is the most enduring focus of political conflict, it is nevertheless often obscured by ethnic, religious, and racial cleavages within particular polities. In the past, Marxists in particular have been predisposed to deny the autonomy and irreducibility of such "subcultural" cleavages, although their domination of the political life of a large number of countries is by now fully clear. One can nevertheless abstract out of the welter of the democratic political experience a discernible rhythm—or dialectic—of Left/Right conflict, which represents at least *one* major theme of their politics. Perhaps there is also a rhythm in the development over time of ethnic or religious struggles, a rhythm intersecting or superimposed upon that of Left/Right conflict. But my concern here is solely with the latter.

The cyclical rhythm is not the effect of a mysterious cosmic law; it rather reflects a pattern of change that is inherent in the workings of a democratic political system in a class-divided society. Political democracy based on universal suffrage was itself originally a demand of the Left introduced into previously authoritarian and hierarchical social orders. In European countries, though not in the United States, it was the central issue around which new working-class and socialist parties organized in the closing decades of the nineteenth century. For the formal, i.e., the legal and constitutional, redistribution of power achieved by universal suffrage to have any consequences in reducing social inequalities, a long period of political mobilization of the lower classes had to take place, a process that is scarcely complete even today in many countries, including the United States. Once, however, parties of the Left have been organized, or the lower classes have been successfully mobilized by older parties, some crisis such as an economic depression, defeat in war, or a split in the ranks of the Right is bound to give the parties of the Left the opportunity to win office, whether on their own or as part of a coalition. They are then able to carry out reforms that constitute at least their minimum program. But the crisis passes or is resolved; the Right regroups while conflicts between moderates and radicals on the Left become more acute; and the discontent of the Left's electoral constituency is temporarily appeased by the limited gains, actual or symbolic, that have been won. The Right then returns to office after successfully persuading a sizable segment of the Left's regular following that a conservative government will not wipe out these gains.

Although American political history has often been regarded as uniquely "consensual" and free of ideological conflict, it fits rather neatly into a pattern of oscillation between periods in which demands from the Left dominate, and those given over to periods of reaction. In any case, whatever truth there may have been in the past to the view that American politics reflected the historical peculiarities of American origins and destiny—the doctrine of American "exceptionalism" as it has sometimes been called—the idea has increasingly lost plausibility. Richard Rovere, one of the more astute observers of American politics, remarked in 1970 that "the Europeanization of American politics proceeds . . . apace."

The periodization of American politics into successive Left and

Right eras was presented at length by Arthur Schlesinger, Sr., in a 1939 article, "Tides of American Politics," revised and expanded in his 1949 book *Paths to the Present*,[4] which attracted a good deal of attention at the time. His son, Arthur Schlesinger, Jr., revived and updated his father's thesis in the late 1950s to argue that the '60s were destined to be a period of reform and innovation favorable to the liberal wing of the Democratic party, in which he himself was an active figure.

The elder Schlesinger divided American history into 11 periods of alternating Right and Left ascendancy—he used the labels "conservative" and "liberal"—from 1765 to 1947, each one averaging 16.5 years with very slight deviations around the mean, except in the period from the Civil War to the end of the nineteenth century. Schlesinger's inferences or "predictions" for the years ahead have been borne out to a surprising degree.

In this century, if we carry Schlesinger's periodization up to the present and modify it very slightly, there are five distinct periods. The progressive era is usually seen as beginning with Theodore Roosevelt's accession to the presidency in 1901 and ending with American entrance into World War I, or, at least, with Wilson's congressional losses in 1918. The period from 1918 until Franklin D. Roosevelt's election in 1932, or, perhaps, until the stock-market crash in 1929, was a period of war-inspired patriotism, postwar reaction (the "Red Scare"), return to "normalcy" under Harding and Coolidge, and complacent prosperity. The decline in the momentum of the New Deal is often dated from Democratic losses in the mid-term elections of 1938, but World War II prolonged and partially revived the ideological climate of the '30s. (Someone has remarked that 1948 was the last year of the '30s.) The Cold War, Korea, Republican victories, and the years of McCarthyism to which these events contributed gave a conservative cast to the '50s. The Left began to recapture some political initiative with the civil rights movement in the South in the late '50s, shortly followed by the rhetoric of the New Frontier and the resounding electoral repudiation of a militant right-wing presidential candidate in 1964. A few years later the "radicalization" of large segments of college youth and intellectuals in response to the Vietnam War created a mood of left-wing insurgency on a variety of fronts.

Since 1968, however, reaction or "backlash" against the black, student, and peace movements has been a salient theme of our politics, exploited by George Wallace's candidacy in the 1968 and 1972 election campaigns, and very closely identified with Vice-President Agnew and Attorney-General Mitchell who were the most publicized figures of the first Nixon administration. The mentality that led to Watergate fed off the mood of backlash.

Wars often appear to mark the beginning or the end or the intensification of particular phases of the cycle. Schlesinger denied that there was "a correlation between foreign wars and the mass drift of sentiments," maintaining that "these conflicts have taken place about equally in conservative and liberal periods, sometimes coming at the start, sometimes at the end and sometimes midway." But surely foreign wars differ in the ideological significance they possess for domestic currents of opinion. Also, their significance has certainly increased since the 1930s. Moreover, as Robert Nisbet has cogently argued, neither nations, continents, nor even units as large as civilizations can be treated as isolated, self-contained "systems" obeying their own internal laws.[5] They are parts of a larger international or supracivilizational environment that interpenetrates them. Wars, international crises, and the issues of foreign policy to which they give rise can therefore neither be ignored as shaping agents of the domestic political process nor invoked as *dei ex machina* to account for internal political shifts. Theories of American exceptionalism, on the one hand, and some Marxist analyses, on the other, have unduly minimized this fact.

In general, the ideological coloration of the perceived national enemy has complicated the impact of wars on the Left/Right dialectic. World War I divided the American Left; the Russian Revolution not only further divided it but gave impetus to the period of postwar reaction and repression that ended the Progressive era. World War II, on the other hand, was fought against nations seen as the very incarnation of the values most bitterly opposed by the Left and did not therefore displace New Deal liberalism and its radical allies. The Cold War and Korea, fought against an enemy laying claim to the ideological heritage of the Left, not only delegitimated the American Left but almost completely obliterated its radical wing. In the '60s, however, the failure and unpopularity of the Vietnam War revived American radicalism and discredited the Cold War. But the fact that responsibility for the Vietnam disaster rested on a liberal Democratic administration created a split on the Left that permitted Nixon's victory in 1968.

The Left, of course, is itself invariably divided into reformist and radical wings, and the shifting balance of unity and conflict achieved by its factions constitutes another dialectic within the larger dialectic of Left and Right. Obviously, the Right is also usually divided between militants and moderates, reactionaries and conservatives, although such divisions have not, I think, played as important a role in the United States as in some European countries.

Metaphors of pendular or tidal movements are misleading when applied to the cyclical rhythm of politics. For the pattern has not been one of mere repetitive oscillation between fixed points. In Schlesinger's words, "a more appropriate figure than the pendulum is the spiral, in which the alternation proceeds at successively higher levels." The classic Marxist conception of the movement of history has also been described as a spiral, combining a cyclical with a developmental or unilinear motion. But to disclose such a pattern in historical events is not to explain *why* it prevails, or *how* transitions from one stage to the next come about. No one who has read Robert Nisbet's brilliant book *Social Change and History* can retain any illusions on this score.[6] One must always ask, "What makes the wheels go around?" in the case of a cyclical motion, or, "What propels mankind upward and onward?"—or, at least, forward in a given direction—if a unilinear trend is exhibited. Neither recurrent cycles, unilinear evolution, nor a spiral course combining them amount to self-sufficient, self-explaining "laws" of change. Schlesinger recognized this in his cyclical account of American politics, but his own explanations of the cycle were brief and vague, scarcely going beyond the assertion of inevitable "changes in mass psychology" resulting from boredom or disappointment with the prevailing phase of the cycle. In trying to account for the cyclical rhythm, Schlesinger also referred to alleged peculiarities of the American people, such as their preference for "empiricism" rather than "preconceived theory," and their belief in the virtues of competition—although he also acknowledged the existence of a similar rhythm in the West European democracies.

In his autobiography, published in 1963 just two years before his death, Schlesinger reported that Franklin D. Roosevelt's adviser, David Niles, once told him that FDR was influenced in his decision to run for reelection in 1944 by Schlesinger's calculation that liberalism would remain dominant until 1948 (based on his figure of a 16.5 years' average duration of each phase of the cycle).[7] Schlesinger also mentioned a preelection column by James Reston in 1960 maintaining that John F. Kennedy "based his campaign on the assumption," derived from Schlesinger's "theory," that a turn to the Left was in the offing within a year or two.[8]

If these stories are true, Roosevelt and Kennedy would seem to have understood the cyclical pattern in far too mechanical a fashion that is vulnerable to Nisbet's strictures. Such efforts to predict the exact duration of periods of the cyclical or spiral rhythm, while they possess a dangerous fascination, do not increase our understanding of it. For a description of the rhythm, however accurate, *explains* nothing whatsoever: in the language of logicians, the rhythm is an *explanandum* rather than an *explanans*—an effect of underlying causes rather than a causal agency itself. Moreover, it is highly likely that in recent decades the rhythm has accelerated as a result of the increasing saturation of modern populations by the mass media. Nowadays a "new" generation seems to come along every five years or so.

An explanation of the rhythm of democratic politics must necessarily be historically specific, because party politics under conditions of mass suffrage are less than a century old even in most of the stable, "advanced" constitutional democracies of the West. Yet it may be possible to formulate explanatory generalizations that transcend the historical uniqueness of particular nations. Furthermore, it is at least worth observing in passing that there is some evidence of a similar periodicity in nondemocratic states. Despotic rulers of absolutist monarchies have often been followed by rulers more responsive to pressures from below. Totalitarian dictatorships undertake "great leaps forward" that are succeeded by periods of relaxed discipline in which "a hundred flowers" are encouraged to bloom. An analyst of Stalin's rule has written of the "artificial dialectic" imposed by the dictator on Soviet society, where rigorous demands for total ideological conformity and the use of terror to deter even the mildest dissent abruptly alternated with periods of greater permissiveness or "thaw."[9]

But an explanation of the rhythm of democratic politics must necessarily be specific to constitutional mass democracies. I shall try to summarize schematically the elements of such an explanation.

1.   The political mobilization of the previously disenfranchised lower classes is a long and slow process, still incomplete in many of the major Western democracies, as indicated by higher-middle- and upper-class as against working-class rates of voting, higher working- and lower-class support for parties of the Right than of upper- and middle-class support for parties of the Left, and the occasional survival of formal and informal barriers to voting imposed on some low-status groups, such as blacks in the American South. Thus even after the winning of full citizenship rights, including the right to vote, by groups previously subject to legal discrimination, "conservative government," in Woodrow Wilson's words, "is in the saddle most of the time."

2.   But Left parties and movements succeed in mobilizing a large enough proportion of their potential constituency to become leading opposition parties. Sometimes they displace older parties, as in the rise of Labour at the expense of the Liberals in Britain. Sometimes they emerge as the first and largest organized mass parties confronting electoral or governmental coalitions of smaller parties of the Right, as on the European continent. Sometimes they partially transform an older, heterogeneous, and factionalized party into a vehicle for the demands of newly mobilized lower-class groups, as in the United States. Sooner or later the Left party wins office, often as a result of a severe economic crisis or the impact of a war (especially a lost one) that discredits an existing government.

It has often been the fate of Left parties to come to power at a time of such acute crisis for the entire society that they are forced

to concentrate on improvised short-run policies to restore or
maintain internal peace, with the result that their long-range
goals of social reconstruction have to be shelved or severely
modified, inspiring accusations of "class betrayal" from their
more militant followers. The Social Democracy in the first and
last years of the Weimar Republic is the classic case. Nevertheless, by coming to office the Left party wins a kind of legitimacy
in the eyes of the electorate that it previously lacked and it is
usually able to carry out at least a part of its minimum program.
But failure to resolve the crisis that brought the party to office,
or the passing of the crisis whether or not the government's
measures are given credit for this; splits between the party's or
government's radical and moderate reformist wings once the
minimum program has been passed; the retrenchment of the
Right during a period in opposition; and a constant factor
—what George Bernard Shaw called "the damned wantlessness
of the poor"—all result in electoral defeat or the "co-optation" of
prominent leaders before the Left party has done more than
institute "incremental," or "token," reforms.

3.   The return of the Right, however, is conditional on its persuading the electorate that it will not "turn the clock back" on the
reforms achieved by the Left. Old issues bitterly contested in the
past by the parties suddenly become obsolescent and periods of
"Butskellism," or even Grand Coalitions between the rivals, become the order of the day, isolating and infuriating the more
militant partisans on each side who may break away and create
splinter or "ginger" groups within legislatures, or "extrapar-
liamentary opposition" movements outside. The Right party, in
an effort to enhance or consolidate its appeal to the constituency
of the Left, may adopt new hybrid, apparently contradictory,
names or slogans designed to suggest that it has outgrown past
hostility to Left policies now in effect, such as "Tory Socialism,"
"Progressive Conservatism," "Christian Democracy," or "Moderate Republicanism"—this last a label favored byPresident
Eisenhower shortly after his first election.
    This recurrent sequence of events is the rhythm, or the
"dialectic," of politically directed change in a democracy. It falls
far short of realizing either the far-reaching hopes of the advo-

cates or the apocalyptic fears of the opponents of universal suffrage in the nineteenth century. Why do parties of the Left become so pallidly reformist and achieve so little in the way of fundamental "structural change" in the direction of their egalitarian ideals? Machiavelli gave the most general answer long before the establishment of democratic institutions:

> It must be considered that there is nothing more difficult to carry out, nor more doubtful of success nor more danger- ous to handle, than to initiate a new order of things. For the reformer has enemies in all those who profit by the old order, and only lukewarm defenders in all those who would profit by the new order, this lukewarmness arising partly from fear of their adversaries, who have the laws in their favor; and partly from the incredulity of mankind, who do not truly believe in anything new until they have actual experience of it. Thus it arises that on every opportunity for attacking the reformer, his opponents do so with the zeal of partisans, the others only defend him half-heartedly, so that between them he runs great danger.[10]

The contemporary social scientist would doubtless put it in different and far less elegant language, but his conclusion would be much the same as Machiavelli's.

Yet the potential electoral constituency of the Left in modern democracies is larger than that of the Right—"God must love the poor people for he made so many of them," Lincoln once re- marked. Popular elections based on universal suffrage give deci- sive weight to the one political resource with which the lower classes are amply endowed—numbers. How does the Right counter this demographic superiority of their opponents? In the first place, the Right possesses a massive advantage with respect to other political resources—wealth, education, social status, traditional legitimacy—and is able to throw these into the bal- ance in election campaigns as well as employing them on an enormous scale to influence government policy between elec- tions. In confronting the electorate, however, the most regular and reliable strategy of the Right is to appeal to nationalist sentiment. Modern nationalism is itself, of course, a product of democratic ideology, born in the wake of the French and American Revolutions. But this very fact has served to enhance its appeal in opposition to the class and antielitist populist appeals of the Left, which has so repeatedly and tragically underestimated the strength of national loyalties in this century.

The Right lays claim to the symbols of legitimacy identified with the past of the nation, indeed with its very existence in a world of competing nation-states, an existence usually achieved by wars of conquest or revolts against foreign domination which usually, though not in the United States, antedated the creation of democratic institutions and the extension of the franchise. Thus parties of the Right tend to wave the flag, to nominate generals who stand "above politics" as candidates for office, and to invoke the need for national unity, in contrast to the divisive appeals of the Left. National leaders of the Right have sometimes engaged in foreign adventurism and even embarked upon limited expansionist wars in order to overcome internal tensions generated by the domestic class struggle. War has often in this sense been "the health of the state," in Randolph Bourne's famous dictum. Parties of the Left, on the other hand, have traditionally been isolationist in the United States, internationalist and anti-imperialist on the European continent, and Little Englanders in Britain.

If events ensure that sooner or later reformist parties of the Left will come to office, and if the return to office of conservative parties is partly conditional on their leaving untouched the popular reforms carried out by Left administrations, then there is *an unmistakable "leftward drift" inherent in the functioning over time of democratic politics.* The existence of such a drift alarms and enrages militants of the Right; its slowness and the many counterpressures to which it is subject disillusions and radicalizes utopians of the Left, who then dismiss parliament as a "talking-shop," the major parties as "Tweedledum" and "Tweedledee," and "The System" itself as a fraud in professing to offer opportunities for change. Militants of both Right and Left are disposed to conclude with Machiavelli that

> Thus it comes about that all armed prophets have conquered and unarmed ones failed; for . . . the character of

peoples varies, and it is easy to persuade them of a thing, but difficult to keep them in that persuasion. And so it is necessary to order things so that when they no longer believe, they can be made to believe by force.[11]

Segments of both Right and Left, in short, are attracted by violent revolutionary or counterrevolutionary shortcuts: in the case of the Right, to arrest and even reverse the leftward drift; in the case of the Left, to accelerate and complete it. The Right calls for a government of "national unity" that will not hesitate to suspend constitutional liberties and suppress the opposition parties, while the Left succumbs to a mood of revolutionary impatience, or "utopian greed." In periods of acute national crisis and distress, a "dialectic of the extremes," to use a phrase of Raymond Aron's,[12] in which each side violently confronts the other, often enough in the streets, may take center stage and threaten the survival of democratic institutions themselves. The last years of the Weimar Republic are, of course, the classic example of such a confrontation.

But even in less critical situations, this dialectic is visible at the periphery rather than at the center of the political arena and often seems to be gaining momentum through the enlistment of growing numbers of partisans on each side. The tactic of Left militants is to attack the entire political system as part of a repressive "Establishment" moving toward "fascism," and the most plausible evidence for this is found in the efforts of militants on the Right to brand their customary political opponents as Communist sympathizers, or dangerous radicals encouraging disrespect for law, insurrectionary violence, treason, or all three. The Left calls for a "popular front" against "repression" and incipient "fascism." The Right reaffirms traditional values and calls for a closing of ranks against the fomenters of public disorder. At the level of rhetoric and public demonstrations, this kind of ultimatist ideological politics was fairly visible in the United States during the late '60s. That it may become at least a permanent sideshow of American politics is one implication of the notion of the Europeanization of American politics to which I previously referred. The dialectic of the extremes reflects an effort, conscious or unconscious, to short-circuit the "normal" pattern of alternating periods of protest and stabilization with its built-in tendency toward a glacially slow "leftward drift."

Democratic conservatives, or "moderates," frequently reject "ideological politics" in favor of a "pragmatic politics" based on bargaining, compromise, and consensus on the rules of political competition. Their suspicion of those on both the Left and the Right who out of impatience with the stately rhythm of democratic politics wish to fracture it by making a forward "leap to socialism" or a restoration of an idealized status quo ante is surely well-founded. But the "ideological" demands of idealists, visionaries, "extremists," prophets, and seers are also part of the democratic political process—sources of "input," as some political scientists would gracelessly say. Without them, the professional politicians would have little to bargain about and strike compromises over. The major political philosopher of democracy, John Stuart Mill, recognized this when he wrote of his brief period of service in the House of Commons:

> If . . . there were any intermediate course which had a claim to a trial, I well knew that to propose something which would be called extreme was the true way not to impede but to facilitate a more moderate experiment. . . . It is the character of the British people, or at least of the higher and middle classes who pass muster for the British people, that to induce them to approve of any change, it is necessary that they should look upon it as a middle course: they think every proposal extreme and violent unless they hear of some other proposal going still further, upon which their antipathy to extreme views may discharge itself.[13]

Mill's tone reflects the relatively serene and civil politics of Britain in the Victorian age when the franchise was still restricted. Out of the experience of the disorder and violence of European mass politics in this century, Albert Camus observed: "Heads must roll, and blood must flow like rivers in the streets, merely to bring about a minor amendment to the Constitution." This is easily read as a despairing or cynical rejection of political effort. But recall that Camus' heroic exemplar of the human condition was Sisyphus. The task of the Left is always Sisyphean.

Movement toward its goals is at best asymptotic. Disappointment is inevitable over the "wantlessness" and fickleness—often sourly labeled "false consciousness"—of the suffering and oppressed the Left seeks to serve. Committed neither in principle nor pragmatically to the world as it is, defined rather by its "project" in the Sartrean sense, the Left is inherently prone to bitter internal struggles over which ends, means, and agencies advance or hinder that project.

The Left is often proclaimed to be obsolete as a result of the very establishment of political democracy, since the voice of the people at any given time so rarely fully affirms the aspirations of the Left. The actual role of the Left is usually the undramatic one, as Barrington Moore, Jr., has recently defined it, of keeping "radical fire" under liberal reforms.[14] The Left might well attribute to political democracy as an ironic motto Galileo's famous aside when forced to recant his belief in the Copernican theory: *eppur si muove*— "and yet it still moves." But unlike the mechanical force of the sun's gravity, the effort and will of men and women on the Left are what keep the system of democratic politics in motion.

Michael Walzer

In Defense of Equality

At the very center of conservative thought lies this idea: that the present division of wealth and power corresponds to some deeper reality of human life. Conservatives don't want to say merely that the present division is what it ought to be, for that would invite a search for some distributive principle—as if it were possible to *make* a distribution. They want to say that whatever the division of wealth and power is, it naturally is, and that all efforts to change it, temporarily successful in proportion to their bloodiness, must be futile in the end. We are then invited, as in Irving Kristol's recent *Commentary* article, to reflect upon the perversity of those who would make the attempt.[1] Like a certain sort of leftist thought, conservative argument seems quickly to shape itself around a rhetoric of motives rather than one of reasons. Kristol is especially adept at that rhetoric and strangely unconcerned about the reductionism it involves. He aims to expose egalitarianism as the ideology of envious and resentful intellectuals. No one else cares about it, he says, except the "new class" of college-educated, professional, most importantly, professorial men and women, who hate their bourgeois past (and present) and long for a world of their own making.

I suppose I should have felt, after reading Kristol's piece, that the decent drapery of my socialist convictions has been stripped away, that I was left naked and shivering, small-minded and self-concerned. Perhaps I did feel a little like that, for my first impulse was to respond in kind, exposing anti-egalitarianism as the ideology of those other intellectuals—"they are mostly professors, of course"—whose spiritual course was sketched some years ago by the editor of *Commentary*. But that would be at best a degrading business, and I doubt that my analysis would be any more accurate than Kristol's. It is better to ignore the motives of these "new men" and focus instead on what they say: that the inequalities we are all familiar with are inherent in our condition, are accepted by ordinary people (like themselves), and are criticized only by the perverse. I think all these assertions are false; I shall try to respond to them in a serious way.

Kristol doesn't argue that we can't possibly have greater equality or greater inequality than we presently have. Both communist and aristocratic societies are possible, he writes, under conditions of political repression or economic underdevelopment and stagnation. But insofar as men are set free from the coerciveness of the state and from material necessity, they will distribute themselves in a more natural way, more or less as contemporary Americans have done. The American way is exemplary because it derives from or reflects the real inequalities of mankind. Men don't naturally fall into two classes (patricians and plebeians) as conservatives once thought; nor can they plausibly be grouped into a single class (citizens or comrades) as leftists still believe, Instead, "human talents and abilities . . . distribute themselves along a bell-shaped curve, with most people clustered around the middle, and with much smaller percentages at the lower and higher ends." The marvels of social science!—this distribution is a demonstrable fact. And it is another "demonstrable fact that in all modern bourgeois societies, the distribution of income is also along a bell-shaped curve. . . ." The second bell echoes the first. Moreover, once this harmony is established, "the political structure—the distribution of political power—follows along the same way. . . ." At this point, Kristol must add, "however slowly and reluctantly," since he believes that the Soviet economy is moving closer every year to its natural shape, and it is admittedly hard to find evidence that nature is winning out in the political realm. But in the United States, nature is triumphant: we are perfectly bell-shaped.

The first bell is obviously the crucial one. The defense of

inequality reduces to these two propositions: that talent is distributed unequally and that talent will out. Clearly, we all want men and women to develop and express their talents, but whenever they are able to do that, Kristol suggests, the bell-shaped curve will appear or reappear, first in the economy, then in the political system. It is a neat argument but also a peculiar one, for there is no reason to think that "human talents and abilities" in fact distribute themselves along a *single* curve, although income necessarily does. Consider the range and variety of human capacities: intelligence, physical strength, agility and grace, artistic creativity, mechanical skill, leadership, endurance, memory, psychological insight, the capacity for hard work —even, moral strength, sensitivity, the ability to express compassion. Let's assume that with respect to all these, most people (but different people in each case) cluster around the middle of whatever scale we can construct, with smaller numbers at the lower and higher ends. Which of these curves is actually echoed by the income bell? Which, if any, ought to be?

There is another talent that we need to consider: the ability to make money, the green thumb of bourgeois society—a secondary talent, no doubt, combining many of the others in ways specified by the immediate environment, but probably also a talent which distributes, if we could graph it, along a bell-shaped curve. Even this curve would not correlate exactly with the income bell because of the intervention of luck, that eternal friend of the untalented, whose most important social expression is the inheritance of property. But the correlation would be close enough, and it might also be morally plausible and satisfying. People who are able to make money ought to make money, in the same way that people who are able to write books ought to write books. Every human talent should be developed and expressed.

The difficulty here is that making money is only rarely a form of self-expression, and the money we make is rarely enjoyed for its intrinsic qualities (at least, economists frown upon that sort of enjoyment). In a capitalist world, money is the universal medium of exchange; it enables the men and women who possess it to purchase virtually every other sort of social good; we collect it for its exchange value. Political power, celebrity, admiration, leisure, works of art, baseball teams, legal advice, sexual pleasure, travel, education, medical care, rare books, sailboats—all these (and much more) are up for sale. The list is as endless as human desire and social invention. Now isn't it odd, and morally implausible and unsatisfying, that all these things should be distributed to people with a talent for making money? And even odder and more unsatisfying that they should be distributed (as they are) to people who have money, whether or not they made it, whether or not they possess any talent at all?

Rich people, of course, always look talented—just as princesses always look beautiful—to the deferential observer. But it is the first task of social science, one would think, to look beyond these appearances. "The properties of money," Marx wrote, "are my own (the possessor's) properties and faculties. What I *am* and *can* do is, therefore, not at all determined by my individuality. I *am* ugly, but I can buy the most beautiful woman for myself. Consequently, I am not ugly, for the effect of ugliness, its power to repel, is annulled by money. . . . I am a detestable, dishonorable, unscrupulous, and stupid man, but money is honored and so also is its possessor."[2]

It would not be any better if we gave men money in direct proportion to their intelligence, their strength, or their moral rectitude. The resulting distributions would each, no doubt, reflect what Kristol calls "the tyranny of the bell-shaped curve," though it is worth noticing again that the populations in the lower, middle, and upper regions of each graph would be radically different. But whether it was the smart, the strong, or the righteous who enjoyed all the things that money can buy, the oddity would remain: why them? Why anybody? In fact, there is no single talent or combination of talents which plausibly entitles a man to every available social good—and there is no single talent or combination of talents that necessarily must win the available goods of a free society. Kristol's bell-shaped curve is tyrannical only in a purely formal sense. Any particular distribution may indeed be bell-shaped, but there are a large number of possible distributions. Nor need there be a single distribution of all social goods, for different goods might well be distributed differently. Nor again need all the distributions follow this or that talent curve, for in the sharing of some social goods, talent does not seem a relevant consideration at all.

Consider the case of medical care: surely it should not be distributed to individuals because they are wealthy, intelligent, or righteous, but only because they are sick. Now, over any given period of time, it may be true that some men and women won't require any medical treatment, a very large number will need some moderate degree of attention, and a few will have to have intensive care. If that is so, then we must hope for the appearance of another bell-shaped curve. Not just any bell will do. It must be the right one, echoing what might be called the susceptibility-to-sickness curve. But in America today, the distribution of medical care actually follows closely the lines of the income graph. It's not how a man feels, but how much money he has that determines how often he visits a doctor. Another demonstrable fact! Does it require envious intellectuals to see that something is wrong?

There are two possible ways of setting things right. We might distribute income in proportion to susceptibility-to-sickness, or we might make sure that medical care is not for sale at all, but is available to those who need it. The second of these is obviously the simpler. Indeed, it is a modest proposal and already has wide support, even among those ordinary men and women who are said to be indifferent to equality. And yet, the distribution of medical care solely for medical reasons would point the way toward an egalitarian society, for it would call the dominance of the income curve dramatically into question.

II

What egalitarianism requires is that many bells should ring. Different goods should be distributed to different people for different reasons. Equality is not a simple notion, and it cannot be satisfied by a single distributive scheme—not even, I hasten to add, by a scheme which emphasizes need. "From each according to his abilities, to each according to his needs" is a fine slogan with regard to medical care. Tax money collected from all of us in proportion to our resources (these will never correlate exactly with our abilities, but that problem I shall leave aside for now) must pay the doctors who care for those of us who are sick. Other people who deliver similar sorts of social goods should probably be paid in the same way—teachers and lawyers, for example. But

Marx's slogan doesn't help at all with regard to the distribution of political power, honor and fame, leisure time, rare books, and sailboats. None of these things can be distributed to individuals in proportion to their needs, for they are not things that anyone (strictly speaking) needs. They can't be distributed in equal amounts or given to whoever wants them, for some of them are necessarily scarce, and some of them can't be possessed unless other people agree on the proper name of the possessor. There is no criteria, I think, that will fit them all. In the past they have indeed been distributed on a single principle: men and women have possessed them or their historical equivalents because they were strong or well-born or wealthy. But this only suggests that a society in which any single distributive principle is dominant cannot be an egalitarian society. Equality requires a diversity of principles, which mirrors the diversity both of mankind and of social goods.

Whenever equality in this sense does not prevail, we have a kind of tyranny, for it is tyrannical of the well-born or the strong or the rich to gather to themselves social goods that have nothing to do with their personal qualities. This is an idea beautifully expressed in a passage from Pascal's *Pensées,* which I am going to quote at some length, since it is the source of my own argument.[3]

> The nature of tyranny is to desire power over the whole world and outside its own sphere.
>
> There are different companies—the strong, the handsome, the intelligent, the devout—and each man reigns in his own, not elsewhere. But sometimes they meet, and the strong and the handsome fight for mastery—foolishly, for their mastery is of different kinds. They misunderstand one another, and make the mistake of each aiming at universal dominion. Nothing can win this, not even strength, for it is powerless in the kingdom of the wise. . . .
>
> *Tyranny.* The following statements, therefore, are false and tyrannical: "Because I am handsome, so I should command respect." "I am strong, therefore men should love me. . . ." "I am . . . etc."
>
> Tyranny is the wish to obtain by one means what can only be had by another. We owe different duties to different

qualities: love is the proper response to charm, fear to strength, and belief to learning.

Marx makes a very similar argument in one of the early manuscripts; perhaps he had this *pensée* in mind.

> Let us assume man to be man, and his relation to the world to be a human one. Then.love can only be exchanged for love, trust for trust, etc. If you wish to enjoy art you must be an artistically cultivated person; if you wish to influence other people, you must be a person who really has a stimulating and encouraging effect upon others. . . . If you love without evoking love in return, i.e., if you are not able, by the manifestation of yourself as a loving person, to make yourself a beloved person, then your love is impotent and a misfortune.[4]

The doctrine suggested by these passages is not an easy one, and I can expound it only in a tentative way. It isn't that every man should get what he deserves—as in the old definition of justice—for desert is relevant only to some of the exchanges that Pascal and Marx have in mind. Charming men and women don't deserve to be loved: I may love this one or that one, but it can't be the case that I ought to do so. Similarly, learned men don't deserve to be believed: they are believed or not depending on the arguments they make. What Pascal and Marx are saying is that love and belief can't rightly be had in any other way—can't be purchased or coerced, for example. It is wrong to seek them in any way that is alien to their intrinsic character. In its extended form, their argument is that for all our personal and collective resources, there are distributive reasons that are somehow *right*, that are naturally part of our ideas about the things themselves. So nature is reestablished as a critical standard, and we are invited to wonder at the strangeness of the existing order.

This new standard is egalitarian, even though it obviously does not require an equal distribution of love and belief. The doctrine of right reasons suggests that we pay equal attention to the "different qualities," and to the "individuality" of every man and woman, that we find ways of sharing our resources that match the variety of their needs, interests, and capacities. The clues that we must follow lie in the conceptions we already have, in the things we already know about love and belief, and also about respect, obedience, education, medical care, legal aid, all the necessities of life—for this is no esoteric doctrine, whatever difficulties it involves. Nor is it a panacea for human misfortune, as Marx's last sentence makes clear: it is only meant to suggest a humane form of social accommodation. There is little we can do, in the best of societies, for the man who isn't loved. But there may be ways to avoid the triumph of the man who doesn't love—who buys love or forces it—or at least of his parallels in the larger social and political world: the leaders, for example, who are obeyed because of their coercive might or their enormous wealth. Our goal should be an end to tyranny, a society in which no man is master outside his sphere. That is the only society of equals worth having.

But it isn't readily had, for there is no necessity implied by the doctrine of right reasons. Pascal is wrong to say that "strength is powerless in the kingdom of the wise"—or rather, he is talking of an ideal realm and not of the intellectual world as we know it. In fact, wise men (at any rate, smart men) have often in the past defended the tyranny of the strong, as they still defend the tyranny of the rich. Sometimes, of course, they do this because they are persuaded of the necessity or the utility of tyrannical rule; sometimes for other reasons. Kristol suggests that whenever intellectuals are not persuaded, they are secretly aspiring to a tyranny of their own: they too would like to rule outside their sphere. Again, that's certainly true of some of them, and we all have our own lists. But it's not necessarily true. Surely it is possible, though no doubt difficult, for an intellectual to pay proper respect to the different companies of men. I want to argue that in our society the only way to do that, or to begin to do it, is to worry about the tyranny of money.

III

Let's start with some things that money cannot buy. It can't buy the American League pennant: star players can be hired, but victories presumably are not up for sale. It can't buy the National

Book Award: writers can be subsidized, but the judges presumably can't be bribed. Nor, it should be added, can the pennant or the award be won by being strong, charming, or ideologically correct—at least we all hope not. In these sorts of cases, the right reasons for winning are built into the very structure of the competition. I am inclined to think that they are similarly built into a large number of social practices and institutions. It's worth focusing again, for example, on the practice of medicine. From ancient times, doctors were required to take an oath to help the sick, not the powerful or the wealthy. That requirement reflects a common understanding about the very nature of medical care. Many professionals don't share that understanding, but the opinion of ordinary men and women, in this case at least, is profoundly egalitarian.

The same understanding is reflected in our legal system. A man accused of a crime is entitled to a fair trial simply by virtue of being an accused man; nothing else about him is a relevant consideration. That is why defendants who cannot afford a lawyer are provided with legal counsel by the state: otherwise justice would be up for sale. And that is why defense counsel can challenge particular jurors thought to be prejudiced: the fate of the accused must hang on his guilt or innocence, not on his political opinions, his social class, or his race. We want different defendants to be treated differently, but only for the right reasons.

The case is the same in the political system, whenever the state is a democracy. Each citizen is entitled to one vote simply because he is a citizen. Men and women who are ambitious to exercise greater power must collect votes, but they can't do that by purchasing them; we don't want votes to be traded in the marketplace, though virtually everything else is traded there, and so we have made it a criminal offense to offer bribes to voters. The only right way to collect votes is to campaign for them, that is, to be persuasive, stimulating, encouraging, and so on. Great inequalities in political power are acceptable only if they result from a political process of a certain kind, open to argument, closed to bribery and coercion. The freely given support of one's fellow citizens is the appropriate criteria for exercising political power and, once again, it is not enough, or it shouldn't be, to be physically powerful, or well-born, or even ideologically correct.

It is often enough, however, to be rich. No one can doubt the mastery of the wealthy in the spheres of medicine, justice, and political power, even though these are not their own spheres. I don't want to say, their unchallenged mastery, for in democratic states we have at least made a start toward restricting the tyranny of money. But we have only made a start: think how different America would have to be before these three companies of men—the sick, the accused, the politically ambitious—could be treated in strict accordance with their individual qualities. It would be immediately necessary to have a national health service, national legal assistance, the strictest possible control over campaign contributions. Modest proposals, again, but they represent so many moves toward the realization of that old socialist slogan about the abolition of money. I have always been puzzled by that slogan, for socialists have never, to my knowledge, advocated a return to a barter economy. But it makes a great deal of sense if it is interpreted to mean *the abolition of the power of money outside its sphere.* What socialists want is a society in which wealth is no longer convertible into social goods with which it has no intrinsic connection.

But it is in the very nature of money to be convertible (that's all it is), and I find it hard to imagine the sorts of laws and law enforcement that would be necessary to prevent monied men and women from buying medical care and legal aid over and above whatever social minimum is provided for everyone. In the U.S. today, people can even buy police protection beyond what the state provides, though one would think that it is the primary purpose of the state to guarantee equal security to all its citizens, and it is by no means the rich, despite the temptations they offer, who stand in greatest need of protection. But this sort of thing could be prevented only by a very considerable restriction of individual liberty—of the freedom to offer services and to purchase them. The case is even harder with respect to politics itself. One can stop overt bribery, limit the size of campaign contributions, require publicity, and so on. But none of these things will be enough to prevent the wealthy from exercising power in all sorts of ways to which their fellow citizens have never consented. Indeed, the ability to hold or spend vast sums of money is itself a form of power, permitting what might be called preemptive strikes against the political system. And this, it seems to me, is the strongest possible argument for a radical redistribution of wealth. So long as money is convertible outside its sphere, it must be widely and more or less equally held so as to minimize its distorting effects upon legitimate distributive processes.

VI

What is the proper sphere of wealth? What sorts of things are rightly had in exchange for money? The obvious answer is also the right one: all those economic goods and services, beyond what is necessary to life itself, which men find useful or pleasing. There is nothing degraded about wanting these things; there is nothing unattractive, boring, debased, or philistine about a society organized to provide them for its members. Kristol insists that a snobbish dislike for the sheer productivity of bourgeois society is a feature of egalitarian argument. I would have thought that a deep appreciation of that productivity has more often marked the work of socialist writers. The question is, how are the products to be distributed? Now, the right way to possess useful and pleasing things is by making them, or growing them, or somehow providing them for others. The medium of exchange is money, and this is the proper function of money and, ideally, its only function.

There should be no way of acquiring rare books and sailboats except by working for them. But this is not to say that men deserve whatever money they can get for the goods and services they provide. In capitalist society, the actual exchange value of the work they do is largely a function of market conditions over which they exercise no control. It has little to do with the intrinsic value of the work or with the individual qualities of the worker. There is no reason for socialists to respect it, unless it turns out to be socially useful to do so. There are other values, however, which they must respect, for money isn't the only or necessarily the most important thing for which work can be exchanged. A lawyer is surely entitled to the respect he wins from his colleagues and to the gratitude and praise he wins from his clients.

The work he has done may also constitute a good reason for making him director of the local legal aid society; it may even be a good reason for making him a judge. It isn't, on the face of it, a good reason for allowing him an enormous income. Nor is the willingness of his clients to pay his fees a sufficient reason, for most of them almost certainly think they should be paying less. The money they pay is different from the praise they give, in that the first is extrinsically determined, the second freely offered.

In a long and thoughtful discussion of egalitarianism in the *Public Interest,* Daniel Bell worries that socialists today are aiming at an "equality of results" instead of the "just meritocracy" (the career open to talents) that he believes was once the goal of leftist and even of revolutionary politics.[5] I confess that I am tempted by "equality of results" in the sphere of money, precisely because it is so hard to see how a man can merit the things that money can buy. On the other hand, it is easy to list cases where merit (of one sort or another) is clearly the right distributive criteria, and where socialism would not require the introduction of any other principle.

- Six people speak at a meeting, advocating different policies, seeking to influence the decision of the assembled group.
- Six doctors are known to aspire to a hospital directorship.
- Six writers publish novels and anxiously await the reviews of the critics.
- Six men seek the company and love of the same woman.

Now, we all know the right reasons for the sorts of decisions, choices, judgments that are in question here. I have never heard anyone seriously argue that the woman must let herself be shared, or the hospital establish a six-man directorate, or the critics distribute their praise evenly, or the people at the meeting adopt all six proposals. In all these cases, the personal qualities of the individuals involved (as these appear to the others) should carry the day.

But what sorts of personal qualities are relevant to owning a $20,000 sailboat? A love for sailing, perhaps, and a willingness to build the boat or to do an equivalent amount of work. In

America today, it would take a steelworker about two years to earn that money (assuming that he didn't buy anything else during all that time) and it would take a corporation executive a month or two. How can that be right, when the executive also has a rug on the floor, air-conditioning, a deferential secretary, and enormous personal power? He's being paid as he goes, while the steelworker is piling up a kind of moral merit (so we have always been taught) by deferring pleasure. Surely there is no meritocratic defense for this sort of difference. It would seem much better to pay the worker and the executive more or less the same weekly wage and let the sailboat be bought by the man who is willing to forgo other goods and services, that is, by the man who really wants it. Is this "equality of result"? In fact, the results will be different, if the men are, and it seems to me that they will be, different for the right reasons.

Against this view, there is a conventional but also very strong argument that can be made on behalf of enterprise and inventiveness. If there is a popular defense of inequality, it is this one, but I don't think it can carry us very far toward the inequalities that Kristol wants to defend. Consider the case of the man who builds a better mousetrap, or opens a restaurant and sells delicious blintzes, or does a little teaching on the side. He has no air-conditioning, no secretary, no power; probably his reward has to be monetary. He has to have a chance, at least, to earn a little more money than his less enterprising neighbors. The market doesn't guarantee that he will in fact earn more, but it does make it possible, and until some other way can be found to do that, market relations are probably defensible under the doctrine of right reasons. Here in the world of the petty-bourgeoisie, it seems appropriate that people able to provide goods or services that are novel, timely, or particularly excellent should reap the rewards they presumably had in mind when they went to work. And which they were right to have in mind: no one would want to feed blintzes to strangers, day after day, merely to win their gratitude.

But one might well want to be a corporation executive, day after day, merely to make all those decisions. It is precisely the people who are paid or who pay themselves vast sums of money who reap all sorts of other rewards too. We need to sort out these different forms of payment. First of all, there are rewards, like the pleasure of exercising power, which are intrinsic to certain jobs. An executive must make decisions—that's what he is there for—and even decisions seriously affecting other people. It is right that he should do that, however, only if he has been persuasive, stimulating, encouraging, and so on, and won the support of a majority of those same people. That he owns the corporation or has been chosen by the owners isn't enough. Indeed, given the nature of corporate power in contemporary society, the following statement (to paraphrase Pascal) is false and tyrannical: because I am rich, so I should make decisions and command obedience. Even in corporations organized democratically, of course, the personal exercise of power will persist. It is more likely to be seen, however, as it is normally seen in political life—as the chief attraction of executive positions. And this will cast a new light on the other rewards of leadership.

The second of these consists in all the side-effects of power: prestige, status, deference, and so on. Democracy tends to reduce these, or should tend that way when it is working well, without significantly reducing the attractions of decision-making. The same is true of the third form of reward, money itself, which is owed to work, but not necessarily to place and power. We pay political leaders much less than corporation executives, precisely because we understand so well the excitement and appeal of political office. Insofar as we recognize the political character of corporations, then, we can pay their executives less too. I doubt that there would be a lack of candidates even if we paid them no more than was paid to any other corporation employee. Perhaps there are reasons for paying them more—but not meritocratic reasons, for we give all the attention that is due to their merit when we make them our leaders.

We don't give all due attention to the restaurant owner, however, merely by eating his blintzes. Him we have to pay, and he can ask, I suppose, whatever the market will bear. That's fair enough, and no real threat to equality so long as he can't amass so much money that he becomes a threat to the integrity of the political system and so long as he does not exercise power, tyrannically, over other men and women. Within his proper sphere, he is as good a citizen as any other. His activities recall Dr. Johnson's remark: "There are few ways in which man can be more innocently employed than in getting money."

V

The most immediate occasion of the conservative attack on equality is the reappearance of the quota system—newly designed, or so it is said, to move us closer to egalitarianism rather than to maintain old patterns of religious and racial discrimination. Kristol does not discuss quotas, perhaps because they are not widely supported by professional people (or by professors): the disputes of the last several years do not fit the brazen simplicity of his argument. But almost everyone else talks about them, and Bell worries at some length, and rightly, about the challenge quotas represent to the "just meritocracy" he favors. Indeed, quotas in any form, new or old, establish "wrong reasons" as the basis of important social decisions, perhaps the most important social decisions: who shall be a doctor, who shall be a lawyer, and who shall be a bureaucrat. It is obvious that being black or a woman or having a Spanish surname (any more than being white, male, and Protestant) is no qualification for entering a university or a medical school or joining the civil service. In a sense, then, the critique of quotas consists almost entirely of a series of restatements and reiterations of the argument I have been urging in this essay. One only wishes that the critics would apply it more generally than they seem ready to do. There is more to be said, however, if they consistently refuse to do that.

The positions for which quotas are being urged are, in America today, key entry points to the good life. They open the way, that is, to a life marked above all by a profusion of goods, material and moral: possessions, conveniences, prestige, and deference. Many of these goods are not in any plausible sense appropriate rewards for the work that is being done. They are merely the rewards that upper classes throughout history have been able to seize and hold for their members. Quotas, as they are currently being used, are a way of redistributing these rewards by redistributing the social places to which they conventionally pertain. It is a bad way, because one really wants doctors and (even) civil servants to have certain sorts of qualifications. To the people on the receiving end of medical and bureaucratic services, race and class are a great deal less important than knowledge, competence, courtesy, and so on. I don't want to say that race and class are entirely unimportant: it would be wrong to underestimate the distortions introduced by an inegalitarian society into these sorts of human relations. But if the right reason for receiving medical care is being sick, then the right reason for giving medical care is being able to help the sick. And so medical schools should pay attention, first of all and almost exclusively, to the potential helpfulness of their applicants.

But they may be able to do that only if the usual connections between place and reward are decisively broken. Here is another example of the doctrine of right reasons. If men and women wanted to be doctors primarily because they wanted to be helpful, they would have no reason to object when judgments were made about their potential helpfulness. But so long as there are extrinsic reasons for wanting to be a doctor, there will be pressure to choose doctors (that is, to make medical school places available) for reasons that are similarly extrinsic. So long as the goods that medical schools distribute include more than certificates of competence, include, to be precise, certificates of earning power, quotas are not entirely implausible. I don't see that being black is a worse reason for owning a sailboat than being a doctor. They are equally bad reasons.

Quotas today are a means of lower-class aggrandizement, and they are likely to be resolutely opposed, opposed without guilt and worry, only by people who are entirely content with the class structure as it is and with the present distribution of goods and services. For those of us who are not content, anxiety can't be avoided. We know that quotas are wrong, but we also know that the present distribution of wealth makes no moral sense, that the dominance of the income curve plays havoc with legitimate distributive principles, and that quotas are a form of redress no more irrational than the world within which and because of which they are demanded. In an egalitarian society, however, quotas would be unnecessary and inexcusable.

VI

I have put forward a difficult argument in very brief form, in order to answer Kristol's even briefer argument—for he is chiefly concerned with the motives of those who advocate equality and not with the case they make or try to make. He is also concerned, he says, with the fact that equality has suddenly been discovered and is now for the first time being advocated as the *chief* virtue of social institutions: as if societies were not complex and values ambiguous. I don't know what discoverers and advocates he has in mind.[6] But it is worth stressing that equality as I have described it does not stand alone, but is closely related to the idea of liberty. The relation is complex, and I cannot say very much about it here. It is a feature of the argument I have made, however, that the right reason for distributing love, belief, and, most important for my immediate purposes, political power is the freely given consent of lovers, believers, and citizens. In these sorts of cases, of course, we all have standards to urge upon our fellows: we say that so and so should not be believed unless he offers evidence or that so and so should not be elected to political office unless he commits himself to civil rights. But clearly credence and power are not and ought not to be distributed according to my standards or yours. What is necessary is that everyone else be able to say yes or nó Without liberty, then, there could be no rightful distribution at all. On the other hand, men are not free, not politically free at least, if *his* yes, because of his birth or place or fortune, counts seventeen times more heavily than *my* no. Here the case is exactly as socialists have always claimed it to be: liberty and equality are the two chief virtues of social institutions, and they stand best when they stand together.

David Spitz

A Grammar of Equality

Equality, wrote Alexandre Dumas the younger, brought kings to the guillotine and the people to the throne.

Like most felicitous phrases, this is no more than a partial truth. New tyrants rather than "the people" often ascended to the momentarily vacated throne; and not simply equality but the stupidity and malevolence of kings,[1] the ambitions of lesser but avaricious mortals, and the effects of changing economic and social systems brought tyrannical rulers to their deserved end. Yet who can deny that the passion for equality played a stirring and vital role?

Whether it *should* have played that role is the contested and more intriguing question; for the case against equality, though it runs counter to the spirit of the democratic age, remains a formidable one. Consider the following:

• Equality requires us to count heads as if each were made out of wood, when in fact some are made of precious metals and others of lesser or even base materials. Still others seem to be no more than empty carcasses held together by tissue and bone. If intelligence and virtue adhere to the normal distribution curve—if, that is to say, in a random group of ten one or two are "brighter" or "better" than the others—it follows that there are few wise and many unwise, or at least less wise. Since in democratic states the quantity rather than quality of minds is politically decisive, it

124

follows too that the less wise will govern the wise. What saves communities from this appalling consequence—if indeed they are saved—is that the wise, precisely because they possess superior intelligence and wisdom, are able to outwit the unwise and persuade them to do the bidding of their betters. But why impose so time-consuming and needless a distraction on the wise? And what if passion so overwhelms the crowd as to render it incorrigible?

- Equality calls upon men and women to do what is psychologi-cally impossible—to love their own children no more than they love the children of a neighbor, to do for their own parents no more than they would for the parents of others, to treat friends no differently than strangers. Ordinary experience attests to the stubborn truth that men and women give preferential treatment to those with whom they have had closest personal ties; it is "unnatural" for them to do otherwise.

As with persons, so with ideas. No man or community will accept the notion that all doctrines are equal, that some doctrines are not to be more favored than others, and that we should "love" or at least tolerate even the most loathsome ideas, e.g., the advocacy of cannibalism or human sacrifice. Is it not, indeed, the meaning of community that it binds persons together precisely because they share certain values and exclude others?

- Equality is incompatible with the necessary arrangements for organizational efficiency, which demand that some sit at the top of the pyramids of power, others at the bottom, and still others at various levels between. Hierarchy is not merely a concomitant of modern technology; it is a principle indispensable to almost every realm of social life, e.g., an army, a university, a hospital, a political system. In our complex world, administration, whether of men or of things, requires organization (or, as Engels put it in 1874, in an essay attempting to discredit the anarchists, "the principle of authority"); which entails ranking; which means inequality (even if not, as Michels argued, oligarchy). It was not without reason that Shakespeare had the Prince of Ithaca say:

Take but degree away, untune that string,
And, hark, what discord follows!

• Equality drives us into an insoluble moral dilemma, and therefore into practices that contradict what we preach. In a world of unequal talents (or diligence, or commitment), equality of opportunity is but a device, though more meritorious than some others, for achieving inequality of results—in power, position, prestige, wealth. To impose equality of results—which is possible in some things, e.g., wealth or income, but not in all things, e.g., status and power—is to limit equality of opportunity. We cannot have both equalities simultaneously, and to opt for equality of opportunity, as in democratic states we purportedly do, is to indulge in open hypocrisy; for we clearly do not intend to follow Socrates' inescapable prescription that children be removed from their parents immediately after birth so that all may be raised alike (by identical nurses and tutors?) and given equal (identical?) chances.

• Equality thus entails a commitment to impossible, certainly wrong values. If we were true egalitarians, we would have to remove the distinctions among people by imposing equality of condition, or at least recognition. Yet we do not really intend to denigrate wisdom, virtue and beauty, achievement and success, by withholding appropriate recognition and applause. We do not really mean to admire stupid or wicked persons, or to esteem failure. At best, we speak of a limited equality, e.g., equality of reward in proportion to one's work or (in some ideal versions) need. We do not seek to treat everyone as if they were the same; for as Hobbes said: If all things are equal in all men, nothing would be prized. Hence we recognize that in certain important respects people are remarkably unlike each other, except perhaps (but only perhaps) at moments of birth and death.

• Moreover, by making equality the ultimate end, when it can never be more than but one among many ends, we make it impossible to come seriously to terms with the problem of conflicting ends, of the need at times to subordinate equality to another value, such as liberty or merit, which in a specific context may impose a higher claim on our loyalty. Thus, it is at least doubtful that Western educators will accept the justification of cheating on an examination recently put forward by a group of students in China: that since knowledge is to be shared, it matters not how this is done.

● To these objections we must add a crucial fact: wherever equality has been proclaimed as an operating principle, it has been subverted by the very people who avowedly espoused it. Thus, despite the American commitment to equality before the law, the rich continue to enjoy marked advantages over the poor, the whites over the blacks. Despite the Christian commitment to the brotherhood of man, most Christians leave fraternal and egalitarian practices to heaven and pursue other practices on earth. Such subversion is deliberate, not accidental. People want it that way. They admire superiority in others; they seek it for themselves; they dream of it for their children. The bitch goddess is sometimes money, but always success; and success means getting ahead of the other, who remains of course—in rhetoric—his brother, his equal.

For these and other reasons, equality (it is still argued) cannot command our exclusive or highest allegiance; perhaps it ought not commend itself at all.

II

On what grounds, then, can the principle of equality be reasonably warranted?

I would argue that there are at least four such grounds:

(1) Equality is not what its detractors generally take it to be.

(2) Equality has an important *negative* function as a protest-ideal as well as a positive content that properly enlists the loyalty of men.

(3) It is a mistake to identify the problems of equality with fatal deficiencies of the principle.

(4) When all is said and done, equality remains an essential ingredient of justice.

Let us consider these in turn.

If equality is not what its detractors take it to be, their criticisms are misdirected; they are launched against an erroneous conception or conceptions of equality. For example:

• Equality does not mean sameness or identity. In Plato's *Republic*, Socrates indicts democracy for "dispensing a sort of equality to equals and unequals alike," fathers descending to the level of their sons, and sons standing on a level with their fathers. But this is a caricature as well as a confusion. Fathers and sons do not stand on the same level, not at least while they relate to each other as fathers and sons, though they might well stand on the same level as citizens in a polling booth or in a court of law. For they are not merely fathers and sons; they are also persons, with rights and interests outside the parent-child relationship. They both need food, but if one is a mountain-climber and the other a scientist they do not require the same kinds or amounts of food. They both think, but not necessarily in the same way; nor do they necessarily share the same opinions. They may resemble each other physically, yet they are different. To say that men are equal is not to say they are identical—in these or other respects, like cleverness or temperament or wit or character. It is rather to say that behind all these differences there is some common substance of humanity that marks them as men, and in terms of which they are truly equal. They are not equal in all respects, only in all *relevant* respects. What these relevant respects are, I shall explore in a moment. Here it is enough to note that equality does not imply or entail identity in all things.

Nor, by the same token, is difference to be identified with inequality. An apple and an orange are different, but they are equally pieces of fruit. Two people may differ from each other in sex or race or religious affiliation or physical strength, but these connote nothing concerning intellectual or moral capacity; nor do they touch the fact that both people, despite these differences, are still human beings.

• Equality is not liberty, though certain kinds of *inequality* may well deprive men of important liberties. To require all persons to work one day each week at menial labor, or to attend religious services on the Sabbath, or to serve in the armed forces is to treat them equally but to deprive them of corresponding liberties. To allow inequality of wealth or power is to allow some men to live well but others meagerly. To permit racial or religious or sexual discrimination is to provide a favored group the liberty to deny equivalent rights to the disadvantaged.

• To treat all men equally is not always the same as to treat all cases equally. It may in fact result in treating those very men unequally. Thus, to give all men the same income is to favor the unmarried man and disadvantage the man with a family. To fine all men the same amount for the same offense is to treat the wealthy man lightly and the poor man heavily. To send each person to the doctor once a year, but no more than once a year, is to care for the healthy but not for those who are ill.

• Equality, while essential to justice, is not identical with justice. It is possible to treat everyone equally yet unfairly, e.g., to give all students an unfair examination, to pay all workers an inadequate wage, to compel all persons to worship in the same faith. It may be just to require that all children be sent to school; it would be unjust to require that all be given the same grade, yet to do this latter might (in sme curious constructions) accord with equal treatment.

• Equality does not demand that I love my neighbor as myself. To the egalitarian love is not *eros* but *agape,* not carnal or sensual love, not even filial love, but rather charity and respect. Hence I am not asked to *love* or admire him; I am asked only to recognize and respect him as a human being like myself. He is unlike me in many ways; he may be better or less worthy than I in many ways; but in certain relevant ways he remains a person no less than myself.

• Nor does equality require the abolition of hierarchy. If organizational and technological imperatives demand that certain individuals sit at the controls while others do their bidding, it does not follow that (say) accident of birth rather than equality of opportunity should be the governing principle to determine who should sit at those controls. Equality is opposed not to hierarchy but to the unjust distribution of place and power within hierarchy. It seeks to contain the range of that distribution and to base it on agreement (and perhaps merit) rather than on ascription.

• Finally, equality, while an ultimate value, is not the only ultimate and therefore not always the overriding value. Life is not a monolithic or unified whole; there are disharmonies and contradictions, diverse needs and strivings that come into collision, tensions between specific equalities (such as equality of opportunity versus equality of result) and between equality and other values (such as liberty). To press for equality in some things is not to press for equality in all things. To contend for equality does not exclude our contending at the same time for other ends too, which is merely to say that this is what it means to be human, that we want many things but cannot simultaneously obtain all of them, so we must choose. To this problem too I shall return.

III

What, then, is equality? To answer this question adequately it is necessary to consider equality both in its negative significance as a protest-ideal and in its positive content as an ultimate value. This last, in turn, must be grasped both as a general concept and as a system (however disharmonious and changing) of specific equalities and corresponding inequalities. I do not apologize for the complexity of such treatment; for equality, like most political concepts, defies simplistic understanding.

The fundamental and perhaps only legitimate defense of inequality is that it is not conventional but natural: it accords with the nature of men, who differ profoundly in intelligence, talent, and virtue; and it accords with the nature of things, which require hierarchy and degree. Hence the principle: the right man in the right place. However, this, as Giovanni Sartori properly notes,

> is an ideal that is never realized, since in its stead what we find only too often is the privileged man in a privileged place. And this is where the demand for equality actually

and rightly starts. The claim for equality is a protest against unjust, undeserved, and unjustified inequalities. For hierarchies of worth and ability never satisfactorily correspond to effective hierarchies of power. . . . Equality is thus a *protest-ideal,* a symbol of man's revolt against chance, fortuitous disparity, unjust power, crystallized privilege.[2]

If the rich and well-born were also the able, if the powerful were also the virtuous and wise, if, that is to say, actual aristocracies were truly natural aristocracies, based solely on merit; or if, to reverse the terms, the able were made rich, the virtuous made powerful, and the naturally best made the actual best, then the demand for equality might lose much of its force and justification. But history gives an emphatic denial to any such shabby claim. Even Santayana,who argued that it is "a benefit and a joy to a man, being what he is, to know that many are, have been, and will be better than he," felt constrained to attack actual "aristocracies" for their artificial rather than natural eminence. And what did Ortega y Gasset mean by the revolt of the masses if not primarily the domination in our time by men of wealth and power but without taste or standards?

It is no easy matter, moreover, to determine who are the naturally best and to devise a method that will accurately select them and elevate them to power. On these questions political writers have been eloquent but also at odds with one another. Blood and race, wealth and power, education and intelligence, strength (especially as demonstrated in military conquest) and athletic prowess, even piety and the mysticism of charisma, even (it must now be said) attainment of celebrity status, whether of the jet set or the Hollywood screen—all these have been put forward as attributes making for *political* virtue and wisdom. But surely not all these define the best. Nor have those who have come to power through these means remained the best—if initially they were the best—very long. Nor do we have gods to decide these matters. If to all this we add, with Edward Bellamy, that what any one man is and does is in large measure the consequence of what society and past generations have bequeathed to him and now, by providing conditions and opportunities, make it possible for him to do, we see that the very notion of merit or achievement is social and not simply personal. In what sense, then, is any man's superiority "natural"?

To raise this question is to challenge the most venerable and established commonplace in writings on equality. Political and social theorists from Plato through Hume and Rousseau to a host of contemporary thinkers have drawn a distinction between two sorts of inequality: natural (consisting, for example, in differences of age, sex, strength, and what Rousseau called "qualities of mind or soul") and conventional (consisting of differences in wealth, power, and honor, all of which emerge from the consent of men). We have already noted that the first rarely leads to or corresponds with the second. What now needs to be remarked is that what have been called inequalities by nature are often revealed, on examination and by experience, to be inequalities by convention. I do not seek to deny that there are some natural inequalities. I only argue that many inequalities that have been called natural in the past are not in fact so. Some people still believe women are by nature morally and intellectually inferior to men, blacks to whites (in Uganda, Asians to blacks), a defeated people to a conquering nation. This tells us a great deal about those who hold such beliefs; it does not alter the objective reality. Individuals vary, but why they do so—whether this is the result of an unalterable heredity or a changeable environment, for example—is not altogether clear. Nor can it be said that virtue and wisdom (Rousseau's qualities of mind or soul) owe nothing to society, or, since they conform to certain standards of behavior which are social norms or rules, are natural rather than conventional. Much remains to be done before we can assert with confidence that a particular inequality is natural and hence, presumably, unalterable.[3]

What is fatal to any justification of inequality, whether natural or conventional, however, is the fact that inequalities are cumulative and self-reinforcing. Inequality in wealth, for example, leads to inequalities in education, housing, medical care, travel, and the like, and, most important, to inequalities in power. To alter unjustifiable inequalities in the face of this "natural" aggrandizement of inequalities is most difficult, and in some measure impossible. Hence equality as a protest-ideal applies not simply to conventional or unjust inequalities but to inequality as a cumulative and self-reinforcing system of inequalities, both natural and conventional.

In turning to equality as a positive ideal, we must make a final point about differences, or ine es. We must ask: Which differences or inequalities are relevant, and relevant to what? Inequalities are specific, not general. The strongest man may not be the swiftest runner, the gifted violinist may be a poor mathematician, the great scientist a bumbling statesman. To be different or unequal in some things is not necessarily to be different or unequal in the important things, least of all in the single most important thing: to be, to live like a man; to seek one's self-development; to be a rational, free, and relatively autonomous human being.

Here we come to the heart of the principle of equality: *in the things that count men are not, and ought not to be, so much different from each other as to matter.* But what are the things that count?

Hobbes, with his usual felicity, answered the question this way:

> Nature hath made men so equall, in the faculties of body, and mind; as that though there bee found one man sometimes manifestly stronger in body, or of quicker mind than another; yet when all is reckoned together, the difference between man, and man, is not so considerable, as that one man can thereupon claim to himselfe any benefit, to which another may not pretend, as well as he. For as to the strength of body, the weakest has strength enough to kill the strongest, either by secret machination, or by confederacy with others, that are in the same danger with himselfe.

> And as to the faculties of the mind, (setting aside the arts grounded upon words, and especially that skill of proceeding upon generall, and infallible rules, called Science; which very few have, and but in few things; as being not a native faculty, born with us; nor attained, (as Prudence,) while we look after somewhat els,) I find yet a greater equality amongst men, than that of strength. For Prudence, is but Experience; which equall time, equally bestowes on all men, in those things they equally apply themselves unto. That

which may perhaps make such equality incredible, is but a
vain conceipt of ones owne wisdome, which almost all men
think they have in a greater degree, than the Vulgar; that is,
than all men but themselves, and a few others, whom by
Fame, or for concurring with themselves, they approve. For
such is the nature of men, that howsoever they may acknowledge many others to be more witty, or more eloquent,
or more learned; Yet they will hardly believe there be many
so wise as themselves: For they see their own wit at hand,
and other mens at a distance. But this proveth rather that
men are in that point equall, than unequall. For there is not
ordinarily a greater signe of the equall distribution of any
thing, than that every man is contented with his share.[4]

It is important not to slight Hobbes's teaching here. Hobbes
advances as an empirical fact—against classical and Christian
thought—what I take to be a first principle of politics: that men
must sleep, and when a strong man sleeps his life is in danger;
hence to protect himself from weaker men he needs either their
assurance that he will be left to awake or protection against them,
and preferably both; hence government, which involves (rests
upon) both force and consent. But to establish and maintain a
government, the strong must persuade the others that it is also
good for them. The appeal must be to the general interest, the
common good. And since the weak are also in danger, what is
common to them all is the fear of death, hence a love of peace,
and a desire for a system of order that will enable them all to live
and to pursue a commodious life. This, whatever their differences of mind, they can all grasp. To this they can all agree. From
all of which it follows that what is common to men is more
important than what differentiates or divides them. Inequalities
of body or mind are thus (in Hobbes's view) trivial, not politically
relevant, because not relevant to their survival as men.

It is true that survival without regard to the purposes for
which men survive—e.g., to live "virtuously"—is not an acceptable end for a classical or idealist philosopher; but since, for
Hobbes, "there is no such *Finus ultimus* (utmost ayme), nor
Summum Bonum (greatest Good), as is spoken of in the Books of
the old Morall Philosophers," this is not a fatal objection. It is

enough that men should be protected against an untimely death and be given an equal chance to attain their ends.

So too with Rousseau, who in pressing the case for equality differs from Hobbes in but two respects: he looks to other, conventional rather than natural, attributes of men; and he does so in normative rather than descriptive terms. Here is the relevant passage:

> By equality, we should understand, not that the degrees of power and riches are to be absolutely identical for everybody; but that power shall never be great enough for violence, and shall always be exercised by virtue of rank and law; and that, in respect of riches, no citizen shall ever be wealthy enough to buy another, and none poor enough to be forced to sell himself.[5]

Clearly, equality does not entail identity, at least not (for Rousseau) in power and wealth. What it does require is moderation—"on the part of the great, moderation in goods and position, and, on the side of the common sort, moderation in avarice and covetousness." It requires that the *range* of differences be contained: that inequality of power shall never enable one man to dominate another, to force him to act against his will; and that inequality of wealth shall similarly be limited to prevent any man from becoming master or slave. Neither a master nor a slave, neither to demean nor to be demeaned—this (for Rousseau) is the essence of equality.

Given these equalities—of ability and of rank—it follows, to invoke Hobbes again, that men may properly have equality of hope in attaining their ends. And if, to return once more to Rousseau, we are told that such equality is an unpractical ideal that cannot actually exist, that its abuse is inevitable, it does not follow that we should not at least make regulations concerning it. Indeed, Rousseau argues, "it is precisely because the force of circumstances tends continually to destroy equality that the force of legislation should always tend to its maintenance."

Central as these considerations are, it is not enough to rest with them. We must go back, if briefly, to Aristotle and forward to John Stuart Mill. I think of Aristotle here not for his distinction between numerical equality and equality proportionate to desert (of this, more later), but for his discussion of the general causes of revolution. What concerns Aristotle is the state of mind which leads to sedition. Here he makes principal the passions for equality and inequality.

> There are some [he says] who stir up sedition because their minds are filled by a passion for equality, which arises from their thinking that they have the worst of the bargain in spite of being the equals of those who have got the advantage. There are others who do it because their minds are filled with a passion for inequality (i.e. superiority), which arises from their conceiving that they get no advantage over others (but only an equal amount, or even a smaller amount) although they are really more than equal to others. . . . Thus inferiors become revolutionaries in order to be equals, and equals in order to be superiors.[6]

If, then, we are to assure stability in a society, we must take account of the attitudes and opinions of men. Whatever the justification or lack of justification for particular views, a polity that ignores what men think or believe runs the risk of disruption. For men fight for what they want or think they want, and they frequently want what they think they are entitled to have. If ordinary men regard themselves as politically competent (as equal), as they do, they will fight, as they have, to obtain an equal voice and an equal position. To deny them that voice is to assure conflict and perhaps revolution. Similarly, if men strive for inequality (i.e., superiority), this too will make for disorder. Moderation in men is then essential for social and political stability, and such moderation can only be achieved where the range of differences does not exceed the boundaries of what is tolerable. Which returns us, inescapably, to equality.

We come, finally, to John Stuart Mill and the liberal conception of man. Here the meaning of (and case for) equality may be briefly stated, for it turns primarily on but two notions: the rationality of man and the importance of individuality.[7] If man—each man—has a mind, he must be free to use it. This entails the right to choose, to decide between alternatives, to determine one's own way of life. It is true that he may choose wrongly, i.e., contrary to what another thinks. But to let that other choose for him makes it unnecessary for him to have, as Mill put it, "any other faculty than the ape-like one of imitation." By surrendering his mind, he surrenders himself; he remains a child. If he is to realize (or retain) his stature as a man, he must be equal in his right to decide for himself. And that he may choose differently from other men is not a risk but a virtue, the indispensable condition for the pursuit of self-development, identity, individuality. Without individuality, in all its rich diversity, what is society but a drab, uniform, and static collection of robot-like beings?

It is true also that, because man lives in society, he cannot be free to make *all* decisions for himself. No society can allow him to decide that he will drive on the left side of the road when others are required to drive on the right, or to kill or steal or otherwise injure his fellowmen at his pleasure. But being in society need not deprive him of the right to share equally in making such decisions. In the language of Thomas Rainborough, a spokesman for the Levellers, "the poorest he that is in England hath a life to live, as the greastest he"; hence the poorest and the richest should share equally in determining the conditions under which they are to live. Every man is to count for one; no one is to count for more than one.

IV

I have spoken thus far of equality as a general concept. In the real world, however, we are confronted not by "equality" but by many diverse and not always compatible equalities. Not all of course simultaneously press for our attention; not all are equally relevant to or applicable in a given situation. But it is sometimes the case that two or more equalities collide; then in choosing one we necessarily limit or curtail another. To which specific equality shall we give priority in a particular case, and why? Moreover, to choose among equalities—to treat men equally in some things (say voting) but unequally in others (say income)—requires a principle or principles of justification other than equality itself. To the extent that this choice between two kinds of equality is derived from other considerations, equality becomes a derivative value. But it is still a choice between two equalities in their own right, and in this respect equality remains an ultimate value. Beyond this, it is also often the case that there are ambiguities and tensions both within a particular equality (say equality of opportunity) and between equality however conceived and other values. We do not live in a tidy world. We are constantly jarred and tormented by incompatible, yet mutually commanding, ideals: honesty and kindness, love and obligation, equality and liberty, or excellence, or heroic achievement. These are the problems—to some the deficiencies—of equality, to which I now turn.

Let us begin with Aristotle's distinction between numerical equality and equality proportionate to desert, for in one form or another this remains perhaps the central problem of equality. According to the first sort of equality, all shall be treated alike; hence a sales tax or uniform wage or price or rent or bus fare is just, and a graduated income tax or differential wage or price or rent is not. According to the second, each shall be treated according to his merit; hence the reverse of the first set of practices would apply; for in these terms to give to the superior no more than is given to the inferior, or to extract from the poor man with a family of four the same rent or tax or price as the unmarried rich but not more meritorious man, is manifestly wrong.

In Yugoslavia some years ago, workers in a factory were bitterly divided over the question whether the same wage was to be given to each worker, on the principle that all stomachs are equal, or apportioned according to each person's contribution, on the principle that some did more, or better, or more important work than others. Apart from the not inconsiderable difficulty in defining each man's "desert," or determining the right proportion, which of the two notions of equality is correct? Why? (It ought to be noted, if only parenthetically, that a further inconvenient problem attaches to the numerical conception of equality here. For in the absence of strict controls over spending, providing for equality of wages or income may soon lead to inequalities of wealth—given the fairly evident fact that some men are frugal and save while others quickly rid themselves of all that they receive.)

Or take the idea that each member of an orchestra shall be rewarded equally for a fine performance. Does this mean giving each player his favorite instrument, in which case one may get a pair of cymbals and another a grand piano, or does it entail giving each player the same instrument (say a violin) or a ten-dollar bill?

Consider the socialist principle of equality: from each according to his ability, to each according to his need. The one place where this principle is almost universally found is, paradoxically, in the family, perhaps the least egalitarian of human associations. Shall we now apply it in the realm of work? If so, what shall we say to the women's liberation movement when a wife demands "appropriate" payment for her labor even though her husband may already earn a sum sufficient to provide for both their material needs? Shall we diminish his (or her) earnings proportionately, or insist that she (or he) work without pay?

And what of the venerable adage, Let the punishment fit the crime? Should it not rather be, Let the punishment fit the criminal, thereby taking into account such factors as age, motive, circumstance, and frequency (or infrequency) of offense? Shall the figure of justice really be blindfolded, or should she (or he) look at each case with clear and searching eyes?

To these and similar questions Aristotle, though he understood the problem, offered no satisfactory answer. With his customary prudence he observed: "Some take the line that if men are equal in one respect, they may consider themselves equal in all: others take the line that if they are superior in one respect, they may claim superiority all round. . . . The right course is (not to pursue either conception exclusively, but) to use in some cases the principle of numerical equality, and in others that of equality proportionate to desert." The difficulty of course is that such a formulation does not tell us which cases properly fall under the one, and which under the other category. But then, no general principle can decide each concrete case; always secondary principles and special circumstances enter into consideration.

Most decisively, these conflicting notions of equality entail a perennial, because irresolvable, paradox: namely, that to treat different (unequal) people equally (the same way) is often to achieve unequal results—e.g., to give a sickly person no more medical care than is required by a robust person is not to produce equally healthy individuals; while to treat different people differently (unequally) may be precisely what is required (as in the given example) to produce an equal result.

From all of which it follows that not mathematics or formal logic but experience, circumstance, and the shared values of a particular people at a particular time will variously determine the outcome. But whether that determination is the "right" outcome remains an open question.

Let us now turn to certain difficulties inherent in a seemingly simple and widely accepted principle: equality of opportunity. Surely if a society is to have hierarchies or pyramids of power —and what society can avoid this?—it is proper that movement up and down the ladder accord with competence or merit. But (and this indeed is a very large but), as already noted: (1) the equal opportunity principle requires conditions that neither our own nor any other society outside the visions of utopian thinkers is willing to provide, e.g., removing children from their parents immediately after birth and raising them in common. Moreover, every actual society is disfigured by discriminatory practices and unjust arrangements that limit or vitiate equality of opportunity. Hence, whatever the rhetoric, the principle is at best approximated but nowhere fully observed. And   (2) even if the principle were to be realized, it would lead, paradoxically, to a nonegalitarian result; for in a differentiated and hierarchical society equality of opportunity is but another mode—even if the "best" mode—of arriving at inequalities of condition, notably of power, status, and (commonly) wealth.

These considerations are alone sufficient to render the principle suspect. But there is, in the view of some critics (oddly enough, critics of the Left rather than the Right), an even more fatal objection to the equal opportunity principle: namely, that it converts life from a cooperative adventure of equal human beings into a competitive struggle of unequal talents, in the course of which not individuals but aspects of individuals are prized, and as a consequence of which losers, who are the bulk of the human race, are denigrated and demeaned.

Consider the following statements:

> When you think of equality of opportunity as the career open to talents, you cease to think of the man who is untalented. . . . The newer conception of merit is not talent but personality, creativity, which includes talent but sets it in its rightful place. Justice consists not in seeing that all start from the same line, permitting all to race, and awarding prizes to the winners, but rather, abandoning the whole idea of a race with prizes, in seeing that each is as far as possible given space, scope, room, and encouragement to employ his free powers in the building of a human life.[8]

> Striving is not for equality nor for superiority; it is for the enhancement of uniqueness. . . . When it is being itself which is valued, then none can be inferior, or superior. . . . People are not [to be] valued in terms of achievement. People are [to be] valued for what they are. . . .[9]

Now in one sense—a very profound sense—these contentions are surely unassailable, for they ask no more than that we recognize and respect the reality (and the rights) of each individual as a living presence. They ask us to set aside the vexing problem of determining the value of a man's talents—often by arbitrary if socially approved standards—and thereby to avoid the consequential division of men into higher and lower orders, into various strata of inequalities. Far more, they ask us to cease judging men as fragmented beings, in terms of their functional roles, and to look at *who* they are rather than at *what* they do. Then it matters not whether a man is a butcher or a doctor, a garbage collector or an engineer. What matters is that he is a man, who happens to perform a certain task for some portion of his time, but who is also a husband and a father, a friend and a neighbor, perhaps a churchgoer and a participant in certain communal activities, but always a total person and a full-time member of the same human race. He is with us, of us, in us. And he counts, not because he is different, but because he is the same.

In these terms the equal opportunity principle, because it leads to and emphasizes differences, inequalities, is destructive of what is most essential to the human enterprise—respect for that which is common to all men, their humanity.

Yet, when all this has been said, can we really abandon the equal opportunity principle? Can we really ignore talent and dispense not simply with differences but with the esteem we attach to differences? In so far as a man is a teacher, or an artist, or a statesman, do we not wish him to be a *good* teacher or artist or statesman? And shall we not esteem the *better* rather than the poorer teacher? Moreover, if in the modern world specialization of function is unavoidable, if organization and consequently hierarchy are *necessary,* then how except through the equal opportunity principle can we assure a just determination of place? It is true, as Michels argued, that organization and hierarchy carry with them a tendency to oligarchy, but the task then is surely to guard against the conversion of that tendency into a reality; it is not to abandon organization and hierarchy, which is in any case impossible. It is also true that the esteem we generally attach to differences and inequalities may often exaggerate (or diminish) the worth of the individual as a total being; but the problem then is not that men are functionally different, and behave toward each other as superiors or inferiors in certain roles, but that *we* (or society) impute a certain value to such differences, and *that* plainly is a matter of reeducation.[10]

The greater difficulty seems to me to lie in another direction. For if deficiencies in existing arrangements and practices militate against the proper functioning of the equal opportunity principle, it follows that those who stand at various levels in the pyramids of position and power do not necessarily belong there. It is then necessary either to correct those deficiencies or, if that is not possible, to shift our attention away from the principle of equality of opportunity to the alternative, perhaps complementary, principle of equality of result. Thus, it was not the doyens of the New Left but a moderate liberal, Franklin D. Roosevelt, who in 1932 proclaimed that "equality of opportunity as we have known it no longer exists," called for "a re-appraisal of values," and set as our task "distributing wealth and products more equitably." In the same vein, in his address on the State of the

Union in January 1944 he articulated what he called "a second Bill of Rights," including the right to a useful job, an adequate income, a decent home, adequate medical care, a good education, and other components of what we now associate with the welfare state.

What is of interest here is the notion that a man's success or failure is not simply the consequence of his innate ability but, in some measure, of the system—its practices, arrangements, and (let it be said) its derangements. Hence equality of result —meaning by equality not identity but the tolerable range of which Aristotle and Rousseau spoke—is the necessary and altogether proper mode of redress. Then, paradoxically, equalization of results provides the conditions that make possible a greater measure of equality of opportunity. So the two principles, far from being intrinsically in opposition, come together as alternative or complementary means to the same end—the achievement of justice in determining fitness and place.

In short, despite all its admitted difficulties, the equal opportunity principle, whether as a working standard to be approximated or an ideal by which a people shall be judged, remains an essential element of any right ordering of social life.

I now turn briefly to the familiar yet still vexing question: Does a commitment to equality endanger other ultimate and equally prized ends, in particular liberty?[11]

This of course is the problem that agitated Alexis de Tocqueville and John Stuart Mill and that concerns not merely conservatives but traditional liberals today. For at one level the answer to the question is surely affirmative. To say that all persons shall behave, or not behave, in a certain way—pay taxes, observe the traffic laws, send children to school, abstain from polygamy or trespass—is to deprive them of corresponding liberties. In this obvious sense *every* law or custom that imposes a uniform requirement is an interference with liberty.

But liberty, like equality, is not a simple entity, like an apple pie, out of which each law cuts an irretrievable piece. Nor is government, through law, the only source of interference with liberty; other men and groups, through force or economic sanctions or other forms of pressure, also interfere with human freedom. To assure a particular liberty, such as freedom of expression, it is then necessary to restrain those nonpolitical powers who might otherwise limit it—on the alleged ground that the speech in question is (say) obscene or subversive or otherwise harmful. Law in that case enters not simply as a restraint but as a restraint on a restraint. All of which is to say that liberty, properly understood, is a complex of particular liberties—of speech, religion, travel, and the like—and of concomitant restraints.

To determine whether the law should restrain or tolerate a social restraint, and thereby secure a particular liberty for some (perhaps only under certain circumstances) but not an apposite liberty for others, is merely to recognize that not all liberties are equally important, or equally desirable. Liberties, like equalities, must be ranked hierarchically; and when we give primacy to one we may well have to surrender another.

In the same way we must choose between conflicting liberties and equalities: between the liberty of parents to raise their children as they see fit, giving them what advantages they can, and equality of opportunity, which requires that all children be treated alike, that no child receive less (or more) than another, and hence that all children be raised in common; between the liberty of an employer to hire whomever he pleases (say only red-haired, white-skinned females) and antidiscrimination laws which in the service of equality require him to employ qualified persons of whatever sex and color; between the liberty of a man to live among "his own kind" and the egalitarian requirement that residential areas be open to all; and so on.

It is not always the case that equality will, or should, prevail over liberty. In the name of individuality, we deny the right of egalitarians to compel hippies to dress and behave as others do. In the name of religious freedom, we deny the right of egalitarians to require all children, including the children of atheists and agnostics, to take religious education in the schools, or, in the case of children whose parents are members of Jehovah's Witnesses, to salute the flag.

Nor is it always the case that liberty will, or should, prevail over equality—witness our antidiscrimination laws.

So when we confront the diverse issues that bedevil us today, whether it be equality versus inequality of result, or conformity versus diversity, we must understand that there is no simple and final resolution. Both liberty and equality, while in one sense ultimate values, are also derivative values; for when there are conflicts among or between them, it is only with reference to another and presumably higher principle that they can be handled. This higher principle is sometimes stability, but since stability is itself justified only when the system is worth preserving, it is generally some conception of justice or the common good.

V

Now every theory of justice—whether it looks to God or nature or tradition or utility or an initial (actual or hypothetical) social contract—is vulnerable to serious criticism; and none, it seems hardly necessary to add, is universally accepted. If we forgo mutual slaughter or the authoritarian imposition of a particular creed, and turn instead to a democratic resolution of this disagreement, we build once again on the principle of equality.

For what counts in democratic states is not the putative truth or falsity of a theory but majority acceptance or belief, and this is the outcome of a process of negotiation, bargaining, compromise, and voting. What is crucial to this process is the question: Who shall participate? If the democratic response is, as it must be, *all,* then all must be equally free to articulate, assess, and judge among alternative policies. Equality and liberty thus again come together in a common cause.

From this standpoint, equality is not, as Isaiah Berlin would have it, simply an ultimate principle that "cannot itself be defended or justified, for it is itself that which justifies other acts—means taken towards its realization."[12] It is rather an instrumental principle that cannot be other than defended and justified, for it is indispensable to the realization of something other than itself—namely, democracy. Those who, for whatever reason, opt for democracy must opt too for at least those equalities essential to democracy. And if among the diverse forms of state democracy is a just regime, perhaps—though I cannot argue this here—the *best* regime, it follows that those equalities (and liberties) appropriate or necessary to democracy are warranted; for to will the end is also to will the means.

But democracy, it may fairly be contended, is itself not an end but a means, a political principle or set of arrangements that must be defended or justified in terms of what democracy does for man. To the extent that this is true, it only reinforces the justice of equality. For what democracy does, as John Stuart Mill so ably argued, is to enable each man both to protect himself and to elevate himself. To protect himself against misgovernment, not by entrusting another with his guardianship but by himself standing up for his rights and interests, by himself exercising his power—of opinion and of political participation, not merely through the suffrage but also by taking an actual part in the government—and thereby sharing, as far as any one individual can, in the making of decisions that govern his life. To elevate himself morally and intellectually, by that very participation, acquiring through discussion and ensuing enlightenment a concern not only for his own selfish interests but for the general good.

Thus democracy, whether as end or as means, vindicates the egalitarian claim.

The case for the justice of equality of course does not rest here. If the end is man, then equality—even if by equality we mean treating different people in the same way—is essential to the very life of man. For however different people may be, in some respects they are the same. They all want to live, and all societies—despite wars and other forms of senseless killings—respect this as a fundamental right. This is why we have traffic regulations and laws against murder, hospitals and safety devices in automobiles and industrial plants, lifeguards on bathing beaches, and the like—all without regard to sex, race, religion, intelligence, and other matters that differentiate persons from one another. Given this equal right to life, it follows that all men are equally entitled to whatever is necessary to sustain and protect life. At a minimum, this means that no man can legitimately be denied adequate food, clothing, housing, medical care, etc. Beyond that minimum, decent and rational men may disagree as to what is required. In most societies today, for example, education—though not of course at the same level in all societies—is recognized as such a necessity.

What is entailed here is the notion of need. Obviously, different people need different things. But just as obviously, *all* people need the same, or the same sorts of things. Equality thus builds on what is common to men, on what is necessary, perhaps even on what is good, for all men. To exclude any individual or group from these rights—to life and the things essential to life—is to deny their humanity. Possibly there are good reasons for denying these rights, or some of them, to particular persons or groups under special circumstances; but in such cases the burden of proof is surely on those who would argue for those exceptions. And exceptions they must remain. No principle is absolute, automatically binding in all cases without regard to circumstances; but without the principle of equality it is difficult to see what sense can be made of "the common" that is at the very heart of what it means to be a man.[13]

Men want not merely to live but to live well. From a moral point of view, this means that they wish to live, if not nobly, at least justly; to do good rather than evil, to act rightly rather than wrongly. It cannot be said that everyone understands precisely the same things by "the right" and "the good." What can be said is that they are generally agreed on at least one principle appropriate to the determination of what is right and good. This is the principle of fairness.

We do not call a race fair when one runner is hobbled by a ball and chain and another is mounted on a horse. We do not call a fight fair when one pugilist's hands are encased in armor and the other in foam-padded gloves. We insist in both cases that those who enter the contest do so on the same terms. We do not recognize as fair a trial where only one party is represented by adequate counsel, safeguarded by the rules of evidence, and given an opportunity to testify in his behalf. We do not call a social order fair that gives only some people the liberty to criticize the government and to pursue their own life-styles. Nor do we consider fair an arrangement that stacks the conditions behind these procedures to the advantage of one party: e.g., where one pugilist is considerably taller and heavier than the other, or where parental wealth is distributed so unevenly that the rich child but not the poor can satisfy his desires or alone have the power to qualify himself so that he may earn them.

From this perspective, fairness as a principle of justice dictates equality.[14] Fairness does not prescribe the "right" result; it requires us to treat people equally in order to arrive at the right result. Or, conversely, it stipulates that no person shall be treated differently from another without just cause; and by just cause I mean not simply reasons—there are always "reasons"—but arguments and justifications that make sense and carry conviction on logical, empirical, and moral grounds. Thus, to say that there shall be no cruelty without just cause is not to preclude (say) punishment for heinous crimes, but to prohibit the arbitrary imprisonment or debasement of "inferior" by "superior" peoples.

This sort of equality—what may be called equality of consideration—is an ultimate end in that it affirms the intrinsic value of every human being. It does not deny that there are differences (inequalities?) among men. It rather insists that such differences do not justify—except for good and sufficient reasons—the withdrawal from some men of those conditions which are required for the development of their varying individualities. It insists that no man is fully human who must bend his knee to a master, who is cast into secondary importance and subjected as a consequence of that label to unjustifiable inequalities. It insists that, whatever the differences among men, what is common to them all is the desire to lead the kind of life each wants to lead; and that, from this standpoint, it does not matter that one is wealthier or more powerful or more prestigious than another; what matters is that each should be equally free, and reasonably able, to be himself, to live as he wishes to live, and not as another wants him to live.[15] What matters is not merely equality in this kind of freedom, but also respect. It is fashionable in certain quarters today to disparage the value of tolerance; but surely tolerance—of each man's rationality, of his right to be different, to live as he thinks best—is essential to his humanity. In this at least all must be equal. And since it is obvious that some limits must always be placed on individual action, those limits too must emerge only from an equal consideration of each man's rights and interests.

In the wisdom of the classical philosophers, justice consists in giving each man his due. This has generally meant treating unequal men unequally, according to their differences. But in another, and I think greater wisdom, justice consists not in looking at what divides men but at what unites them, what is common to them all. And what is common to them all is their equal integrity as human beings. It may well be that a full theory of justice must attend not to one or the other of these conceptions but to both. In that case all must still be treated equally in those respects in which they are equal. Equality does not require more.

VI

We can now see where the newer critics of equality—Daniel Bell and Irving Kristol,[16] among others—have gone wrong. They are of course much too sophisticated and insightful not to have dwelt on legitimate concerns or not to have taken account of some of the more obvious objections to their positions. Nevertheless, it remains the case that they have not come adequately to grips with the nature and complexities of the specific equalities they treat; they have tended to confuse the specific equality they condemn with the whole of equality; and, most important, because they have sought to build on what divides rather than on what unites men, they have not understood the necessity of equality for the maintenance of community.

Thus, when Bell pleads the cause of meritocracy, he does not fully face up to the deficiencies of the equal opportunity principle in actual societies, and the implications of such deficiencies for the notion of personal achievement. When Kristol worries about the nature and implications of a greater measure of equality in income, and of the costs entailed by a redistributive policy, he neglects the costs entailed by the maintenance of existing, unjust practices and confuses this particular equality with the whole of equality. When they both, along with many others, argue against equality of result, they do not confront the fact that inequalities of result create privileges that vitiate equality of opportunity and thereby render inequitable the results that have in fact emerged and will continue to emerge, and that society must then intervene to redress or even (perhaps) cancel out those privileges so as to restore—or newly establish—an initial equality of opportunity.

All too often these newer critics contest not equality but a caricature of equality. No serious liberal or socialist thinker has ever held to a notion of absolute equality. None, to my knowledge, has ever maintained that equality must apply to all things—to cards in a deck, pictures in an exhibition, ideas in the marketplace. None, to my knowledge, has ever maintained that equality precludes our distinguishing old from young men, or young men from children, when drafting soldiers into the army. Nor has any serious liberal or socialist thinker failed to recognize the tensions and conflicts among equalities, or between equality and other values, such that choices must be made and some equalities set aside. This is precisely why, for liberals and socialists, equality is so important; for in making those choices all men must equally share.

All men must share, for all are members of the community. Now a community embraces partial associations, like a university or a corporation, but it transcends them. For it builds not on those aspects of the individual relevant to the association—his special aptitudes and talents—but on his wholeness as a person. A community, unlike a corporation but like a family, does not recognize degrees of membership; it does not value an individual only as a means, as an instrument to the fulfillment of the association's purpose; it values him as an end. Consequently it respects and cares for him as an end. As such, he is equal—equal in his humanity, and in the rights and freedoms appropriate to that humanity.

Whatever the limits of equality, whatever its difficulties, this then remains true: without equality properly understood and constantly held in view as *a* (but not of course *the*) first principle, there can be no community, and hence no individuality. And without these there can be no just society.

Mark Kelman

The Social Costs
of Inequality

For most radicals, the problem of poverty and the problem of inequality have been connected. Whether they had a theory of the exploitation of the working class or a gut sense that price-gougers and sweat-shop operators stole the bread of the poor, radicals have long felt that many were badly off *because* a few were so well off. This view has for some time been under attack, with the result that the issue of equality has also seemed to fade.

According to neoclassical economics and its philosophical derivatives, inequality as such is acceptable, as long as it also serves to raise the level of those at the bottom. All manner of inequality-producing economic arrangements are justified by this presumption, from incentive bonuses to entrepreneurial profits to interest on capital. More immediately, such policies as investment tax credits and accelerated depreciation, though clearly most beneficial to those at the top, are lauded because they lead to economic growth which, in turn, may raise the real income levels of the poorest members of society.

The neoclassicists also attack the goal of equality by hexing it with their worst curse: it is *inefficient*. If increasing inequality raises the Gross National Product, they say, the lot of even the poorest can then be improved by some redistributive taxation.

All but the most rabidly Ayn Randist disciples urge that the government establish a "negative income tax" program to share some of the copiously growing income with the impoverished; but they demand that the rates for the rich not have a disincentive effect that would increase equality at the cost of lower total national income.

Radicals have failed to mount an adequate counterattack on either of the two key assumptions the neoclassicists make. (1) Are the "economic incentives" really necessary for overall economic growth—or are the institutions inegalitarian and hierarchical merely to maximize the income of the elite? (2) Does the *well-being* of the poor improve in proportion to their changing real income if the rich get disproportionately richer—or does *inequality itself* hurt the poor?

This essay will concentrate on the second of these questions, presuming, solely for the sake of argument, that "economic incentives" are necessary to growth. It will argue against the proposition that growing inequality is perfectly acceptable as long as the real income of the poorest members of society is increased.

In all fairness, neoclassicists do concede that there are some costs to inequality per se. Consumption, it is acknowledged, has externalities or neighborhood effects. If you and I both consume more goods but I continue to consume less than you, I may feel no better off. A Winter '72 *Public Interest* article, "Does Money Buy Happiness?," confirmed this bit of economic theory. Although the *relatively* well off seem to express satisfaction in all manner of public opinion polls and pyschological tests, there seems to be no evidence that people get happier as a society gets richer or that people were happier in richer societies than in poorer ones. In other words, merely raising everyone's income level does not change anyone's satisfaction with his economic lot.

Economists often explain this "neighborhood effect" in a most unflattering way: a textbook example is that a poor person with a black-and-white television set still feels deprived because he knows there are color television sets around. But this "envy" explanation is not at all adequate. For a start, in purely economic terms, different infrastructures inflate the needs of the poor in increasingly rich societies so that those left out of growth are directly hurt. With no stream nearby, a washing machine becomes a necessity. Dispersed job markets make expensive transportation part of the production cost for the poor worker who requires it for work. More important, social relations and structures in poor societies may make perfectly acceptable certain activities that would be a burden in a rich society. For instance, milling grain or weaving clothes may not seem a *task* to an Indian peasant; for the "richer" yet relatively more deprived ghetto-dwelling American, a lack of money to buy processed food or clothes off the rack is quite a deprivation since making these items would scarcely fit into an urban culture.

Some neoclassicists would also concede that there are sociopolitical costs to inequality as such. Deferential behavior, and an associated dehumanization and loss of self-esteem, clearly arises from discrepancies in economic position rather than from lack of goods or from poverty. Antidemocratic political corruption grows out of the existence of inequality: both offering and accepting bribery is based on the expectation of becoming *better off* than your neighbors, not just "well off."

But I am most interested here in pursuing a point that is vehemently denied in neoclassical theory: *that a real growth in income for the poor may not even enable them to obtain more of some of the most essential goods if there is a concurrent increase in income inequality.* The poor will obviously be able to get more of some services and goods (that is, after all, what a rise in real income means), but they may not get more of all kinds of goods, and those goods from which they are excluded may be among the most important.

II

What is economic growth? It is a product of increases in hours worked and in productivity, an increase in the output of tangible goods and services. If we say that people in the poorest class have experienced a real income growth from, say, $1,000 to $2,000 a year, we mean that they can consume twice as many goods of identical quality or twice as many hours of equally efficient service.

For ordinary items like food, the process by which economic

growth leads to the procurement of goods can be described quite simply: with their additional income, people go to the store to buy food. Since there is only a given, fixed amount of food in the stores at a single point in time, they will bid up the price on this existing stock of food. This increase in price will make food production unusually profitable and divert some of the society's resources into the production of food until its price drops down again to the lowest possible cost of production (including a "normal" rate of profit).

But for certain goods this process could not occur. For example, unique goods, like an authentic signed Rembrandt, are in completely inelastic supply. Assume that at Time I there are two art lovers earning $1,000 a year, one (X) willing to spend his total income on the Rembrandt, the other (Y) willing to spend half. The wheels of technical progress spin and, at Time II, each man finds himself with an income of $3,000. Man Y surmises that this income should give him his Rembrandt plus more clothes for his family. But there is still only one Rembrandt, and he is still outbid. More clothes, yes, but no more Rembrandts.

For goods in totally inelastic supply, price is not fixed by supply cost, even in the long run; it is fixed by demand. Ordinarily, if five items costing $1 each are offered at Time I and there are five buyers willing to pay $10 (as well as a sixth willing to pay $9.99), the price will be $10, but production will increase immediately till demand=supply=cost, perhaps brings about 50 buyers and the 50th buyer is willing to pay only $1. If the supply is fixed at five, though, the price will remain $10; it will remain as far above cost as the demand price for the number of available goods.

If we assume, just for argument now, that there is some good G in fixed supply which poor people are willing to spend a very large proportion of their income for, their ability to obtain the good depends upon the *relative* income (and preferences) of the richest class. If the poor cannot get such a good, their "income" is devalued; it is as if we were given $10,000 but allowed to spend it only in a store selling bubble gum. We could certainly get a lot, but we couldn't get very much *satisfaction*.

Assume there have been two shipwrecks, each with 1,000 people and one doctor who can give 50 hours of medical care, to be distributed by economic criteria alone, in the week before the rescue ship comes. In one shipwreck, 90 percent of the victims have the same amount of money, say $1,000, and 10 percent have $1,999. The 100 most injured are willing to give all their money for treatment, the next 800 are willing to give 50 percent, and the last 100, who are slightly wounded, 10 percent. The doctor will treat the 100 most wounded for one half hour each for a fee of $1,000 per person. In the second shipwreck, 90 percent of the passengers have $2,000, 10 percent have $50,000. Assuming injury is distributed randomly so that 90 of the most injured are relatively poor, the richest 10 percent will still be the only ones treated since they will all outbid even those "poor" willing to spend 100 percent of their income. Even the slightly wounded will offer $5,000 for the doctor's time. Though the "poor" are richer in the second shipwreck, they are less able to obtain a good in fixed supply.

In the extreme form I have presented, only totally nonhomogeneous collectors' items and Veblenesque goods (those whose rarity is the basis of their value) would be considered in completely inelastic supply, and these are hardly very important cases. But the fact is that of the four basic consumption items—housing, medical care, clothing and food—the first two partake, each in its own way, of this supply inflexibility, *so that the mass access to them is determined by the degree of inequality rather than the real levels of income.* I will draw the case in detail for medical care, and suggest outlines for a similar case in the housing and education markets.

III

No serious observer could claim that the supply of medical care is constant. Supply can be raised through an increase in the number of doctors, longer working hours for current practitioners, and wider use of paraprofessionals. While there is a considerable time lag in the first and most vital of these methods, because of the long training period involved (if one wanted to double the total supply of physicians by 1990, one would now have to increase the size of medical-school entering classes by 400 percent) there is every reason to believe that, on the supply side, the medical market is relatively "normal," i.e., entry is induced by excess profits.

The problem, though, is that demand is not independent of supply. With any conceivable level of output expansion, demand will expand to exceed it. The ambiguous nature of health and the uncertain delivery of medical care create a situation akin to permanent excess demand, a situation requiring rationing. When demand exceeds supply, two rationing systems are possible in the market. In an egalitarian society, the good is rationed according to a preference based on need, i.e., the severity of the disease. In the inegalitarian society, price is set by the price the rich can pay. Since everyone is willing to spend high portions of her or his income to obtain medical care, a widening spread of income will simply exclude the bottom portions of society from private medical care. If, as I think is the case, the demand for medical services by the rich is limitless within conceivable supply constraints, an attempt by the poor to procure medical care by raising the proportion of their income they are willing to spend on medical care will merely cause further price inflation and higher doctor's incomes for the rich will simply up their bids to retain their share of medical care. Such a process has gone on in all "free medical markets": in the late 1960s, America and Canada spent 8.2 and 9.7 percent respectively of GNP on health care, compared to 6 and 7.1 percent for nonmarket Britain and Sweden. Yet the poor received, according to all measures, far better medical care in the latter two countries.

For an ordinary good, demand functions are discrete and independent, i.e., one knows pretty well what one wants and what price one is willing to pay for it before one knows whether it is available at that price. Medical care is not like that at all, for two main reasons.

First, the demand for medical care is based more on "treatability," a supply factor, than on "disease." In some important sense, people are always sick. The average lower-middle-class male between the age of 20 and 45 experiences over a 20-year period approximately one life-endangering illness, 20 disabling illnesses, 200 nondisabling illnesses, and 1,000 symptomatic episodes: an average of one new episode every six days. When one gets older, it gets worse: as the body ages and chronic disease arises, there is hardly a moment when every part of the body feels perfectly fine. The decision to see a doctor, then, is based in large part on a judgment of his potential effectiveness. People live with arthritis, backache, coughs, allergies because there is not much that can be done for them, just as they once lived with infectious diseases, tuberculosis, etc. And though people *pay* for a great deal of medical care for certain kinds of cancer, heart disease, and nerve disorders, they're not buying anything but reassurance that all was done that could be.

Second, the patient has next to no idea what it is that he wants, in terms of product. While he would like to feel better, the patient has no idea what procedure should be employed. If the doctor says surgery, it is surgery. "Shopping around" is not very relevant in medical practice: it is far too expensive, time-consuming, and often impossible to elicit a number of opinions—besides, the consumer couldn't judge among them anyway. Even if you do look around, most doctors, as a result, tell you to do what *your* doctor says, because the state of medical technology is generally so uncertain that only missionaries and fanatics are particularly sure of their own opinion in complex or chronic cases.

The suppliers' market response to this uncertain demand is simple: establish practices where there are rich people and sell them as much medical care as you care to provide. The pattern of the medical market in the United States today fits this model appallingly well:

• According to the 1970 Census, egalitarian Standard Metropolitan Statistical Areas (SMSAs) have a higher median family income than inegalitarian ones ($10,800 to $10,500), but in 44 of 59 cases,[1] above-median egalitarianism is associated with below-median physician supply (doctors per 100,000 population) and below-median egalitarianism with above-median physician supply. The four poorest, extremely inegalitarian SMSAs (Albuquerque, Oklahoma City, Phoenix, and Tacoma), all with family incomes averaging under $10,000 a year, have a median of 179.7 physicians per 100,000 people, compared to 111.4 for the eight richest egalitarian SMSAs, all with median incomes over $11,000. Only 2 of 13 observations cross medians. While there is the mediating factor that the inegalitarian SMSAs are to some degree "regional" centers or sites of medical schools, the explanation seems insufficient: Detroit and Toledo, which fit the same bill but which are egalitarian, have 138.6 and 134.9 doctors per 100,000 people respectively. The mechanism by which doctors locate in areas where there are rich people to fill their practices is probably not direct: med-school graduates hardly check Gini indices of income equality. But research grants, expensive machinery at hospitals, and "nice" neighborhoods where doctors live are all more likely to be found in inegalitarian SMSAs.

Within SMSAs as well, doctors will choose to go where the rich are: some ghetto areas of New York have less than 10 doctors per 100,000 people while the SMSA as a whole has well over 200.

Once they are set up in rich areas, there is no reason to believe they cannot fill their time. The rich simply learn to go to the doctor for symptoms the poor would ignore. A relatively old but dependable study of an upstate New York city, Earl Koos's *The Health of Regionville,* divided the population into three socioeconomic classes and asked respondents which of a list of symptoms should be called to the attention of a doctor. Only two symptoms were checked as needing attention by less than 75 percent of Class I respondents. Class III respondents checked ten items less than 25 percent of the time and only three symptoms, all related to unexplained bleeding, were checked by more than half of the respondents.

While no good figures for prices or hours worked are available by neighborhoods, simple observation indicates that doctors in Great Neck or White Plains or Newton have no trouble filling their appointment books. Both prices and utilization are extremely high though the supply of physicians in these towns is many, many times above any conceivable national level. A check of the telephone directory indicates that there are roughly 750 physicians per 100,000 inhabitants in Great Neck, more than five times the national average.

• The real income of the American poor has shot up since the Depression, yet there seems to be little reason to believe that their access to medical care has increased significantly. While the number of physicians has doubled since 1931, the absolute number engaged in primary care has *declined.* In 1931, fewer than 20 percent of physicians were engaged in specialty care; by 1967, the figure was 61 percent. What occurred was that the expansion of medical-care supply resulted not so much in an expansion of patient visits as in an expansion of the "quality" of care—i.e., of costliness of care for the rich. Specialists generally provide high-cost, very high-price medical care for more uncertain diseases, while primary care tends to handle the more certain, cost-effective areas of medicine: antibiotics for infection, prenatal checkups for expectant mothers, treatment of injuries. In much the same way, hospitals have done very little to improve the quality of their community services—a 1970 *New England Journal of Medicine* study showed that emergency-room care was effective in only 27 percent of cases—while they have overinvested in fancy, technologically advanced machines. 30 percent of the hospitals equipped to do closed heart surgery had *no* such cases in the year they were studied by the President's Commission on Heart Disease, Cancer, and Stroke.

• Doctors, taking advantage of consumer ignorance and uncertainty, sell their particular service whether it is needed or not. A 1965 study by the Kansas Blue Cross Association found that while populations were homogeneous there were three- to four-fold variations in surgical rates for the population of different areas, because there were large differences in the number of surgeons and hospital beds in the different regions. Similarly, for 23 hospital regions in New York State, the urban population's appendectomy rate was 8.11 per 1,000, the rural population's 3.44 per 1,000. The corresponding mortality rates were 5.26 for the urban population and 3.94 for the rural! Tonsilectomies, costing $150 million and 300 lives a year, are generally considered worthless. Estimates that one-third of hysterectomies are completely unnecessary prompt the common comment that the indications for the operation are two children and $400.

The vast overprescription of antibiotics that is frequently pointed to also reflects the fact that doctors feel they've got to give something to their many patients who come "not feeling well," but who have untreatable virus infections. Likewise, the prescription of skin creams and antibiotics for acne by dermatologists, of various combinations of ups and downs for imprecisely diagnosed depression, and the ungodly speed with which a stomach ache is greeted with a GI series are all basically attempts to delude the rich into thinking that their untreatable diseases are being attended to. It's hardly fraud: the doctors are indeed doing the best they can in most cases. And, on the part of the patients, it's not stupidity but reasonable risk-taking. If you've got a lot of money and you're sick, trying anything is not always a bad idea.

The result of a market distribution of medical care in an inegalitarian setting is very simple: the poor can try to spend more of their income for medical services, but the rich will still get a disproportionate share of the doctors. Not only can they give the doctors more money (for their vastly higher relative incomes permit them to outbid the poor even when they are willing to give only small portions of their income for treatment, i.e., when the ailment is particularly trivial); but their neighborhoods are far more pleasant places for doctors who themselves are generally upper-middle-class in background. In a permanent excess-demand market, rural and ghetto areas simply cannot attract doctors; part of an administered supply is incredible discretion over location by the suppliers.

Unless accompanied by a decline in inequality, a growth in real income for the poor would not necessarily procure more medical care for them: doctors would simply spend more time treating more abstruse, hopeless, or imaginary illnesses in more technically sophisticated ways in the enriched pockets of wealth.

IV

Supply inelasticity is a problem in other important markets as well. Housing supply is extremely inelastic in the short run as leases preclude immediate unit subdivision and zoning laws and small landholders unwilling to sell hold up density changes by blocking multiple dwellings. Furthermore, construction itself is quite time-consuming. In addition, housing supply expansion is dependent upon two key factors outside the housing market itself: credit rates and transport and infrastructure development. Even in the long run, housing is dependent on "locations" that are intrinsically somewhat scarce.

While space limitations preclude a full detailing of the process, suffice it to say that inelasticity has roughly the same results in housing as were outlined in the case of the unique Rembrandt: i.e., the relatively poor get squeezed out even if they get richer. The stock of housing stays fixed even after the relatively rich bid up the price to maintain "their" space in times of population growth, and the poor have to squeeze together to match the bids of the rich for the remaining space.

Of the 62 Northern SMSAs that I checked, 34 diverged considerably from the median equality figures. All indications are that the presence of an unusually rich class does dramatically increase the *price* of housing as the relatively rich bid to hold on to housing for themselves and the poor must match their bids. In the 17 most inegalitarian SMSAs, the median value (price) of housing was 1.80 times the median family income (the average was 1.85) while in the 17 most egalitarian SMSAs, the median was 1.48 and the average 1.54. Only one egalitarian SMSA had as high a housing value/income ratio as the median inegalitarian SMSA.

While there is no perfect measure of the cost of building housing, permit valuations are fairly good since they account for land and construction costs. According to the basic model I drew, price should most exceed cost in the inegalitarian SMSAs since the relatively rich set the price for housing demand with their bids on the limited supply good. This is in fact the case: the median ratio of housing value (price) to permit valuations (cost) is 1.43 for inegalitarian SMSAs and 1.08 for the egalitarian ones.

Extreme overcrowding, too, is related to inequality rather than levels of income, just as would be expected from my model. Seven of the 62 SMSAs I observed have greater than median equality and very low (under $10,000 a year median) family income. The median proportion of units with more than one person per room in these SMSAs is 6.2 percent, the average 6.8. Of our 17 extremely inegalitarian SMSAs, 11 have median incomes over $10,800, yet their median proportion of units with more than one person per room was far higher, 6.9 (the average was 8!). Similarly, rich egalitarian SMSAs have a 6.6 median and an average of 6.8—the poor inegalitarian SMSAs have a 6.9 median and a 7.8 average.

One might imagine that the general preference for housing is greater in the inegalitarian SMSAs and that the poor ratios of housing price to income and to cost are merely based on higher general demand rather than higher inequality and the associated housing bids of the relatively rich. This is simply not true, though: the median vacancy rate in the egalitarian SMSAs is 1.26 percent of units compared to 1.41 in the inegalitarian SMSAs. Similarly, the higher population growth that characterizes the more inegalitarian SMSAs does not explain their poor performance. The five fastest growing of the 17 egalitarian SMSAs all grew faster in the 1960s than the five slowest inegalitarian ones; nonetheless, the ratio of housing price to median family income is far lower (1.59 to 1.9) and there is overlap in only one of ten cases. Similarly, the median price-to-cost ratio in the fast-growing egalitarian SMSAs is 1.35 compared to 1.48 in the slow-growing inegalitarian ones.

In the case of education, I will be even sketchier. If we assume that education is an accreditation rather than a training process—i.e., if we assume that one needs a college degree not to be able to handle a businessman's job but to distinguish oneself from the multitude with mere high school degrees—then a growth of real income will not increase the poor's chance of getting the real output of schooling accreditation. They can buy *more* years of schooling as their incomes rise but never so many as the relatively rich who, in an increasingly inegalitarian regime, continuously have even more to spend. Equality of opportunity, then, depends on equality of condition as well as the elimination of poverty.

The fact that obtaining medical care, housing, and education requires not only a change in real income levels but a narrowing of inequality has many implications.

Most immediately, recognizing that America is an inegalitarian society, it requires us to abandon any "flat grants" strategy of dealing with poverty. The mainstream of economic

thinking holds firmly to the notion that the only poverty program we need is a negative income tax. If we give the poor some
money, they'll get what they want. This position is consistent
with a fairly justified faith in consumer choice and a thoroughly
foolish faith in the perfection of markets.

Since none of the "flat grants" people want to give the poor
enough of rich folks' money to change the basic shape of the
income-distribution curve, their efforts will be largely useless in
getting the poor shelter, medical care, or economically reward-
ing education. What will occur, instead, is that the poor will
obtain more of those goods that are in elastic supply and the
visible paradoxes of American poverty will simply intensify:
dilapidated units will have refrigerators and color TVs and the
poor mother dying in childbirth because she never had a prenatal checkup will be buried in rather nice clothes.

What is needed (short, that is, of what is really needed, a
restructuring of all property relations so that income is distributed more equally), is that government supersede the market
and provide medical care, housing, and education according to
nonmarket criteria.

The implications of this article, though, go much further than
simply attacking the rapidly growing school of anti-inter-
ventionists, as important a task as that is.

The traditional place of inegalitarian incentives in economic
theory must be called into question. The trade-offs between
growth and equality must be weighted more toward equality, for
the welfare cost of growing inequality may well outweigh the
gain of higher productivity. Since the poor spend a higher
proportion of their income on vital goods than do the rich, any
change that raises their relative price hurts them (in much the
same way as the superrich would be better off if the price of
yachts dropped relative to bread, even if their income stayed the
same). Confiscatory taxation at the top, then, would probably
have good effects even if the money were burned rather than
spent on meaningful social programs. In underdeveloped
societies particularly, the use of vastly inegalitarian development
schemes such as land consolidation must be looked at with great
suspicion: not only will access to the many supply-inflexible
goods in such societies be rationed in a more skewed direction

but the destruction of the positive cultural underpinnings implicit in economic restructuring will be tremendously harmful. If development has very uneven economic benefits, it may well be destructive.

Altogether, when one considers the social costs of inequality and an inegalitarian economic system—in terms of alienation of the lower classes from the society at large, crass materialism, and cut-throat competitiveness—and if one then realizes that its immediate *economic* costs are quite substantial as well, a commitment to egalitarianism becomes an urgent commitment.

Robert Lekachman

The Conservative Drift in Modern Economics

American intellectual conservatism, as Joseph Epstein observed, has become a tendency to be interpreted as well as resisted by radicals. Our contemporary conservatives, like their English predecessors, are skeptical about human behavior and disposed to doubt that social behavior and disposed to doubt that social and economic arrangements are susceptible to drastic improvement. With considerable ingenuity, conservative social scientists have argued that government intervention out of benevolent motive into free market processes usually generates unexpectedly malevolent consequences. Thus the conservatives judge most of the social experiments of the 1960s to the failures, less because of fraud and maladministration, and more because New Frontiersmen and Great Societarians were foolishly utopian in their expectations and unwisely Rousseauist in their view of the possibilities of human perfectibility.

The relationship of economists to this intellectual trend is an odd one. The Chicago economists, led by Milton Friedman and George Stigler, have long preached a free market message as legitimate heirs to Henry Simons and Frank Knight who two generations ago created the Chicago tradition. Possibly the most creative economist of his time (it is a professional scandal that a

Nobel prize has not yet come his way), Friedman has proposed education vouchers and a volunteer army, measures supported by the Nixon administration, as well as a negative income tax which surfaced as the central element of the now defunct Family Assistance Plan.

In their profession, the Chicago school is a minority, albeit an increasingly influential one. What of the mainstream professionals, the Keynesians and post-Keynesians who have dominated the journals and the graduate departments and staffed Washington agencies? What have they been up to? Let me recall two events. In 1972, the portion of a major Brookings Institution study of the federal budget, which attracted most attention,[1] was a relatively brief evaluation of manpower training, compensatory education, health care, and similar Great Society initiatives. The volume's senior author, Charles Schultze, had been Budget director during the Johnson years and his coauthors had also occupied Great Society posts. Here they emphasized the difficulties inherent in the measurement of the consequences of social policies, the scanty information available to the designers of such policies, and the consequent urgency of more rational selection of priorities. Cautious experiment, accompanied by constant evaluation, is much preferable to the funding either of programs yielding small results or of large untested new ventures. Coming from a Democratic government in exile such as the Brookings economists, this qualified but unmistakable concession of past error has been of considerable intellectual assistance to the Nixon administration, which for its own reasons has harbored deep resentments against community action, legal services, subsidized housing, job training, and other subverters of the work ethic.

The second event is more recent. On January 11, 1973, President Nixon announced the end of the Administration's moderately successful experiment with Phase II wage-price controls and their replacement by a vaguely designed and even more vaguely described set of Phase III controls. The immediate reaction of Walter Heller, Gardner Ackley, and Arthur Okun —three liberal economists who had served during the eight Kennedy-Johnson years as chairmen of the Council of Economic Advisers—was applause for the President's initiative. On

January 13 the *New York Times* headlined their response: "3 Democratic Economists Back Phase 3 Structure and Principles." The subhead noted that "Heller, Ackley and Okun are joined by Dr. Burns, Who Voices Full Support." Arthur Burns of course is the impeccably conservative economist at the head of the Federal Reserve System. Moderate economists were of similar opinions. Henry Wallich, once on the Eisenhower CEA, declared that "In the long run, the fewer controls the better, and I applaud them for deciding that the long run is now." After all these cheerful statements, stock market, currency market, and corporate price behavior were, to write temperately, distressing. A new run on the American dollar, apparently led by American multinational firms and banks, caused a second devaluation. Food prices surged upward. Industrial materials began to ascend at annual rates in excess of 12 percent. George Meany rumbled before Congress that labor in its impending negotiations would demand full protection against higher prices. By the end of March in a speech that mingled Vietnam and food prices ("beef with honor" in Mary McGrory's apt words), the President reluctantly announced retail and wholesale freezes on the price of beef, pork, veal, and lamb.

Like the Brookings budget survey, this story is exemplary not so much as another disclosure of the inadequacies of eminent economists, in this instance as forecasters (though the *Times* headlines certainly do make that point), but as an excellent insight into the economic cast of mind. What led the economists astray was not the absence of native wit, but the presence of good graduate-school training. The graduate schools teach new technique but old wisdom. As far in the past as 1848, John Stuart Mill insisted that "only through the principle of competition has political economy any pretension to the character of science." In his period Mill was far from a conservative. On the contrary, he argued in favor of steeply progressive taxes on inheritances, identified the virtues of zero economic growth, and seriously questioned the impact upon factory workers of production organized purely in the interest of maximum profit. Through thick and thin, however, Mill clung to the merits of market rivalry and the importance of preserving competitive incentives.

Thus it has always been. In our day, George Stigler has praised the education of young economists in these terms:

> He is drilled in the problems of *all* economic systems and in the methods by which a price system solves these problems. It becomes impossible for him to believe that men of good will can by their individual actions stem inflation, or that it is possible to impose changes in any one market or industry without causing problems in other markets or industries. . . . He cannot believe that a change in the *form* of social organization will eliminate basic economic problems.

Their training, concluded Stigler with approval, transforms economists as social scientists into conservatives. As amateur politicians and apprentice campaign strategists, economists naturally but *nonprofessionally* advocate all manner of preferences for large social change. It was an economist who invented McGovern's demogrant. Nevertheless, economists, when they inspect wages, prices, budgets, and interest rates, perceive complexity and uncertainty. Always they fear the general equilibrium dislocations which may attend the best-intentioned tinkering with any part of the system. Thus economists of all stripes are skeptical of economic controls: they distort market reactions and interfere with the delicate competition of sellers for customer favor and employees for jobs. The sooner the controls come off, if, mistakenly, they are applied, the better.

This emphasis upon markets explains Brookings uneasiness about recent social reform. Although liberal economists favor various government interventions in the interest of the poor, black, and otherwise vulnerable, they are necessarily suspicious of the quality of government action simply because market tests do not typically apply. How can the analyst evaluate alternative arrangements for medical care, pre-school education, urban renovation, manpower training, and so on in the absence of market prices and free choice among competing products by the customers of their parents?

Such skepticism is reinforced by the professional aspiration to avoid value judgments (=nonmarket conclusions uttered by human beings). A fair example is the computation of Gross

National Product and the other national income measures. The 1973 edition of Samuelson's *Economics* defines Gross National Product "as the sum of final products such as consumption goods and gross investment." This is to say, the statisticians in principle simply add up the price tags on consumer goods, hours of medical and legal consultation, new machines and structures, and increases in business inventories. They nobly refrain from judgment on the biological or social merits of the items which enter into the grand total. Comparisons of GNP from one year to the next do not, for example, ask how the new goods and services are distributed among rich, poor, and middling families. From a theoretical standpoint, such a question is irrelevant because economists now believe that there is nothing "scientific" they can say about the psychic enjoyments of different persons. Interpersonal comparisons are *verboten!*

In modern times economists have liberated themselves from the durable Benthamite proposition that as vessels of pleasure and pain human beings are approximately equal and the further postulate that satisfaction diminishes as the quantity of possessions and income rises. As late as the 1920s, A. C. Pigou, Alfred Marshall's Cambridge successor, was arguing on strictly Benthamite grounds that economic changes that promoted income equality also increased economic welfare. A dollar taken from a rich man hurts him less than a dollar removed from a poor man and, by easy extension, a dollar more for a man who starts with only a few implies a quantity of joy greater than the pain endured by the millionaire who surrenders that dollar. But if, as contemporary economists insist, no scientific method exists for comparing the feelings of different people, then there can be no scientific demonstration that one distribution of income and wealth is better (or worse) than any other distribution. Lester Thurow's brilliant *Public Interest* (Spring 1973) essay "Toward a Definition of Economic Justice" demonstrates how hard it is for an excellent technician of egalitarian disposition to harmonize technique and ethical principle. Rather painfully, Thurow does so in the course of arguing that consistent application of free market principles necessitates less inegalitarian distribution of income. Economists were in a stronger polemical posture when their technique was less intricate and their distributive principles were more boldly avowed.

Attachment to market models and reluctance to render ethical judgments entails important consequences. Economists cannot as professionals unite in support of (or opposition to) *any* set of arrangements for the distribution of income and wealth. But in much better professional conscience, they can join hands on behalf of measures that promote freer markets and more efficient use of human and natural resources. Almost all economists are free traders. With diminishing fervor, they advocate antitrust and open access to crafts and professions. As men of practical policy whose central professional value is efficient operation of the economy, economists can readily urge budgetary and monetary initiatives by Congress and the President which promote high rates of growth and full employment of men and material resources. Even here a caveat ought to be uttered. Excessive enthusiasm on the path to full employment often entails inflation which, for economists, may damage efficiency as much, though differently, as unemployment. The Phillips curve, named in honor of its English inventor, explicitly relates rates of unemployment and price rise. To economists, the apparatus conveys the message that painful trade-off, either of price stability or employment, must be made.

The last spell of euphoria on the part of economists about the state of their discipline occurred in the wake of successful national pursuit of high growth and employment. The 1964 tax, advocated by Heller, Tobin, Okun, Ackley, and their colleagues, was remarkably successful as a tool of economic stimulation. In his March 1966 Harvard Godkin lectures, Walter Heller uttered these proud words:

> Economics has come of age in the 1960s. Two presidents have recognized and drawn on modern economics as a source of national strength and Presidential power. Their willingness to use, for the first time, the full range of modern economic tools underlies the unbroken U.S. expansion since early 1961—an expansion that in its first five years created over 7 million new jobs, doubled profits, increased the nation's real output by a third, and closed the $50-billion gap between actual and potential production that plagued the American economy in 1961.

Moreover, achievement was intellectual as well as material:

> Together with the gradual closing of that huge production
> gap has come—part as cause, part as consequence—a
> gradual, then rapid, narrowing of the intellectual gap be-
> tween professional economists and decision-makers. The
> paralyzing grip of economic myth and false fears on policy
> has been loosened.

Heller's eulogy was intoned at just about the last date when an
economist could point with plausible pride to a pleasing combination of high employment, steady growth, and reasonably
well-behaved prices. Lyndon Johnson's ill-fated attempt to support simultaneously an ever bigger war and an increasingly
expensive set of social programs overheated the economy and
generated an inflation that in 1973, seven years after its incep-
tion, has not yet been tamed.

II

It would have been reasonable to anticipate from the Nixon
administration some disgust with the economists aroused by
both their failures and their "successes." For if Walter Heller
accurately praised the profession for its role in the mid-1960s,
then critics had an equal warrant to complain of the meek
fashion in which Ackley, Okun, and Schultze administered an
inflationary regime from 1966 through 1968. Here quotation
marks surround successes because these were the social programs that tax cuts, rapid economic growth, and larger tax
collections had made possible. These were also on the whole
measures the President disliked or detested. If economists were
implicated in the design of the War on Poverty, Model Cities,
and other disturbers of the status quo, so much the worse for
them and their colleagues. Probably no student of Mr. Nixon's
political history would have been startled if he had staffed his
official family with the businessmen and accountants who were
so prominent in the Eisenhower regime.

Instead the President surrounded himself at least as closely as
his Democratic predecessors with economists in positions of

prominence, among them George Schultz, successively secretary of Labor, director of the vital Office of Management and Budget, and in the second Nixon administration simultaneously secretary of the Treasury. White House counselor, and chairman of the Cost of Living Council, Herbert Stein who in 1973 began his fifth year as member and chairman of the Council of Economic Advisers; Arthur F. Burns, the first economist to head the Federal Reserve System; and James Schlesinger, who moved as chairman of the Atomic Energy Commission to the directorship of the Central Intelligence Agency. By sympathy, association, and training, these men are conservative. Schultz and Stein are members in good standing of the Chicago free market cult. Schlesinger is a veteran of Rand systems analysis. The independent Arthur Burns venerates the work ethic, hates to spend public money, and evinces more sympathy for the ideas of his old friend Milton Friedman than chairmen of the Federal Reserve have displayed in the past.

Indeed examined critically even the economists' 1964 tax cut triumph says as much about the profession's conservative hierarchy of values as about the capacity of economic analysis to promote social improvement. Within the Kennedy administration, the argument about how best to stimulate a sluggish economy centered on the relative merits of lower taxes and larger social spending. From New Delhi, Galbraith urgently reiterated the message of his *Affluent Society*—the private sector is bloated and the public sector starved. Among economists, Galbraith is generally held to be an excellent polemicist and a superior writer but a poor technician. Within the New Frontier certainly it was tax reduction fervently advocated by Walter Heller which won the President's favor. Kennedy's decision in late 1962 to propose a package of tax reforms and tax reductions implied postponement at best of new public spending initiatives and narrowing of the revenue sources of such programs in the future. Choice of tax reduction as the instrument of business expansion has had the fiscal consequence of reducing the 1973 tax receipts of the federal government by approximately $45 billion—if the 1962 rates were still in force. At the same time, regressive social security payroll levies have risen $40 billion. As a direct result of policies advocated or accepted by liberal economists and their congressional allies, poor people pay more and their affluent neighbors less. Along the way, the tax reforms have been repeatedly jettisoned.

Let it be said yet again that Walter Heller, Arthur Okun, and Gardner Ackley are sincere friends of the poor, black, and deprived. They are on public record in favor of progressive taxation, loophole closing, and a wide variety of federal interventions on behalf of the needy. Okun reacted to President Nixon's plan to dismantle some 115 categorical grant programs in the 1974 budget with the comment that it was "impeccable economic and intolerable social policy." How then did these economists and their colleagues find themselves in such disrepair that President Nixon could plausibly advance budget limitations (mostly created by tax cuts sponsored by liberal economists) as an excuse for reducing social expenditures? Why were the liberal tools—full-employment budgeting and revenue-sharing —so readily converted into conservative weapons?

Much of the answer is to be found in standard economic ideology. I noted earlier that economists find most attractive the "scientific" objectives of efficiency, growth, and free choice. Although some economists are egalitarians, still others uneasy about GNP increase as an unequivocal community boon, and probably a substantial majority (of Americans in general as well as economists) distressed by the persistence of poverty amid general plenty, economic science fails to justify these generous sentiments. Since conventional wisdom holds there is no scientific way to compare the satisfactions of different people, it is possible that economic welfare will be enlarged by subsidizing Nelson Rockefeller as a Bedford-Stuyvesant welfare mother of five. Again, although economic growth notoriously generates pollution, overcrowding, destruction of viable ethnic neighborhoods, demolition of architectural landmarks, clogged highways and overpopulated beaches, and assorted emotional distempers attendant on disruptive change, professional economists and national income statisticians have only recently come around to taking the first steps in modifying the national-income accounts to accommodate these malign side-effects of growth.

For as presently computed, the national income measures exaggerate year-to-year improvements in economic welfare because they deliberately avoid judging the consequences of "free" market operations. If businessmen produced only two classes of output—pollutants and antipollutants, Department of Commerce statisticians would routinely total the price tags on the items classified under each rubric and call the result Gross National Product. Although careful statisticians refrain from identifying as synonymous GNP and economic welfare, Presidents, lesser politicians, and ordinary folk inevitably do so interpret annual celebrations of ever-larger GNP. The first serious attempt to cope with the disamenities of growth occurred in 1972! William Nordhaus's and James Tobin's "pioneering study" (the words are Paul Samuelson's) put their objective in these words:

> Our adjustments to GNP fall into three general categories: reclassification of GNP expenditures as consumption, investment, and intermediate; imputation for the services of consumer capital, for leisure, and for the product of household work; correction for some of the disamenities of urbanization.[2]

What an odd subject it is, to be sure, that could ignore until only yesterday leisure trends, the changing significance of work within the home, and the emergence of new disamenities as well as the persistence of old ones! The profession has been equally tardy in its concession of the extent to which private entrepreneurs fail fully to "internalize" some of their costs. Paper mills which pour foul odors into the air and foul chemical wastes into adjacent streams have long imposed upon individuals and communities the expense of cleaning themselves, their possessions, and the municipal water supply. As economists now belatedly explain, these costs can readily be shifted back to the polluters ("internalized" according to professional jargon) if Congress and state legislatures compel the polluters to install efficient cleansing devices or purchase expensive licenses to pollute. The receipts from the latter might finance public facilities and compensate individuals for protecting themselves against remaining pollution.

Failure adequately to measure the costs of growth carries with it persistent overestimate both of the extent and the benefits of growth. Even according to their own favored criteria, economists have done badly. It is old doctrine that markets allocate efficiently only when the producers and sellers are engaged in genuine competition, and the pattern of consumer demand accurately mirrors the tastes and preferences of buyers. The American economy departs significantly from both of these structural arrangements. In real life, price competition, at the heart of free market requirements, proceeds, if at all, under a large variety of limitations. The auto industry is paradigmatic of the behavior of the concentrated industries. Ford, Chrysler, and General Motors jostle each other for market shares in ways that do not include the prices they charge their dealers for comparable models, fuel economy, safety, or antipollution.[3] The limited actual competition in this market focuses upon style, advertising, and meretricious frivolities of design.

Oligopoly is the dominant style of manufacturing organization, but far from the only limitation upon price competition. Tariffs and quotas limit imports, narrow consumer choice, and raise the prices of rival domestic products. In the construction trades, strong unions limit the entry of new labor. Professional licenses serve much the same function. Patents narrow the ambit of legal rivalry. From the economists's standpoint, each of these market imperfections distorts efficient allocation of resources and generates the wrong answers to the signals given by the customers.

Matters are no better on the buying side of the supply-demand equation. It is again a familiar proposition among economists that market purchases accurately reflect consumer preferences under two conditions: the customers freely express their own desires,[4] and they bring with them the dollars they have earned by productive effort. If all income were earned, people would be richer or poorer according to the differing estimate free markets make of their skills and talents. Talented performers realize more income and cast more dollar votes when they go to market.

The pretty picture is crucially marred by the reality of inherited wealth. The child of a millionaire has contributed nothing to GNP. Nevertheless, the accident of birth confers many dollar votes upon him. Because the rich are always with us, "free" markets furnish numerous luxuries that consume resources otherwise available for use in the fabrication of necessities and comforts for people of more modest income. The prices of the luxuries are lower and those of the necessities higher because of this resource diversion.

If economists were faithful to their own conclusions, the pursuit of efficiency, growth, and free choice should make the profession partisans of radical change in the central institutions of contemporary capitalism. Economists of all people should be militant antitrusters, enemies of national trade unions, foes of occupational licenses and professional credentials, bigoted free traders, and, like Mill, eager by inheritance taxation to diminish the distortions of free markets occasioned by accumulations of inherited wealth. Be it said in their honor that only the Chicago economists have consistently spelled out the full implications of the economists' central valuations.

III

Under the circumstances, the response of establishment economics to concrete issues such as the domestic plans of the second Nixon administration is necessarily limited and peculiarly disembodied. Consider, as a representative example, Dr. Alice M. Rivlin's "A Counter-Budget for Social Progress."[5] Now at the Brookings Institution, Dr. Rivlin served the Great Society as assistant secretary of Health, Education, and Welfare in charge of program evaluation. She identifies "plenty of reason to be outraged by this budget if one believes the Federal Government ought to be substantially increasing, not decreasing, its efforts to improve opportunities for the poor and to increase social services for everyone." She then gives the devil his due: "With some important exceptions, the social programs the President cut were outdated or inequitable or only partially effective."

Unfortunately most lay readers of Dr. Rivlin's highly intelligent argument would be constrained to concede that her second point is more effectively argued than the adverse judgment on the budget thrust contained in her initial point. She has no trouble at all demonstrating that some existing programs lacked equity, others were "unnecessarily costly," and still others poorly designed actually to diminish hunger, improve the delivery of health services, reduce pollution, or alleviate other human ills. Economists know about efficiency.

The "counter-budget" of the title is based less on economic analysis than on a set of political judgments:

> . . . there is general agreement [how can she be sure?] that the solutions should remain within the existing framework of American government. The radical Left talks glibly about "overthrowing the system," but never says what would replace it—and the radical left does not have enough political clout to be taken seriously anyway. The old Socialist solution—nationalizing major industries as a means of equalizing incomes—does not attract reformers any more. Socialism isn't considered radical, just quaint. Who thinks any useful social purpose would be served by having the Federal Government running U.S. Steel or General Motors? Nor does one hear serious proposals any more for direct provisions of social services by the Federal Government. A national health service and a national education system once sounded like brave new ideas to reformers; now they sound like unwieldy superbureaucracies.

After eliminating several generations of radical proposals, Dr. Rivlin sketches three strategies which she finds attractive: tax and cash transfers; subsidies to low-income individuals for the purchase of housing, college training, medical insurance, and the like; and grants to localities to enlarge their "capacity to render services."

The drift of this analysis is, according to taste in nomenclature, mildly liberal or mildly conservative. On the Right, Friedmanite structural change is to be avoided. So, at least equally, are the various redistributions of power and wealth that are the staples of radical prescription. In Brookings hands, economics becomes the ally of minute, incremental change. The "system" is realistically accepted. And although Dr. Rivlin, like her colleague Joseph Pechman, has harsh words to say about tax inequity, there is really no reason why the beneficiaries of present arrangements should not also claim their rights as leading actors in the system. Economic theory as presently construed by practical men and women is a poor weapon against the rich.

Accepting the prevailing political climate, mainstream economists concentrate on immediately available possibilities. In a conservative period, when the chances of egalitarian action are low to zero, the economists, whatever their politics, have congenial work to do. Their virtuosity in cost-benefit analysis helps them sort out the weaker from the stronger social initiatives of the recent past, compose endless interpretations of the successes (few) and the failures (many) of job training, compensatory education, housing subsidies, and community action, and accept, when opportunity knocks, employment in the citadels of the Nixon administration.

No more than conservatives should liberals and radicals applaud inefficiency or shut their eyes to the waste of public funds. The point, however, is by now familiar; efficiency is almost the only scientific value that economists are educated to identify. As Stigler rightly maintained, by the time a young economist has been thoroughly socialized en route to his doctorate, he is burdened by the complexity of economic affairs, convinced that alteration of anything in the economy affects everything else, and deeply indoctrinated with a preference for small, marginal change of a kind that, not entirely coincidentally, economists since 1870 have been comfortable in interpreting.

His teachers inform him that he has no right to judge the quality of the items that enter into GNP. He may not utter interpersonal comparisons of the utilities of rich and poor persons. It must be a tribute to their residual good sense that economists in such large numbers are to be found on the side of progressive social change and mildly egalitarian redistributions of income, wealth, services, and power. For in the end, marginalism inhibits, paradoxically, even the structural shifts that appear to be dictated by the valuations of conventional theory. Economists have retreated from antitrust and nationalization, not in very many instances because they are in the pay of General Motors. or ITT, but because a genuine rearrangement of the industrial landscape would upset the economy after a fashion only to be guessed at, and therefore to be avoided.

That patron saint of Anglo-Saxon economics Alfred Marshall adopted as his motto *"natura non facit saltum"*—nature makes no leaps—and neither, his *Principles of Economics* at length insisted, ought societies. Establishment economics relies ultimately upon political and pecuniary markets to define the arena within which it can safely operate. Political markets are congressional, presidential, state, and local contests used by rival politicians to present themselves and their programs to the inspection of the electorate. As citizen, the typical economist probably voted for George McGovern. As social scientist, he has to be aware that the contrary preference of 62 percent of the voters has and, moreover, ought to have an impact upon the choice of national policy and the allocation among competing objectives of federal resources. Since as an economist our hero has nothing to say about the character of the voters' choice, he ought to cultivate his own garden.

In economics this moral is repetitive. The lesson is much the same out here in the factories and supermarkets. People do buy more copies of *Playboy* than of the *Public Interest* or *Dissent*. In the rating game Marcus Welby consistently does better than BBC dramas on public television. Boone's Apple Farm Wine sells considerably better than real wine, and so on. Who is the economist to judge his fellow citizens? If he presumes to try, he does no more than express his own elitist prejudices. Hence still, despite signs of change, the official national income statistics remain an idiot's measure of economic welfare—a record of activities, beneficial and harmful, trivial and important, free and coerced. Even when economists are uneasily aware of the imperfections of existing markets, the concentrations of economic power in defiance of economic theory, and the inequities of great wealth, their preference for tiny readjustment, and their desperate dependence upon markets as the only institution with which they are trained to cope, prevent them from advocating important change.

Why shouldn't Richard Nixon hire economists? By ideology, they ought to be comfortable in any administration. On the one hand, they affirm the legitimacy of the political market. On the other, they join strong affections for efficiency with self-denying ordinances that inhibit analytic judgment of the quality of private output, the equity of present distributions of income and wealth, and the realities of the concentration of economic power.

One ought then to absolve of any charge of inconsistency

Great Society economists who initially presided over and now negatively evaluate Lyndon Johnson's wars on poverty, racial discrimination, and assorted social ills. The 1964 presidential election issued Lyndon Johnson a set of instructions which the economists helped him to carry out. Reassessing their political preferences, the voters in 1968 and more strongly in 1972 gave Richard Nixon a different set of instructions. With utter propriety, economists can assist this winner in his effort to interpret and follow these instructions. Waiting in the wings, Great Society economists can usefully employ themselves in the making of efficiency judgments of their previous handiwork.

If, come 1976, Edward Kennedy, Walter Mondale, or some as yet unidentified savior returns the country to Democratic stewardship, the economists will gladly accept new definitions of political reality and new opportunities for incremental change. The economists who, among the social scientists, have probably changed their basic attitudes least, support themselves with a comparatively consistent set of intellectual values. The only trouble is that it amounts to an ideology inherently hostile to significant change and implicitly friendly to all handy status quos.

Gus Tyler

The Politics of
Pat Moynihan

(From the New Leader, April 2, 1973, pp. 6-10.)

In the course of serving with distinction in the subcabinets of
Presidents John F. Kennedy and Lyndon B. Johnson and the
Cabinet of President Richard M. Nixon, Daniel Patrick (Pat)
Moynihan has shown himself to be a man of many parts: enthusiast, moralist, Talmudist, sociologist, publicist. As a glandu-
lar enthusiast, he likes to be in the thick of things and prefers to
believe where *he* is is where it's at. As moralist, he is prone to
identify his allies with virtue and his opponents with vice. As
Talmudist, he spins syllogisms to suggest an eternal inevitability
to his sometimes transient conclusions. As sociologist, he taps
updated research and sophisticated insights to fortify and footnote his commitments. And as publicist, he is a sheer genius in
promoting his plans—and himself. Now, in *The Politics of a
Guaranteed Income* (New York: Random House, 1973), his book
on the rejected Family Assistance Plan (FAP), Moynihan reas-
sembles this impressive array of talents to compose an intriguing
political fugue with two central themes interwoven in startling
counterpoint.

His first motif is that FAP—a "quantum leap" in social

181

policy—was killed by a coalition of people with mean motives: Liberal Democrats did not want to give a credit line to a Republican president. Southern Democrats did not want to emancipate their poor from economic exploitation or political intimidation. Conservatives did not want to pamper the undeserving poor. Social workers did not want to lose their pay or prestige: there was "money in poverty" and "power . . . through control of community agencies." Militant black mothers of the National Welfare Rights Organization (NWRO), the "aristocracy of welfare recipients," did not want to share their goodies with the less fortunate poor. The American Federation of State, County and Municipal Employees did not want to lose jurisdiction over numerous welfare bureaucrats. Even George McGovern was more interested in wooing blue-collar votes for his presidential ambitions than in caring for the politically apathetic poor.

Moynihan's second motif is that standing against these unholy uglies was Richard Nixon, whose "attitudes were much closer to those of welfare recipients themselves," who "proposed to spend more money for the direct provision of the needs of low-income groups than any President in history" and who was determined to "fulfill the promises of the 1960s." Although he knew that FAP was politically risky, he was still bent on going ahead with it, courageously "leaning toward FAP not least because of the risks involved." In his crusading role, of course, Nixon had the spur and savvy of Moynihan.

The overriding "irony"—a favorite Moynihan word—of this contrapuntal composition is that "good guys" come out looking bad and vice versa. Perhaps meant to be an *apologia pro vita sua* (1969-71), the book will no doubt reinforce the conviction of many liberals that Moynihan is another "lost leader" who left them just for a ribbon to pin on his coat. If so, they do him (and others of his tendency) an injustice, for he began to evolve a Nixonian concept of public policy for the '70s *prior* to Nixon's first election. And it runs like a pedal point through the present opus, giving the entire work durable dimensions for debate that range far beyond the relatively narrow, limited flap over FAP.

As early as 1967, addressing an audience with established liberal credentials (Americans for Democratic Action), Moynihan argued warmly for a liberal-conservative alliance to check the lunacy of the New Left. But he did not merely suggest a coalition that would preserve order against disorder. He set down the programmatic precepts for a new (Disraelian?) conservatism: (1) Though the federal government is a handy device for "redistributing power and wealth," it is a "highly unreliable device for . . . providing services." (2) The initiative for social policy should be shifted from the federal government to the cities and states, the source of "a preponderance of social programs . . . in the 20th century." Underlying these precepts was a philosophy of politics asserting "the limited capacities of government to bring about social change."

Quite appropriately, Moynihan's ADA speech was reprinted by Melvin Laird in *The Republican Papers.* For an incoming Republican administration inclined to undo the federal programs and agencies built up by Democratic presidents from FDR to LBJ, the Moynihan thesis was singularly useful: Here was a statement from a certified liberal proposing to dismantle the "welfare state" in the name of "redistributing wealth and power" to the people.

The Family Assistance Plan was Moynihan's attempt to apply his philosophy. Above all else, he saw FAP as a form of income redistribution, designed to move more money downward to the poor. In the process, it would give the impoverished a greater say over their own destinies by getting the federal bureaucrats off their backs. They would finally have a share of the wealth and power!

Yet, if that is what FAP was all about, the Nixon administration totally misrepresented the proposal to the American people. As the President publicly and repeatedly explained it, FAP was a way to get the welfare loafers off their unethical duffs. "I will put it very bluntly," Nixon said in 1970. "If a man is able to work, if a man is trained for a job, and then he refuses to work, that man should not be paid to loaf by a hardworking taxpayer in the United States of America." The press took its cue. "Able-bodied unemployed fathers on relief," editorialized the New York *Daily News,* "and mothers of school-age children on FA rolls would be required to take work or job training." Holmes Alexander wrote: "This means in plain language that the poor may have to work-or-starve, and that 'dependent children' will no longer be the excuse by nonearning parents."

In short, as advertised by the White House and the media, FAP was a plan to turn shirkers into workers. Nixon had set the tone in his August 8, 1969, nationwide television address: "What America needs now is not more welfare but more workfare." This was to be achieved by stick and carrot. If you did not work on a job or take job training, you would be punished by the withdrawal of funds; if you earned money on your own, you would be allowed to hold on to 50 cents of every dollar you made, up to a set sum.

According to Moynihan, the widely publicized workfare-not-welfare line was pure hokum, a sales pitch to peddle FAP to the country, especially to conservatives. The work-or-starve provisions of FAP, he says, were more *lenient* than existing regulations written as amendments to the Social Security Act in 1967. These get-tough rules had not been effective from 1967-70 and were hardly likely to succeed at a time when the unemployment rate had—under Nixon—nearly doubled. The earnings "incentive" (keep 50 percent of what you earn) was equally phoney. After deductions for Social Security taxes and other costs incident to a job, Milton Friedman calculated, the earner would end up with no more than 28.5 cents out of every hard-won buck.

Actually, as former conservative Senator John J. Williams (R.-Del.) proved while quizzing a star White House witness, Robert Patricelli, in many instances the *more* an FAP recipient earned, the *less* he or she would get. If income went beyond a given "notch," the family would lose Medicaid, or rent subsidy, or low-income housing, or day care for the kids—items worth hundreds or thousands of dollars. The disincentives to work inherent in FAP were dramatically revealed during a crucial exchange between Williams and Patricelli before the Senate Finance Committee:

Williams: If they increase their earnings from $720 to $5,560 under this bill, they have a spendable income of $6,109, or $19 less than if they sit in a rocking chair earning only $720. Is that not correct?
Patricelli: That is correct. . . .

Williams: They are penalized $19 because they go out and earn $5,500. Is that correct?
Patricelli: That is correct.
Williams: What possible logic is there to it?
Patricelli: There is none Senator.

In his 1969 TV broadcast Nixon also indicted the present welfare system because its unequal standards in different areas lure "thousands more into already overcrowded inner cities as unprepared for city life as they are for city jobs," and because it creates "an incentive for desertion," since "in most states a family is denied welfare if a father is present—even though he is unable to support his family." FAP, he claimed, would check the flow of dependent families into cities with higher welfare benefits and would reunite broken families.

In reality, Moynihan abundantly demonstrates, FAP would do nothing of the kind. It would not end the unequal welfare payments from state to state; it would only establish a minimum (about $1,500 for a family of four) and mandate states paying above that level to maintain existing standards. In addition, Moynihan is too knowledgeable a sociologist to ignore the fact (although he mentions it only in passing) that the great flood of the uprooted from soil to city in post-World War II America was brought on by a "green revolution" in agricultural productivity which, combined with a federal policy of subsidizing curtailment of production, forced some 20 million rural Americans to choose between starvation and the city. As for bringing families back together, Moynihan reports that "under FAP, no less than with AFDC, any low-income family with an employed head could substantially increase the 'cash flow' through its various pockets and pocketbooks by the simple expedient of breaking up and putting the women and children on welfare."

In other words, as "welfare reform" FAP was blatant huckstering: It could not force people to work; it would provide no serious incentive to work; it would not check the flow from rural poverty to urban dependency; it would not help hold families together.

What, then, was FAP all about? To Moynihan, it was a

"guaranteed income." To Nixon, at least in his public statements, it was not:

> This national floor under incomes for working or dependent families is not a guaranteed income. Under the guaranteed income proposal, everyone would be assured a minimum income, regardless of how much he was capable of earning, regardless of what his need was, regardless of whether or not he was willing to work. I opposed such a plan. I oppose it now and I will continue to oppose it.

Robert Finch, then secretary of HEW, reinforced the President's disclaimer: "The most widely discussed question is whether Family Assistance is really in fact a 'guaranteed annual income' and to this question I can emphatically answer 'no.' . . . Under Family Assistance, income is not provided regardless of personal effort or attitudes."

Moynihan's explanation is that the political exigencies surrounding FAP required the White House to present the proposal as welfare reform (which it was not) and deny it was a guaranteed income (which it was). Simultaneously, in speaking to social workers and other liberal groups, Moynihan argued that FAP was really a guaranteed income plan intended to redistribute wealth in America. He maintains that both Nixon and he knew exactly what they were doing: The President was selling the idea to the right wing ("boob-bait for the conservatives" is what William F. Buckley Jr. called it); Moynihan was selling it to the left wing. The conservatives were supposed to be taken in by Nixon's rhetoric and thus back the bill. The liberals were not expected to believe Nixon but to support FAP as a guaranteed income scheme. In fact, everything came out topsy-turvy. The conservatives saw it as payment for nonwork while some liberals saw it as "forced labor."

Moynihan, however, is not content to portray FAP merely as a form of guaranteed income—a cause in which he, as moralist, has earned well-deserved kudos. As enthusiast and publicist, he calls it "the purest embodiment of income redistribution," a system that "will abolish poverty for dependent children and the working poor." Despite the genuine merits of FAP, in truth it would not have come anywhere near ending poverty and was a burlesque of income redistribution.

FAP "guaranteed" an income of only $1,200 for a family of four. The base guarantee was originally $1,500, but if the head of the family refused to take a job or job training the family was to be penalized $300, reducing the base to $1,200. Either way—$1,200 or $1,500 or even $1,600—that family would still be living in painfully abject poverty on its $23 or $30 a week. Since Moynihan proves convincingly that raising the base would have escalated costs prohibitively, FAP could only have helped a little. To claim that this small lift would have effectively ended poverty is a bad case of delusion.

The claim that FAP was serious income redistribution is equally illusory. The beneficiaries at the bottom would have received their crumbs of redistributed "wealth" almost exclusively from the nonwealthy. Given that the FAP ceiling "would have reduced benefits to some welfare families," part of the money would have come from other families presently *on welfare*. The rest of the cost would have been picked up by the nonpoor, near-poor, and not-so-poor who bear the major burden of the Federal tax load. Nothing in the bill would have significantly touched the top 2 percent who own about 40 percent of the wealth, about 75 percent of the privately held corporate stocks, about 85 percent of the bonds, and about 99 percent of the municipal bonds. Indeed, these top holders were granted even more than their usual tax privileges through Administration-sponsored business "incentives." In view of the way it was to be funded, FAP was far less a means of redistributing wealth than of reshuffling poverty.

By dressing up FAP as a grand plan to "abolish poverty" through "income redistribution," though, Moynihan is not simply indulging in an understandable exaggeration. He is pushing a policy on how to deal with the problem of the poor and dependent. His solution is simple: Give them money! "If what the poor lacked was money, giving it to them directly was, on the face of it, a reasonable response: direct, efficient, and immediate." This seemingly incontrovertible idea is the keystone to what Moynihan calls his "income strategy." He sees FAP as a "quantum leap" not because of the sum involved (estimated at only $4 billion the first year and less later on), but because it is "nonincremental." And it is this allegedly revolutionary aspect of FAP—its jump to a galaxy of nonincremental policies, to something different—that makes Moynihan's book much more than the discussion of a legislative proposal Nixon once made and soon forgot.

To those acquainted with New Deal/Fair Deal/New Frontier/Great Society programs, the idea of an income strategy is not new. What is new—and a booby trap for the poor—is substituting it for a "service strategy."

When the National Recovery Administration organized whole industries to set a floor on wages in 1933, that was an income strategy. Section 7a of the NIRA, encouraging collective bargaining to raise the wages of employees above the floor level, was an income strategy. The Fair Labor Standards Act of 1938, setting federal minimum wages at 25 cents an hour, was an income strategy. Work and make-work projects, such as the FERA, WPA, PWA, CCC, CWA, were all devices to put income into the hands of those who did not have it. So were unemployment insurance, old-age pensions, aid to the blind and handicapped and, most relevantly, aid to dependent children. The Full Employment Act of 1947 was a sweeping resolve to provide incomes to everyone who wanted to work by making jobs available to all.

But the income strategy that preceded Moynihan's FAP more than a full generation was never viewed as something contrary to a services strategy. There were just too many services that low- and middle-income families could not purchase, despite steady and higher incomes: items such as education for their children, decent housing, medical care, job training, legal counsel, job placement, or adequate protection against discrimination. To meet these crying needs, the government had to provide schools, housing, Medicare and Medicaid, legal services, employment offices, day care, etc. The services strategy became a vital ingredient of income strategy, for there was no point in giving a family money to buy services it could not afford even with a few added bucks.

The original FAP combined income with a services strategy. A vital part of the proposal was a major service—the day care program. Testifying on FAP before the House Ways and Means Committee, then Labor Secretary George Schultz gave day care top priority: "If somebody asked me what is the most important thing in this whole plan, I would say it is the idea of quality child care. . . . This is what I would put my emphasis on." The emphasis made sense: If mothers were to go to work, some provision had to be made for their children; if dependency was not to become self-propagating, quality care for youngsters would be needed at some point to break the poverty cycle.

Nixon added his voice: "Many of the problems of poverty are traceable directly to early childhood experience . . . if we are to make genuine, long-range progress, we must focus our efforts much more than heretofore on those few years which may determine how far, throughout his later life, the child can reach." The New York *Daily News* got the message: "Day care centers would be set up, where mothers at work or in job training could leave their children to be cared for during working hours." Yet when Congress did pass a comprehensive child care development bill, with a meager $2 billion appropriation that included day care centers, the proposal was vetoed by President Nixon on the grounds that it was substituting "communal" for familial forms of child-rearing.

As for Moynihan, he began to turn his back on the services strategy long before he joined the Nixon administration. The 1966 Coleman Report on education convinced him that monies put into Headstart, Compensatory Education, or even the Elementary and Secondary Education Act of 1965 were a waste—much input with no measurable output. Only 10 weeks after Nixon took office, Moynihan sent him a memo suggesting how FAP could be used as a strategy to reduce other services: "The Family Security System would enable you to begin cutting back sharply on these costly and questionable services, and yet to assert with full validity that it was under your Presidency that poverty was abolished in America." (In plain talk: Give them that $1,600 and knock out those useless services—like Headstart, etc.) Nixon could buy his place in history as the noblest warrior against poverty at bargain rates. "The cost is not very great," counseled Moynihan, "*because it is a direct payment system*. The tremendous cost of the poverty program comes from *services*."

While the debate over FAP revolved around its merits per se, the real question should have been whether FAP was a *part of* or a *substitute for* the welfare state. As a part of it, it has great merit; as a substitute for it, it is a bitter hoax.

The same logic holds for revenue sharing, a concept Moynihan repeatedly describes as part of the income strategy scheme. It was originally proposed by Democrat Walter W. Heller when he was chairman of the Council of Economic Advisers, as a way of using the federal taxing power to aid hard-pressed local governments. The idea was to make *more* money available. Under Nixon, however, revenue sharing became a substitute for categorical grants supplied by Washington to the states for a wide range of defined projects, like education, housing and social services. Heller has denounced the Nixon proposals as "an excuse for a fiscal cop-out." Robert Wood, former Secretary of HUD, calls it a "shell game," in which whatever "shell you look under, the Federal funds you thought were there have vanished." Using Moynihan's phraseology, *The New York Times* noted: "The so-called 'service approach' to ending poverty is not being launched. . . . The effect is that the Administration has cut-and-run from the War on Poverty."

As practiced by Nixon, revenue-sharing is quite consistent with the philosophy Moynihan outlined in his 1967 ADA speech. It gets the Feds out of services, turns the initiative over to what Nixon calls "grass-root government," and reduces the total involvement of government in the process of social progress —thereby recognizing "the limited capacities of government to bring about social change." Praising an early Republican proposal for revenue-sharing, Moynihan observes that it was superior to the Democratic version in that the GOP would provide for "an automatic pass-through of Federal revenues to cities and counties and subdivisions. Each unit of local 'general purpose' government would receive an amount 'based on its share of total local revenue raised in the state.' Once again there would be a reward for extra effort."

In other words, if some subdivision "raised" more, it would be given more. Concretely, wealthy Scarsdale or Beverly Hills would receive more per capita than Bedford-Stuyvesant or Watts, not because of their "extra effort" but because of their added riches. Such a formula would guarantee to affluent subdivisions that they would be rewarded in line with the Biblical injunction: "To them that hath shall be given."

More recently, Moynihan carried his philosophy one step further by declaring that New York City "Must permit *communities* to levy some taxes." On the face of it, this sounds democratic: "power to the people." In practice, the rich neighborhoods would raise funds to provide for their services while the poor communities would continue to languish in poverty.

Although Moynihan's book gives the impression that it is the full story of the battle over the Family Assistance Plan, it is really only a truncated presentation. It runs to the end of the 91st Congress, where the bill was killed in the conservative-minded Senate Finance Committee. (It had passed the House with the full support of the liberal Democrats—a fact that almost gets lost in Moynihan's account because of his general animus against liberals.) But the battle was resumed in the 92nd Congress, under the leadership of liberal Democratic Senator Abraham Ribicoff. Reviewing Moynihan's book in the *New Republic,* Ribicoff notes that the author "left at half time," and that if he had "stayed for the third and fourth quarters of the game—or even chronicled it—he would have seen that it was the failure of support from President Nixon that sealed the doom for welfare reform."

This should not come as a surprise to Moynihan, though he would probably point the finger at some of those around Nixon rather than at the President himself. "Within the White House, and the Administration," records Moynihan, "there developed a group that wished to see FAP defeated." This group did not really make itself heard on Capitol Hill "until FAP, wholly unexpectedly, passed the House." Up to then, the White House had been expecting the bill to lose, which would allow the Republican president to claim credit for his "liberal" proposal and blame the Democratic House for its defeat. When the House "unexpectedly" passed the measure, this "somewhat nebulous White House group did have an impact among senators who wished to believe what such persons would intimate, namely that the

President's support for the legislation was waning, or even that he had never really supported it to begin with." Presumably, while Moynihan knew about these FAP finks, Nixon did not —or, knowing, Nixon did nothing to correct the misimpression his aides were spreading.

On March 2, 1973, a headline in *The New York Times* reported: PRESIDENT FORMALLY DROPS PLAN FOR GUARANTEED ANNUAL INCOME. In a press conference, HEW Secretary Caspar Weinberger explained why by echoing "a comment made by John D. Ehrlichman": "Many people in this administration were never really comfortable with the idea." Now that these people have his credo in hand—"that [federal] government is best that governs least"—they don't really need him at hand with his "guaranteed incomes."

Murray Hausknecht

Caliban's Abode

PROSPERO:
> A devil, a born devil on whose unfortunate nature
> Nurture can never stick; on whom my pains
> Humanely taken, all, all lost, quite lost;
> And as with age his body uglier grows,
> So his mind cankers . . .
>
> *The Tempest*

Celebrated as the cradle of civilization, the source of civility, change, and progress, the city has also been damned as the locus of evil, and for many Sodom and Gomorrah are still the archetypal urban communities. These themes run together with traditional political ideologies: liberals and radicals are generally favorable and conservatives take the dim view.

Today the fit between the latter's ideology and reality seems better than ever. It is difficult to discover in modern American urban life those virtues cherished by conservatives; the contemporary city appears to justify their worst apprehensions about the long-term drift of a liberal society. This may account for the attraction urban ills have for the conservative: he contemplates them with the relish of a fundamentalist preacher gazing upon a sinner.

There is something of this in Edward Banfield's influential book *The Unheavenly City*,[1] which perhaps explains why some

193

remnants of the New Left have demanded that it be banned in schools and universities. It is more likely, though, that these difficulties come from the nature of his arguments which in many ways reflect, from the opposite end of the political spectrum, the simplicities of the New Left. The book is about major American preoccupations: a walk through the city streets discloses poverty, deteriorated housing, crime, delinquency, segregation, addiction—the whole gamut of problems in what seem to be more concentrated forms than ever before. To the questions of why, and what can be done, Banfield provides clear answers that apparently flow from the best of modern social research. At a time when any answers, much less unequivocal ones, are in short supply, his analysis is likely to seem attractive and persuasive. But it also resonates, as we shall see, with some darker currents running through American consciousness that make his perspective additionally seductive.

In a previous work Banfield said of a Chicago official,

> His remarks about Puerto Ricans and Negroes also won him support from "reactionaries." Those remarks were misinterpreted of course—Rose himself was not prejudiced, and did not like those who were—but if he had seen fit to do so, he could have phrased what he had to say so that there would have been no possibility of misinterpretation.[2]

Banfield, too, can and has been read as a "racist" by those who want him banned. But that does him an injustice and misses the real political import of his position. His "prejudice" is of a more fundamental kind than vulgar racism; his prejudgments concern the necessary structure of a human community.

Banfield's fundamental proposition about the city is that "its characteristic form and most of its problems" are the result of its population, particularly the lower-class population. "If the lower class were to disappear . . . the most serious and intractable problems of the city would disappear with it." Each class has a "distinctive psychological orientation," and that of the lower-class person involves an inability "to discipline oneself to sacrifice present for future gratifications" largely because of an inability "to imagine a future." A contrast with the upper class highlights some of the details.

An upper-class individual defines himself in relation to "the future of his children, grandchildren, great-grandchildren" and is also concerned about the future of the "community, nation, or mankind." He is self-confident about his ability to shape the future through his own actions, and he realizes that this entails a sacrifice of present gratifications for future returns. He, therefore, inhibits any self-indulgent impulses toward sex or violence lest these damage his "provision for the future." Since he also believes in the value of "self-expression," his behavior may occasionally resemble that of lower-class persons, but "whereas the lower-class individual is capable *only* of present-oriented behavior, the upper-class one can choose." His positive evaluation of self-expression is probably linked to his tolerant, "perhaps even encouraging view of unconventional behavior in sex, the arts, and politics." At the same time he "deplores bigotry" and "abhors violence." He also possesses a strong sense of responsibility to the community and frequently decides to serve it.

At the opposite extreme stands the lower-class person "living from moment to moment." He is far from self-confident; his future is "fixed, fated, beyond his control: things happen to him." He is "radically improvident" and anything "he cannot consume immediately he considers valueless. . . . His bodily needs (especially for sex) . . . take precedence over everything else—certainly any work routines." His occupational career consists of a ceaseless drift from one unskilled job to another. He is bedeviled by "feelings of self-contempt" and is inclined to be "suspicious and hostile, aggressive yet dependent." He tends to remain unmarried and has no attachment to "community, neighbors, or friends . . . he belongs to no voluntary associations . . . and does not vote unless paid to do so." The lower-class man is constantly searching for "action" and this probably contributes to making "lower-class life extraordinarily violent." Banfield claims, however, that lower-class violence is better accounted for by the high incidence of mental illness rather than class subculture.

A significant portion of the lower class is black, but it is class rather than race that is important here. The problems of these people are not primarily those of racial prejudice, though it undeniably exists. What appears to blacks as racial prejudice is in reality "class prejudice or, at any rate, class antipathy . . . much of what appears to whites as 'Negro' behavior is really lower-class behavior." So, for example, the ghetto riots of the sixties were not "political" phenomena; rather, they were either "rampages . . . outbreak[s] of animal—usually gang, male animal—spirits" or "the foray for pillage . . . and here also boys and adults of the lower class are the principal offenders." In other words, wherever there are large concentrations of "boys and young men of the lower class" as there are in black neighborhoods, the necessary conditions for riots exist. It follows, then, that "it is naive to think that efforts to end racial injustice and eliminate poverty, slums, and unemployment will have any appreciable affect upon the amount of rioting that will be done in the next decade or two."

Banfield's stress on class subculture resembles the emphasis of the "culture of poverty" theorists. While not denying that such a culture exists, Banfield goes beyond it, so to speak:

> Extreme present-orientedness, not lack of income or wealth, is the principal cause of poverty in the sense of "the culture of poverty." Most of those caught up in this culture are unable or unwilling to plan for the future, or to sacrifice immediate gratifications in favor of future ones, or to accept the disciplines that are required in order to get and to spend. . . . Lower-class poverty is "inwardly" caused (by psychological inability to provide for the future and all that this inability implies).

In short, poverty is "the effect rather than the cause" of the culture of poverty.

On the other hand, it is not exactly clear what poverty is. If it means "destitution . . . lack of income sufficient to insure physical survival," then no one in the city is destitute. If poverty is defined as "want . . . lack of enough income to support 'essential welfare,' " there is very little of it in the city. Want involves a standard of "basic needs" and these

> do not change much from one generation to the next (if they do they are not basic!), neither does a culture's idea of what constitutes a "decent," worthy, respectable, etc., mode

of life. Therefore want can be defined by a standard that changes so slowly as to be for all practical purposes fixed.

Banfield quotes a standard laid down by the economist Alfred Marshall in the 19th century and suggests that it can still serve today: " 'a well-drained dwelling with several rooms, warm clothing, with some changes of underclothing, pure water, a plentiful supply of cereal food, with a moderate allowance of meat and milk, and a little tea, etc. . . . .' " By this standard there is little want. The poverty that people are so exercised about is really a matter of relative deprivation; that is, people *feel* poor, they suffer not from a "lack of income but from a lack of status." In theory it is possible to remedy this by such schemes as the negative income tax, but these schemes probably would not work since "the lower-class person prefers near destitution without work to abundance with it." Thus here, as with other problems such as unemployment, little can be done, though this does not mean that

> calamity impends. Powerful accidental (by which is meant, nongovernmental and, more generally, nonorganizational) forces are at work that tend to alleviate and even to elimi-nate the problems. . . . One powerful accidental force at work is economic growth.

Although the notion of class seems central to Banfield's analysis, in a very real sense he is not talking of class at all. Less paradoxi-cally, Banfield's concept of class is quite different from what is commonly understood by it in most social and political analyses.

In contemporary usage class refers to the position of people relative to "the means of production" or similar "life chances"; that is, class refers to social fate as it is determined by the economy of the society. People commonly situated find ways of adapting to or coping with the exigencies of their situation and, therefore, a common economic fate gives rise to distinctive pat-terns of life or a "subculture."

Herbert Gans, one of Banfield's primary sources on class subcultures, notes that "Classes are strata-with-subcultures that grow out of the national economy and society."[3] The subcultures "are *responses* that people make to the *opportunities* and *deprivations* they encounter."[4] Classes, then, are not given by God or Nature; they emerge out of conflicts for control over property and political power. These conflicts produce systems of inequality that determine the kinds of lives men can lead. But the inequalities of today need not be the inequalities of tomorrow: what is produced by human action can be changed by human action. In this understanding of class, people are connected with the economic realities that underlie their lives. To talk of class as merely "distinctive psychological orientations" is to divorce personal lives from the realities that influence them, hide the inequalities that rule those lives, and obstruct a perception of the possibilities for changing the social structure and, thereby, the lives of men.

Banfield's use of the term "culture" has a similarly tendentious quality; it serves further to shroud reality in mystery. The label "cultural" implies that patterns of thought and behavior cannot be explained by racial or psychological theories. A further implication, one upon which Banfield's entire analysis rests, is that culture exerts an independent affect on behavior. "Deferred gratification" may originate as a way an emerging class copes with a hostile social and political environment, but it can eventually become part of a moral code to which everyone is expected to conform. As a "value" it becomes a motive of individuals through "the socialization process," and socialization, in turn, insures that culture and personality are integrated and mutually reinforcing, thus functioning as a force for social inertia.

Unfortunately, cultural realities are not so straightforward and uncomplicated, though Banfield would like us to believe it is all this simple. Not all group responses to exigencies are cultural in the sense that they are so deeply embedded, culturally and psychologically, as to be highly intractable to change. Some patterns are strongly valued, while others exist at more superficial levels because circumstances permit no alternatives: the experience of middle-aged, unskilled workers at the poverty line suggests that their future will be as bleak as their past. Their response—to live in the present—is a "cultural" one, but it could change fairly rapidly if circumstances would permit future payoffs for present self-denial. Banfield's use of "culture" does not, however, allow for these essential distinctions.[5]

There is an additional complexity. Any description of a sub-culture inevitably emphasizes distinctive characteristics; it ignores or minimizes aspects of a subculture shared with other groups which motivate actions in ways different from what is assumed to be the main thrust of the subculture. Put differently, a subculture is not a consistent whole but an entity shot through with conflicting elements: "commitment to values, norms, and other cultural themes may often involve ambiguity, ambivalence, and the simultaneous holding of alternative or contradictory beliefs."[6] What appear to be strong impulses to action under one set of circumstances may be severely weakened by a change in circumstances.

For more is at issue here than academic thrust and parry. Concepts define the world for us, and our understanding of reality goes a long way to determining what policy and action we are willing to back. Class and culture emphasize that men's lives are the result of historical forces, that the style and quality of life are not fixed by nature or the supernatural. What some would have us see as permanent is, in reality, impermanent; social and cultural realities change through human action. Forces flowing from class and culture are far less inexorable than those immanent in biological structure. To raise, as Banfield does, the specter of class and culture as implacable forces with an unbreakable grip on people is nothing less than a process of mystification.

If concepts are perverted to make reality seem something other than it is, we find something of the same process when we raise an empirical question: To what extent does Banfield offer a valid description of the "inward" nature and behavior of the lower-class person?

While his description is based upon a fairly large and familiar body of social science research data collected over the past two decades, there are some major difficulties in the way Banfield chooses to use the data. As he himself points out, not all his statements have the same status vis à vis known fact:

> Most of the statements about time horizons . . . are empirical. . . . The main proposition, namely, that individuals and cultures have differing time orientations toward the future

is of this character. . . . Some propositions, however, are *implications* of the main proposition; they are themselves deductive . . . arrived at from premises that have been inductively established. No "data" support the statement that present-oriented persons are unconcerned about the welfare of their grandchildren yet unborn; such a statement follows from the meaning of present orientation.

By the same token there is no evidence supporting the proposition that future-oriented persons are concerned about their potential grandchildren, to say nothing of upper-class people who worry about great-grandchildren. Since no one claims a lack of concern about sons and daughters in the lower class, the only empirically supported proposition left is that members of all classes are concerned with their children's welfare. An unexciting conclusion to be sure, but certainly a better basis for prudent social policy than one drawn from dramatic but factually unsupported propositions.

There are other peculiarities in the use of data. In contrasting the effects of "disincentives" to work, Banfield notes that raising the income tax rate does not seem to have much affect on the motivations of the middle class. But "low-income earners" react differently: "That they will not work when welfare payments are as much or more than they could earn is to be expected, of course." This carries a citation from the McCone Commission Report on the Watts riot which notes that grants under Aid to Families with Dependent Children were greater than what could be earned at minimum-wage jobs. Banfield then states, "it also appears that many poor persons will not put forth effort to get 'extras' once they have been assured of a level of living which, while extremely low, seems to them to be 'enough.' " This is followed by the further proposition that "the higher the floor that is put under incomes, the greater the number of workers who will see no reason to work." The one empirical datum in the course of this argument is only tangentially related to it. The finding that welfare payments are sometimes higher than earnings at minimum wage does not tell us whether it does *in fact* act as a disincentive, under what conditions, and for how many it will be a disincentive. Not only are the two inferences unsupported, but they have no factual base. There is, of course, the further difficulty of whether the two types of disincentives mentioned are comparable.

Some of the difficulties of relying upon unsupported inference is illustrated by data gathered by a survey of AFDC mothers in six counties of Wisconsin including Milwaukee: over half the respondents had positive attitudes about working, and "most AFDC recipients would like to work if their children could be taken care of, especially younger women or women with recent employment." Having preschool children, which might seem an excellent rationalization for a lack of interest in jobs, turned out, on the contrary, to be associated with "the desire to have a job." Although Banfield claims that class rather than race is important, in this sample, at least, race does seem to have some sort of independent effect: "71 percent of the blacks want a job either 'very much' or 'somewhat' as compared with 50 percent of the whites in Milwaukee." Only "one-third of the Milwaukee respondents had previous experience with AFDC," and the "percentage of white women who were repeaters was higher than for black women."[7] One wonders whether T. H. Huxley's remark about Herbert Spencer applies to Banfield as well: "Spencer's definition of a tragedy was the spectacle of a deduction killed by a fact."

Sometimes the reported facts, when traced to the source, do not have the same meaning or significance that Banfield's text gives them. The latter reads: "The incidence of mental illness is greater in the lower class than in any of the others. Moreover, the nature of lower-class culture is such that much behavior that in another class would be considered bizarre seems routine." Three sources are cited in a footnote.[8] One, a study of the families of delinquent boys, confirms after a one-page survey of the literature the association of "poverty and pathology." A citation from Myers and Roberts is for part of their discussion of the importance of money in the lower class and the psychological stress its lack entails. The only possible instance of "bizarre" behavior found here is in a quotation from an interview: "In fact everybody in our family has to worry about it [money] except my old man when he gets drunk." The page cited from a monograph by Hollingshead and Redlich occurs in the chapter, "Paths to the Psychiatrist." On page 172 they note that while "perception of the psychological nature of personal problems is a rare trait in any class" it is most frequently found in the upper strata. Consequently, "more abnormal behavior is tolerated" by the lower strata "even though the behavior may be disapproved by class norms." On page 174 the following paragraph runs to the top of page 175, the page cited by Banfield:

> Although the patient presents a lifelong history of hostility, suspicion, and extreme lack of consideration of others, so far as we are able to determine neither his family nor others in his environment—even when his behavior became violent— considered him a "psychiatric problem" . . . people in all strata have blind spots regarding psycho-pathological implications of unusual behavior or even deliberately avoid thinking about them. The lower-stratus patient will attribute his troubles to unhappiness, tough luck, laziness, meanness, or physical illness rather than to factors of psychogenic origin. The worst thing that can happen to a Class V person is to be labeled "bugs," "crazy," or "nuts." Such judgment is often equal to being sentenced for life to the "bughouse." Unfortunately, this sentiment is realistic.

The remainder of the page contains two case histories of "compulsory promiscuous" behavior of a middle-class and a lower-class girl. Now, at minimum, a somewhat different picture of the problem of "abnormal behavior" and class emerges from this discussion than from Banfield's statement that is presumably based on it.

Similar questions can be and have been raised about the factual basis of the central thesis: lower-class individuals are incapable of deferring gratifications. The research literature indicates that in the lower class there is a distinct tendency not to defer gratifications—although this pattern is found not only in the lower class.[9] A major difficulty with the data, though, is assessing its significance. Banfield sees "deferred gratification" as one of those autonomous cultural patterns that remain "for all practical purposes fixed"; that is, unaffected by changes in material conditions. But it is equally plausible, on the basis of what we know, to see the persistence of the pattern as a functional adaptation to severely restrictive life situations.

Consider some of the conditions that must prevail if such a pattern is to become established and continue: an orientation to time that makes connections between present and future behavior demands some freedom from constant preoccupation with meeting pressing immediate needs—shoes for the children and next month's rent. Concentration on the present may be needed for survival in the present. To be oriented to the future requires some reasonable basis for believing that present behavior will result in a better future. And even if low-income earners could subject themselves to extra deprivations by adhering to the bourgeois virtue of regular savings, the money they would put in the bank could not make as much difference to their children's education, say, as investment programs of highly paid executives.

Even if one could save significant amounts, the opportunities one is saving for must be present in the future. Traditionally American workers have dreamed of becoming small businessmen, but a small business comes to seem a less and less viable alternative in a modern economy. If these necessary conditions are not present it is difficult to see how one can reasonably expect lower-class persons to defer gratifications. What would one say of the rationality or even the mental health of those who persistently deferred pleasures in the face of only slim chances of future payoffs?[10]

In fact, fewer and fewer people in all classes seem to be denying themselves present pleasures. Support for the existence of the deferred-gratification pattern used to be found in Kinsey's report that middle-class people began having sexual intercourse at a later age than those in lower strata.[11] Today this pleasure does not appear to be unduly postponed in any class. Between 1960 and 1970 consumer installment credit rose from $43 billion to $101.2 billion.[12] Even discounting for inflation, this suggests a rapidly declining rate of deferred gratification.

If large numbers of people in all classes are choosing only one type of behavior, how valid is it to talk of the existence of a pattern of a deferred gratification that distinguishes one stratum from another? The lower class, in short, is being reproached and condemned for not conforming to a pattern of behavior that is probably disappearing in the rest of the society.

Banfield is aware of critical assessments of the data but chooses not to discuss them. Given this glorification of self-denial along with his penchant for unsupported inferences and his conception of class and culture, there seems to be an insistent perverseness in his approach. But "perverseness" suggests mere idiosyncracy where, in fact, we are dealing with a modernized version of an older ideological bias.

Class and race are classificatory concepts. Race categorizes in terms of biological givens, traits beyond control or change except through long-term evolutionary processes. Members of a class possess mutable characteristics that change with changes in society. *But if a class is defined in terms of psychological orientations rather than social location, then structural change becomes for all practical purposes an irrelevant consideration.* (Banfield is aware, of course, that many psychological traits change relatively quickly, but any changes in orientations like present-mindedness, he emphasizes, "must occur very slowly" because they are rooted in culture.) This means that the logical status of Banfield's concept of class comes to be equivalent to that of race: the thought and behavior of members of a class, as with members of a race, are unrelated to the nature of the society. Just as racist dogma focuses on the fixed biological constitution of man as the source of behavior, so Banfield's class concept directs attention to the relatively immutable "inward" traits of individuals. Banfield's formulation is thereby to be seen as a species of conceptual alchemy.

His idea of class has, for some, its ideological attractions. A traditional function of race has been to justify and defend inequality and domination. But race has fallen on hard times, and as a result Banfield's formulation comes to seem attractive to the kinds of minds who would earlier have been drawn to race. His "class" converts an idea antagonistic to the meaning and implications of race to the political and ideological ends served by the latter.

But for the transmutation to work a somewhat similar operation must be performed on the concept of culture. This concept developed, in part, as a reaction to that of race: cultural anthropologists were committed to demonstrating that the culture concept was a better explanatory notion than race. Since what had to be explained seemed to be relatively persistent and fixed in the history of a society, and since the societies under examination were in fact slow to change, the consistent and mutually reinforcing elements of culture were stressed, elements producing consensus and stability.

Once race was supplanted as the dominant intellectual orientation, and attention focused on modern societies, the conception of culture as a unitary and consistent whole could no longer be maintained. The idea of "subculture," for example, was partially a consequence of the realization that the culture of a modern society was not a unitary whole—as one moved from group to group one expected to find differences, contradictions, counterpushes and pulls. Culture, therefore, is a source not only of order and stability but of disorder and change, and what is true of culture as a whole is true of subcultures as well. A more complex picture of subculture emerges from descriptions by those not committed to a perception of social reality as fixed and unchanging:

> A constant source of frustration to most lower-class individuals is their awareness that despite the surface validity of the self they present, their behavior is not consistent with some of the standards of the larger society which they have internalized, often in spite of themselves. . . . Seeking to become a valid person in a more conventional way remains attractive even though the probability of success may be low.[13]

This suggests that a view of the lower-class person as one who, for example, is "engaged in an unremitting search for sex" may be a highly oversimplified version of a more deeply textured reality. The lower-class person shares moral aspirations and qualities with others in the society. But those who see no contradiction between justice and inequality *must* distinguish strata in terms of their moral qualities:

Man is so built that he cannot achieve perfection of his humanity except by keeping down his lower impulses. He cannot rule his body by persuasion. This fact alone shows that even despotic rule is not per se against nature. . . . To take the extreme case, despotic rule is unjust only if it is applied to beings who can be ruled by persuasion or whose understanding is insufficient: Prospero's rule over Caliban is by nature just.[14]

If, on the other hand, Prospero and Caliban as moral beings are more like than unlike, Prospero's order will be called into question.

Nor may Caliban claim, according to this view of the "just society," that his material needs are not being met by that order. Where once the inequities he might have railed against could be justified by recourse to the differing needs of superior and inferior racial stocks, today one refers to the "basic needs" of fixed and unchanging cultural milieus. By the standard invoked by Banfield, one which he says "changes so slowly as to be for all practical purposes fixed," Prospero's order is the best of all possible worlds. Thus the transmuted concepts of class and culture perform the ideological tasks once fulfilled by baser intellectual coinage.

The Unheavenly City is oriented to the needs of a policy-maker who is finally admonished not to be too active. Banfield recommends to his notice the beneficial consequences of such "accidental forces" as "economic growth"—a modern, secular version of "the divine hand" that used to produce the harmonious society. But in an age when even a Republican president recognizes the prophetic voice of Keynes, one wonders whether any future-oriented policy-maker, duly concerned about the "community, the nation . . . mankind," could in good conscience accept so backward-looking a view of man and society as that offered to him by Edward Banfield.

David K. Cohen

Does IQ Matter?

In the late 1960s a social fact began to take shape: liberal social programs were "failing." The observations on which this notion was based varied from impressionistic reporting about local CAP agencies to detailed statistical studies of Headstart, and many of these observations were fallible. But whether or not the evidence was correct, the social fact was true. By 1970 it was widely believed that liberal social programs had failed, and that belief is itself a reality of no mean consequence.

The response of intellectuals has been varied, and not entirely predictable. Some have taken the view that the appearance of failure is due essentially to the absence of serious effort: many of the programs in question, they argue, existed only rhetorically, or embryonically, or marginally, so that no one could reasonably expect success in the first place. On this view, the problem was not with liberal goals or program impact, but with a failure of implementation.

Others have suggested problems with the Great Society strategy of relying heavily on education and training. Questions have been raised about the notion that eliminating educational inequality will reduce other social and economic inequalities. On this view the problem is not with liberal social goals or program implementation, but with the strategies upon which the programs rested: it is suggested that education and training may be less helpful than more direct redistribution.

Still other commentators have pushed matters further. Instead of attacking the assumptions underlying a particular egalitarian strategy, they question the assumptions of egalitarianism itself. Some have focused on the idea that society is less malleable than might have been assumed, suggesting that there may be "limits of social policy" embedded in the social structure. Others have explored the notion that man is less malleable than might have been believed, suggesting that human nature may be resistant to liberal social goals.

The boundaries among these rather loose tendencies are far from distinct, but differences in their popularity are not. Disproportionate attention has been given to the last line of thought, and especially to the notion that education has failed to reduce inequality because of genetic differences between advantaged and disadvantaged segments of the population. A few years ago, in an essay in the prestigious *Harvard Educational Review*, Arthur Jensen reviewed the evidence on group differences in intellectual ability and school achievement; everything showed large and consistent gaps among groups. On the average, children whose families were poor or black did much less well on tests than children whose families were well-to-do or white. Jensen also pulled together a considerable body of research which suggested that differences in intelligence among individuals seemed to be caused more by heredity than by environment. And finally he ventured the idea that heredity may explain intellectual differences among groups just as well as it appeared to account for differences among individuals.

A few years later, H. J. Eysenck, a British psychologist, brought out a book which purported to subject Jensen's work to a critical assessment.[1] Although there is little indication of such an assessment in this pot-boiler, it does support Jensen's appraisal of the research, as well as his speculation concerning the genetic sources of racial differences in IQ. Finally, in 1972 Richard J. Herrnstein, a Harvard psychologist, published an essay in the *Atlantic Monthly* which generated quite a stir. Herrnstein broadened, refined, and defended arguments laid down earlier. He maintained that what IQ tests measure is an important and stable human attribute. He marshaled evidence that IQ differences among individuals are mostly accounted for by genes, not by environment. And he pressed the idea that intelligence is an increasingly powerful influence on intergroup differences in status, wealth, and power in advanced industrial societies.

None of these works was presented as an expressly conservative polemic. Indeed, all three claimed scientific dispassion, academic freedom, and bemoaned the negative reaction their words provoked. Whatever one may think of these claims, the most restrained assessment one could plausibly make is that the drift of all this work is distinctly conservative. For one thing, in somewhat different ways each of these three authors questions the traditional liberal notion that stupidity results from the inheritance of poverty, and suggests instead that poverty may result from the inheritance of stupidity. For another, it is not clear that research on such questions can be morally or politically neutral. Such work requires, at the very least, a working assumption that society might want to take alleged genetic differences into account in making judgments about the worth of citizens. This is hardly a self-evident assumption, and in fact is one which historically has been congenial only to the most conservative tendencies in social thought and action.

As this suggests, the arguments themselves are nothing new. The heritability of IQ first became a major public fixation in reaction to the turn-of-the century deluge of poor European immigrants; it bubbled to the surface once again just after the Brown decision in 1954, when racial mixing in public schools seemed to loom on the horizon; and not surprisingly it reemerged when the disappointing results of recent school-improvement programs for the poor became known. As this little chronicle may suggest, recent attention to the subject is not wholly the product of scientific interest. While the heritability of IQ holds a constant fascination for psychologists and demographers, most of the time they are the only people who care enough about the matter to mention it. Only when there are broader issues involving ethnic or racial minorities—in which the character of the culture, or the allocation of public resources, or the composition of society is at stake—does the relationship between genes and IQ reach the front page of anything other than arcane professional journals.

But while this may improve our understanding of recent interest in the deficiencies of the poor as a social phenomenon, it doesn't say much about the arguments themselves. Almost reflexively, one wants to know whether heredity *does* account for most individual differences in IQ, and whether it also is to blame for group differences in social and economic status. On the other hand, it seems in some respects morally obscene to enter into such matters as though they were science, when a persuasive argument can be made that inherited differences in the moral and personal attributes of groups (if there be such things) should have no public significance in a fair society. But clearly, America is not so fair so that such distinctions are irrelevant, and it thus seems plausible to take up the issues as a matter of fact. Does the available evidence suggest that liberal social reform may founder on the intellectual deficiencies of the poor?

Of all the issues, the role of heredity in causing differences in individual IQ has been the most thoroughly probed. One way of approaching it has been to compare the intelligences of identical twins who have been raised in different environments. Since identical twins have the same genetic endowment in all respects, any difference in their IQ's that are not due to errors in measurement would presumably be traceable to differences in environment. Studies show that somewhere between twenty and forty percent of the variation in the IQ's of twins can be attributed to variations in their environment—the rest is presumably due to heredity.

Another approach has been to compare the intelligence of unrelated children reared together. Since their genetic material can safely be assumed to have nothing in common, any relationship between their IQ's would probably be the result of environmental similarity. Studies of this kind have yielded roughly the same results as the twin studies.

This evidence is nothing to sneeze at, but it might easily be misinterpreted. For one thing, genes and environment may interact in ways which would lead to overestimates of genetic influence: a child with a low IQ will probably be treated accordingly, while a brighter child would get more stimulation. This could enhance the bright child's IQ while depressing the dull child's; in studies of the sort summarized here, such environmental effects would all be marked down to heredity. The magnitude of these effects might be as much as twenty percent of the variation among individual IQ's.

Another problem with the twin studies has to do with the distribution of environments. Identical twins reared apart are nearly as rare as hen's teeth, and constriction in the range of their environments might overstate the importance of heredity. The environments studied do not fully cover the available extremes in the U.S. or Britain, and there is some dispute about how adequate the representation of environments was.

Suppose, for example, that instead of going to a moderately advantaged foster home one twin had been placed in a super-enriched environment, absolutely booming and buzzing with the stimulation that psychologists regard as brain food. Would his IQ have shown astounding gains? We don't know very much about the effects of changing the intensity of environments or of reversing inequalities in their distribution. The experiments that have been conducted suggest that certain varieties of stimulation can produce considerable IQ gains in disadvantaged children. Some of them, in fact, have produced gains of roughly the same magnitude as the gap which on the average separates the IQ of blacks and whites. These programs have often involved highly structured pre-schools or home-visiting programs designed to improve parents' effectiveness as teachers. They generally last about nine months or a year, but often the effects don't persist much longer. Evidence from most experiments indicates that as the experience recedes into the past the effects diminish. This is no surprise, for experiments, unlike families, usually last only a few months. No one knows what would happen if the experiments were more intense, or if they lasted for nine years instead of nine months. And for the immediate future, at least, these questions will remain unanswered.

One important point about all these studies, then, is that they show the malleability of IQ. But another is that the results are still compatible with findings on the relative influence of heredity and environment on IQ. For to say (by way of example) that genes seem to account for 60 percent of the variation among individuals' IQ's is not to say that 40 percent of anyone's IQ is malleable. No one knows whether there is a "ceiling" on environmental effects or not, or what it might be.

All of this should be enough to persuade any sensible reader that the issue will not soon be resolved. Indeed, it would be astonishing if people ever stopped arguing about the relative influence of heredity and environment on individual IQ differences. Hereditarians will always point to evidence which shows that (things being what they are) more of the variability in IQ is explained by heredity, and environmentalists will always be able to point to evidence which encourages the belief that if environments were radically altered, their relative importance might increase and IQ's might be sharply changed. Since these phenomena are not mutually exclusive, and since experiments to test the limits of environmental effects are unlikely to be devised, the argument will probably continue for the next thirty years in much the same terms as it has for the last thirty.

The question of chief interest here, of course, is not that of individual but of group differences. The sources of such differences, however, are not nearly so well illuminated by research. That there is a substantial gap in test scores between classes and races seems clear. What people want to know is whether the gap is a result of difference in heredity or environment, but the answer is hard to get at. The same conditions which make for interest in the question—the existence of large differences in both measured ability and social achievement—make it very difficult to decide where cause ends and effect begins. It is hard to figure out whether poverty causes low IQ or low IQ causes poverty, because they tend to occur in the same groups. The very groups which are continually suspected of being genetically underendowed with respect to IQ have also been socially underendowed with respect to environment. This means, for example, that the full range of environmental differences available to native Wasps in the 1920s were not available to immigrant Italians, and as a result it would have been well-nigh impossible to find comparable samples of Italians and Wasps on whom to conduct research.

The same holds for blacks and whites today. One can investigate the relative influence of heredity and environment among blacks, just as in the studies of white children summarized earlier. But such studies of black children would only tell us how much of the IQ variation among blacks themselves is due to heredity; they would not tell us how much of the gap in test scores between the races is due to heredity and how much to environment. We can imagine ways to get around this problem: study unrelated black and white children who were raised in the same home; or study a population of black and white adults who have had the same environments; or (as one wag has suggested) find several pairs of identical twins who have been reared apart, making sure that each pair consists of one white and one black twin. But simply listing the examples reveals the problem: securing blacks and whites with the same environments is only a little easier than securing blacks and whites with the same natural parents. The environmental differences America has created between blacks and whites are profound and ancient, and they can be expected to endure for some time. Until such differences have become a thing of the past for at least some blacks, it is hard to see how respectable research can be done on the sources of the racial IQ gap. It is likely, however, that by the time such social equality is attained, either the environmentalists will be proved right by the disappearance of the IQ gap, or the very fact of social equality will cause everyone to lose interest in the question. Who now cares whether Italians have lower or higher IQ's than native white Americans?

Oddly enough, in most of the arguments about genes and IQ over the past thirty years much greater attention has been paid to the relative importance of circumstances and heredity than to figuring out exactly what IQ means, or what it is good for. Most people with very high IQ's seem very smart, and most people with very low IQ's seem very stupid. But people in between —which is where almost everyone is—are full of surprises. The fact that the tests can distinguish extremes so evident in everyday life inclines one to believe they measure something important. The fact that things get unclear in the middle, however, should make one dubious as to the value of the measuring-stick for most of everyday life.

What do IQ test measure? Some people naively believe they provide a summary index of a general human ability to cope, but this would appear unlikely: think of the psychologist next door who nearly became unhinged trying to put together a hi-fi kit, or of the university sociologists who lost their shirts running a consulting firm, or of the computer freak who is incapable of writing an intelligible English sentence.

← FRED

There also are psychologists who believe that IQ tests measure one dimension of some more general and unified underlying intelligence. Perhaps, but at the moment it is hard to know. Psychologists are not in agreement on the elements of this underlying intelligence, and available research shows that sometimes the elements in question are connected only weakly or not at all. Since IQ is about the only thing psychologists have learned to measure with much validity or consistency, good research on the relation between IQ and other aspects of intelligence or personality is not plentiful.

Finally, there are people who think that intelligence is simply the ability to perform well at whatever one's social situation seems to require. This is obviously true in some ways, but the notion has limits. Does it make sense to say that Lewis Strauss was smarter than Robert Oppenheimer? Or to argue that a high-school student who flunked out and then became a successful numbers runner is just as smart as the valedictorian of his high school who couldn't get a job after graduation? Intelligence may not be timeless and unitary, but the relativist view is not without some problems.

No doubt this debate could go on forever—in fact it probably will—but most people would not wish to pursue it. They assume a social definition of intelligence; they care about not a psychological construct, but a social phenomenon. Indeed, many of those who worry about the proper definition of IQ do so chiefly because they think it is becoming the central criterion for distributing the good things of life. People care about IQ because they regard it as the basis on which society's rewards and punishments are allocated; they believe that America is becoming a society in which status and power are more and more handed out on the basis of brains.

This view is so widely held that it has become a sort of secular catechism. It certainly is repeated often enough, and in many different connections. Radicals attack America for allocating rewards on the basis of technical talent rather than need or human value; liberals bemoan the fact that discrimination has kept members of minority groups from competing on their own merits—i.e., technical talent; Jews fear the demise of merit standards in employment and education, but blacks attack the standards themselves as racist. Conservatives used to attack merit standards too, on the ground that some things were more important than merit or intelligence, but this argument no longer has enough credibility to be used in defense of privilege. It is now employed only on behalf of the poor, which suggests how widespread is the belief that meritocracy is upon us.

In the light of this concern, the fuss over IQ is indeed as important as Professors Eysenck and Herrnstein believe it to be. However muddy the tests or biased their results, they exist; in a meritocracy of the sort we are said to have, such tests would undoubtedly be a major criterion for the allocation of rewards. The basic question, then, is how much, IQ counts in America in terms of status and power.

Perhaps the best place to begin is the schools. That is where IQ is supposed to have its greatest impact, because it is in schools that children get on the various educational tracks which are presumed to play a considerable role in their chances for wealth and status later on. Really bright children are supposed to be routed into college preparatory work, and really not-so-bright children into vocational courses. Those in between are assigned to "general," business, or similar curricula. Then everyone graduates or drops out, goes to work or to college, and moves on to his appointed niche.

This picture is far from being wholly false, but it is by no means as true as most educators make it out to be. Take, for example, one of the most critical decision made during a child's school career: the kind of high-school program he will follow. In a perfectly meritocratic system based on IQ this decision would rest exclusively on one's test score. In a perfect caste system the decision would rest exclusively on one's inherited status. In the United States things are much more confused. According to studies of what causes curriculum assignments of high-school students, measured ability is only one among several influential factors; others include the social and economic status of a student's family, his own aspirations for a career, and the degree of encouragement his parents have offered to those aspirations. The most comprehensive studies suggest also that these causes are not wholly independent; children from higher status homes, for example, typically have higher test scores and aspirations. The studies also show that the cumulative effects of these latter three influences on placement in high school are at least of equal importance to measured ability.

Of course, a good deal happens to children in school before they even reach the point where decisions are made about their high-school curriculum. They are graded and grouped from the very beginning, and this undoubtedly has some impact—if not on how children regard themselves at least on what the teachers think about them. But the assignment of children to ability groups, like the assignment to curricula, seems to be determined by all sorts of things in addition to IQ. And grades too seem to be influenced as much by the attitudes of the children, their behavior toward authority, and their general demeanor as by their test scores.

But the most important point is that all of these factors together—ability, aspirations, inherited status, etc.—account for less than half of the actual variation in the assignment of students to one high-school track or another. A majority of the differences among students in this respect, in other words, are caused by something other than either status or brains. This is not as odd as it might seem. Some of the differences probably arise from mistakes in assignments—bright children who want to go to college but lose out because of a slip or who are incorrectly assigned because of a perverse teacher. Some of the differences probably are caused by variations in family attitudes and motivation, which seem to have a considerable impact on schooling decisions quite independently of parents' status or children's ability; lots of poor parents push their children very hard, and lots of non-poor parents don't. And some of the differences probably are caused by variations in deportment or motivation, or the encouragement students get from teachers, or other factors that usually go unmeasured. In short, if we consider only measured intelligence or inherited status, we cannot explain most of the variation in students' track placement in high school.

One can also examine the role of IQ in college attendance. Here, after all, is one of the great divides in American life. A college degree is regarded increasingly as the only sure way to gain access to the good things in this society, and certainly college entrance is the goal toward much of the school's work. How great a role does IQ play here?

If we look only at the relative influence of tested ability and inherited social and economic status, the available evidence does not show that college entrance is chiefly determined by academic ability. In fact, the relative importance of these two influences seems to be roughly equal. Consider, for example, a high-school senior whose family is in the lowest fifth of the population with respect to both social status and test scores. Not only is this young person less bright than at least 80 percent of all high-school seniors, but his family is less affluent than at least 80 percent of American families. In the early 1960's, he had roughly one chance in ten of entering college the year after high-school graduation.

By way of contrast consider his friend down the street, similarly situated with respect to family circumstances, but in the top fifth of the ability distribution. His family is poorer than over 80 percent of the population, but he is smarter than over 80 percent of all high-school seniors. He had roughly six chances in ten of entering college the year after graduating high school.

A comparison of these two seniors reveals that among poor students, when family circumstances are roughly the same, more brains means a much better chance of going to college.

Do IQ and status operate in the same way for more advantaged students? Consider two seniors who come from families in the upper fifth of the distribution of social advantages and economic status. If one of them fell in the bottom fifth of the ability distribution (stupider than 80 percent of his peers), he would have roughly four chances in ten of going to college. If the other fell in the top fifth of the ability distribution (smarter than 80 percent of his peers), he would have nine chances in ten of going to college. This comparison reveals that brains are a help at the top of the social pyramid, just as at the bottom: rich boys and girls with high IQ's go to college more often than rich boys and girls with low IQ's.

A comparison of the first pair of students with the second pair reveals that getting rich (moving from the bottom to the top of the social pyramid) is nearly as big a help in increasing a student's chances of going to college as getting smart (moving from the bottom to the top of the IQ distribution). More precise analyses of the data on college-going confirm the impression gained from these examples: measured intelligence is of slightly greater influence on college attendance that inherited status. This is a great deal different from a world in which going to college is wholly determined by family position, but it is far from a world in which going to college is wholly determined by intellectual ability.

Once again, however, these comparisons do not reveal what must be the most important fact—namely, that ability and status combined explain somewhat less than half the actual variation in college attendance. As in the case of curriculum placement, we must turn to other factors—motivation, error, discrimination, chance, and family encouragement or lack of it—to find likely explanations. Existing research provides support for the idea that these other factors do play a role (although it does not afford comprehensive estimates of their relative import-ance).[2]

Thus, while academic ability or intelligence is important to educational success, other factors, measured and unmeasured, seem to have more weight in determining who gets ahead in American schools. But this in turn raises an absolute swarm of problems. If test scores are only moderately important, should steps be taken to increase their influence? Or would relying more heavily on test scores in order to lessen the influence of social inheritance leave less room for people to be selected on other criteria, such as motivation? If the influence of inherited status on selection ought to be reduced, how great should the reduction be? In a perfect meritocracy, after all, the objective would be to remove the effect of any social advantages parents had achieved on the life-chances of their children—but what sort of society would that be? Would it be consistent with nuclear families? Does anyone want a society in which every child has an equal chance to be a clamdigger or a cardiac surgeon, subject only to IQ differences? The idea seems bizarre, for it suggests a social rat-race which would make the Great American Status Scramble look like a party game for retired schoolmarms. And if a perfect meritocracy seems like a perfect neurotic nightmare, then just how much, or how little, of an educational advantage would we want families to be able to pass along to their children?

Anyone who thinks about these questions for more than ten seconds will realize that no easy answers are available. More equality in education would be a good thing, and it is sensible to suppose that this implies some effort to reduce the influence of social and economic inheritance on school success. But we have no well-formed conception of how much the impact of families ought to be reduced, or how much of a role IQ ought to have in reducing it. Nor, indeed, is it clear that IQ should bear that burden at all. Distributing rewards in accordance with IQ scores, after all, is not the only known device for reducing social and economic differences, even in education.

Of course, one's view on these last issues will depend in part on the role one thinks intelligence actually plays in the allocation of adult status and power. If it turned out that IQ was crucial, it would be hard to maintain status and power. If it turned out that IQ was crucial, it would be hard to maintain that it ought not to be the principal means for discriminating among school children. So before going any further with these questions about meritocracy in schools, it might be wise to find out just how important IQ is once people get out of them. I will deal with occupational status first, because that is what seems to fascinate most writers on the subject.[3]

One way of looking at this question—as Eysenck and Herrnstein did—is by pointing to the average IQ's of people in different occupations. Manual laborers turn out on the average to have lower IQ's than professors of theology, and this is assumed to mean that IQ is an entry requirement for these occupations. But simply presenting the gross differences begs all the basic questions. First, the averages don't reveal the considerable dispersion of IQ's within occupational groups which reveals that there are lots of people in working-class jobs whose IQ's are in the same range as those in higher-status occupations, and vice versa. But more significantly, listing IQ differences among occupations only tells us that differences exist; it does not tell us how important IQ was in getting people into those occupations. A satisfactory account would require that we know the IQ's of people in different occupations, but it would require other information as well. We would need to know, for example, how far people got in school and what social and economic advantages their parents had, because these might have had a real impact on their own occupational status as adults, to say nothing of affecting their IQ's. Armed with evidence of this sort—which is hard to come by because it covers almost the entire life-cycle—we would compare the relative importance of IQ and other influences on the sorts of jobs adults wind up with. Now there is, in fact, a good deal of research which shows that people who stay in school longer wind up on the average with higher status jobs, and that on the average people who begin life with more social and economic advantages wind up with more of them as adults. But when researchers try to assess the relative importance of education and social inheritance they begin to part company. Some argue that staying in school is a considerably more important influence on occupational attainment than inherited status; others think the opposite is true. The former category of researchers tend to think of America as a relatively open society, in which schooling serves as a vehicle of social mobility from one generation to another. Researchers in the second category tend to think of America as a relatively closed society, in which the schools mostly transmit the same status from parents to children. Since both things are manifestly true to some degree, and since the evidence is not entirely adequate to resolve the matter, the argument will continue for some time. But what is important for our purposes is not how much mobility there is, or to what extent schooling contributes to it; rather we want to know whether IQ itself has an effect on occupational status apart from these two influences.

The available evidence suggests that it has little or no independent effect on the sorts of jobs people wind up with as adults, all other things being equal. IQ does help moderately and indirectly, because it has a moderate influence on how long people stay in school, and the length of their stay in school affects the sorts of jobs they get. But once the influence of schooling is taken into account, IQ appears to have no independent relation to occupational success. If a meritocracy is a society in which intelligent people do well regardless of their parents or their schooling, America is not such a society.

To make this concrete, consider several adults who differ in every aspect under discussion here—jobs, IQ's, length of stay in school, and social and economic backgrounds. The differences in their inherited status and in the length of time they stayed in school account for a fair proportion (somewhat less than half) of the differences in the status of their jobs. Since those who have higher IQ's will have stayed in school somewhat longer, IQ can be said to have a moderate effect on occupational status. But when people with equal amounts of schooling are considered, differences in their IQ's turn out to account for none of the differences in the status of their jobs. Having a higher IQ is no help in getting a higher status job for people who have the same educational attainment and the same social and economic background. In addition, there is an abundance of studies showing that the grades of college students are not related either to their income or to their occupational status once they get out of college; similarly, research on what differentiates good from bad workers (within broad occupational categories) shows that workers who produce more or who are rated highly by their supervisors generally do not have higher test scores, although they do tend to have "better" attitudes, greater "motivation," better "deportment"—in effect, more of the attributes which also seem to make for success in school.

Thus, the process of selection to occupations in America does not appear to be more than mildly dependent on IQ. And here too, as in the case of high-school placement and college entrance, recent research has shown that IQ, schooling, and inherited status together account for less than half of the variation in the occupational attainment of white American males. More than half of the differences in the job status of American men is explained neither by their IQ, nor by how long they went to school, nor by the social and economic advantages (or burdens) they inherited. Some of these unexplained differences are undoubtedly due to errors in the ways sociologists measure things, but others are probably due to such imponderables as enterprise, motivation, chance, and preferences unrelated either to brains or to economic background.

That, however, is not the end of the matter. Whatever the evidence may suggest about the modest influence IQ presently exerts on occupational selection, the popular mythology is that it is much greater now than it was fifty years ago. America, we are told, is a "knowledge society"; we are moving into a post-industrial age, in which talent will rule. Yet when we turn to

historical evidence concerning the role of IQ in occupational
selection, once again we find little support for such claims. If IQ
were becoming a more important force in occupational selection
we would expect the IQ averages of people in any occupation to
have become more similar over time: the IQ's of professional
people should have grown more nearly equal as merit selection
proceeded, and the same would be true of blue-collar workers.
But the fragmentary evidence we have suggests this is not true:
the dispersion of IQ's within occupational categories for native
American whites seems to have remained pretty stable over the
last four or five decades. Similarly, if IQ were becoming more
important we might expect the IQ level of intellectually demand-
ing occupations to rise, and the level of undemanding jobs to fall.
But no such development seems to have taken place. Finally, if
IQ were becoming more important to adult success, we would
imagine that the main instrument by which IQ makes itself felt in
America—schooling—would have become more important to
getting a job. But according to the historical evidence concerning the effect of schooling on occupational attainment over the
past four or five decades, education seems to bear no powerful
relationship to the job one gets today than it did earlier in the
century.

Now all of this evidence is partial, and subject to a variety of
caveats. But the striking thing is that nowhere can we find any
empirical support for the idea that brains are becoming increasingly more important to status in America. Of course, this by
itself is not incompatible with the observation that "knowledge"
is an increasingly central aspect of life. For one thing, measures
of occupational status are based on opinion surveys in which
random samples of the American people are asked about the
relative prestige of occupations. Thus, the "importance" of intellectual work would appear to change only if people thought its
prestige was changing. But in general public attitudes toward
the relative prestige of various occupations have changed very
little over time, so that paradoxically intellectual work could be
becoming more important, in fact, even though it was not reflected in the measures used by sociologists. No one has ever
actually set out to measure how much more important technological and scientific work is now than in 1920, and probably
no one ever will.

But even if we assume that brains are becoming more important or powerful (a dubious notion in my view), other things are changing as well. Fifty years ago most Americans never finished high school, and only a tiny percentage went on to college. Now almost everyone finishes high school, and more than one third go on to some form of post-secondary education. This means that lots of ordinary people who would never have had the chance to be doctors or teachers or engineers fifty years ago, have the chance today. If brains are becoming more powerful at the same time as schooling becomes more universal (and thereby opens up opportunity through the power of certification), the two tendencies may cancel each other out. Of course I am speculating here, but this suggests how complicated the relationship among intelligence, status, and power may be; some social forces may intensify the connection at the same time as others weaken it.

If, then, we measure adult status by way of occupational prestige rankings, and merit by IQ, America does not appear more than mildly meritocratic. At the same time, there is evidence of considerable mobility and openness to movement up and down the social ladder. But there is no reason to believe that IQ has grown more important to that movement during the past five or six decades. This does not mean that the symbols of learning—or its apparatus—have not become more important. Indeed, it is clear that the length of time one stays in school is more relevant to occupational attainment than is raw IQ. Rather than a meritocracy based on intellect we may be creating a "School-ocracy," in which the importance of schooling is based on a variety of non-intellectual factors. Employers may use the school system as a behavior-screening mechanism, on the theory that certain kinds of work require certain kinds of personalities. This would explain why schools place so much stress on deportment, and why they screen out youngsters who have a hard time sitting still for long periods of time, or who don't have the right appearance; these tend to get tracked to lower-status school work and to lower-status jobs. Students who have "better" manners, who behave "properly," who accept authority, and who look the way they should, tend to be routed into higher-status school work and occupations. This screening system may or may not accord with the actual behavior which is required in various sorts of occupations, but it does seem to fit what people think is required.

Another cause of the connection between schooling and adult success may be that schools are becoming the principal vehicle for "professionalizing" occupations. Especially in the marginal and semi-marginal professions, adding educational requirements for certification and licensing is a way of enhancing the standing and respectability of a given line of work in the eyes of its practitioners and clients. It also is a way of persuading people that the occupation in question is up-to-date, modern, and in touch with the latest wisdom. And it often is a way (as with teachers, for example) of getting a bigger paycheck. But whatever the explanation, the additional educational requirements cannot be said to have much relation to job performance.

When schooling becomes necessary to later occupational standing for essentially non-intellectual reasons, various unhappy consequences can result. One is the subversion of the intellectual and academic purposes of educational institutions, and breeding contempt for what they do; another is the creation of an occupational selection system in which the ability to glue one's pants to the seat of a chair for long periods of time becomes a prime recommendation for advancement. The ability to sit still is useful for many purposes, but among children it may not be related to the ingenuity, enterprise, and cleverness which a lively society would want to promote. Under such a system of occupational selection we are as likely to produce an unhealthy accumulation of boredom and discontent as we are to create a dangerous concentration of intellect among the wealthy powerful.

Developments like these are the more distressing because of the greater uniformity they promise, both in what people do and in how they think about it. Such uniformity has not always characterized American society. There is evidence, for example, of ethnic differences in the role that schools have played in promoting occupational mobility. Studies of European ethnic groups show that during this century all of them made substantial increases in occupational status, but that they did so in rather different ways. The children of Russian immigrants (which means Jews for the most part) completed more years of school, on the average, than children from other groups. In addition, educational attainment had a much stronger relationship to the later occupational attainment of these children than it did for children from other groups—which probably means that a disproportionate number of Jews went into occupations which had substantial educational requirements. Not all nationalities had the same experience; Italian and Polish children, for example, tended to complete fewer years of school than those of some other groups. But for Italians and Poles education was not an important influence on later occupational gains. Ethnic variations in the importance of schooling suggests underlying differences in the avenues that various groups have taken to higher social and economic status. And these different avenues probably reflect cultural and historical differences from group to group with regard to the sorts of work which were known and esteemed in the parent country. They even may have been indicative of ethnic differences in the "talent for school," for there were very considerable IQ differences among the European immigrant groups which roughly correspond to their success or failure in school. But the important point is that to the extent that schooling is made an unavoidable requirement for occupational entry or advancement, it may close off genuine cultural differences in occupational values, and irrationally stifle alternatives which might otherwise flourish. To the extent that success in a homogeneous system of schooling becomes the *sine qua non* of entry to occupations, cultural diversity in conceptions of success and worthy work may be diminished. It is hard to think of any good which could possibly come from that situation.

In a sense, however, all the attention to the relative status of occupations is misleading. It is easy to understand why intellectuals might be obsessed with the question, but it is important in the discussion of meritocracy only because of the assumption that jobs which require brains wield more power than jobs which don't. If it turned out that people with high IQ's did not really have more power than ordinary folks, there wouldn't be very much left for one to argue about.

Normally when intellectuals write about this question they bemoan the fact that people like themselves have little power and influence. Indeed, they have mourned this situation for so long that most Americans who regularly read what intellectuals write probably concluded long ago that anyone who has power was either a knave or a fool. As a result, it comes as something of a surprise to hear that intellectuals are in danger of having too much power. But if holding political office, for instance, is an index of power, it is hard to see any cause for alarm, for there certainly is no evidence of an undue concentration of raw IQ among the ranks of government officials. Politics, however, is only one of the several sources of power and influence in America. Wealth is another, but it should come as no great surprise to learn that a high IQ is not the main requirement for being rich. People with more schooling do tend to have somewhat higher incomes, but the relationship between the two is not nearly as strong as the relationship between schooling and occupational status. Partly this is due to the fact that lots of jobs with rather high status—preaching, teaching, and the like—don't come with substantial salaries, and lots of jobs with rather low status, like being a plumber or a machinist, do. There also is the fact that spending decades in school is a condition of employment in most of the high-status but low-paying jobs, but not a condition of tenure in the others. And finally, doing well in school is not yet a prerequisite for inheriting money.

There are other ways of attaining power, or at least influence. The people who write for newspapers and talk on television offer one example, and the "experts" who work for congressional committees and executive agencies offer another. And university professors who spend half their lives traveling to consultations with government officials or corporate managers offer yet another. Still, one is at a loss to imagine why professors should be either brighter or more powerful than they were fifty years ago. One is equally puzzled over the idea that journalists are either smarter or more powerful—certainly a modest stint of watching television would not lead anyone to conclude that the medium is in peril of being taken over by people with dangerously high IQ's. Finally, anyone who imagines that "experts" with high IQ's have a great future in public life ought to visit his nearest government and see how it works. Most government business turns not on the technical skills that experts do monopolize, but on ethical and political considerations. Experts have had to relearn this lesson every few years since the Progressive era.

Let us try to summarize the conclusions of all this. First, America is not a meritocracy, if by that we mean a society in which income, status, or power are heavily determined by IQ. All the evidence suggests that IQ has only moderate impact on adult success, and that this impact is exerted only through the schools.

Second, America seems on balance not to have become more meritocratic in the course of the 20th century. All the evidence suggests that the relationships between IQ and income and status, and schooling and status, have been stable. While opportunity has opened up for great segments of the population, the criteria for advancement seem to have involved many things other than IQ.

Third, something we often incorrectly identify with IQ—namely schooling—seems to be a more important determinant of adult success than IQ. If getting through school is a mark of merit, then America is moderately meritocratic. But then, in a society in which education is rapidly becoming universal such a conception of merit may lose its meaning.

Among all the many factors which cause poverty, then, low intellectual ability is not terribly important. Being stupid is not what is responsible for being poor in America.

insufficient implementation is cause of failure of social programs.

Edwin M. Schur

Crime and the
New Conservatism

According to Edward Banfield, one of neoconservatism's leading spokesmen, crime is largely a matter of lower-class "propensity." The masses, it seems, have a distinctive, "preconventional" morality, in which "the individual's actions are influenced not by conscience but only by a sense of what he can get away with."[1] Banfield does "not deny causal importance to alienation, poor housing, inferior schools, and the like," yet he dismisses the relation between such "objective" social conditions and crime, precisely because it is so deep-seated and elusive. More amenable to control, he claims, are those "situational factors" that help to determine an individual's incentive to commit crimes. Indeed, the policy-maker must take the city's potential for crime as a "given" and concentrate on short-term factors that affect the potential offender's "cost-benefit calculus."

Thus the presumably hyperactive ghetto youth should be offered alternatives to violence (Banfield mentions boxing, skiing, even parachute jumping!) and more opportunities to "make a few bucks" here and there. (Serious efforts to improve employment and income levels seem to be less important since crime involves "people who live in the present" and who therefore only "want small amounts now.") At the same time, we should raise the costs of contemplating crime by increasing the likelihood of offenders being caught and swiftly punished. Potential crime victims can take various preventive measures to reduce opportunities for crime. When all else fails (because, according to Banfield, some individuals have so little "ego-strength" and are so present-oriented that no set of incentives will curb their propensity to crime), imprisonment—of potential as well as actual offenders—will be necessary. Calling for "a gradation of abridgments of freedom, more or less onerous ones to be imposed upon the individual as his behavior raises or lowers the probability of his committing serious crimes," Banfield ultimately sees justification for preventive detention of those deemed to have a high probability of committing crimes in the future. "In any event, if abridging the freedom of persons who have not committed crimes is incompatible with the principles of free society, so, also, is the presence in such society of persons who, if their freedom is not abridged, would use it to inflict serious injuries on others."[2]

Although there is no single unified neoconservative position on crime, Banfield's views are typical in several respects. Skeptical of the liberal's ability to produce social progress, and often citing the quite sound sociological proposition that some crime is inevitable in any society, the new conservative has abandoned the effort to head off crime through basic socioeconomic and legal change. Convinced that major socioeconomic ills have already been substantially ameliorated, he is likely to turn to some explanation of crime oriented toward the individual (Banfield's "propensity" approach is one version, genetic theories are another). He also believes that we can spot in advance the potential troublemakers. Such prediction is the conservative's major strategy for crime prevention—and is seen as a much-preferred alternative to directly confronting crime-generating social conditions. But basically, the conservative emphasis is on control rather than prevention. Crime comes to be viewed as a managerial problem rather than a reflection of social malaise.

For the new conservatives, the crime issue is a "natural." Despite the vagaries of crime statistics (even Banfield admits that "there is reason to think that the rate of violent crime in the metropolitan area as a whole has declined steadily over the last century to a level about one-third lower"[3]), public preoccupation with criminality is, as we know, enormous. At a time when many left-liberals, including those well aware of the structural roots of crime, nonetheless share with other citizens a strong concern about violence in the streets,[4] the short-term control orientation of the conservatives has a special appeal. More police, more efficient courts, or even more effective "treatment" programs for offenders strike the man in the street as direct answers to the crime problem. Under such circumstances it is difficult for people to appreciate the wisdom of the President's Crime Commission (a far from radical body) in concluding that, "unless society does take concerted action to change the general conditions and attitudes that are associated with crime, no improvement in law enforcement and administration of justice . . . will be of much avail."[5]

Public fears about crime are often exaggerated, unfocused, and significantly colored by other social attitudes. Studies have shown, for example, that citizens with the lowest objective risk of being victimized (i.e., those in low crime-rate areas) are more concerned about the problem of crime than those whose risks are greater, and also that "concern about crime is at least in part an expression of resentment of changing social conditions, especially efforts to eliminate racial injustice."[6] To those who deny the nation's failure to eliminate economic injustice and to satisfy legitimate black aspirations, and who view the racial disorders of recent years not as a "manifesto" calling attention to such failures but rather as an indication of the law-breaking propensities of ghetto-dwellers (Banfield writes of "rioting mainly for fun and profit"), such a situation is ripe for exploitation.

Disillusionment with liberal rhetoric and social welfare measures permit the neoconservatives to argue with some surface credibility that crime defies social solution. This argument would be more persuasive if a meaningful attempt had been made to eliminate poverty and inequality (at a minimum, along the lines of the Kerner Commission recommendations), but this of course has never been done. It is certainly true, as the experience of "socialist" countries has shown, that the problems of crime can never be fully eliminated, whatever the type of regime. But it is also true that the nature and extent of these problems always reflect the structure, values, and moral tone of the societies in which they occur. By insisting that we already have achieved a just social order, neoconservatism impedes the kinds of change that in the long run could help to minimize crime.

Crime backlash and neoconservative views tend to reinforce each other. The move in various jurisdictions to reinstate the death penalty, President Nixon's determination to attack crime "without pity" by instituting harsh penalties and reducing the discretion of federal judges, and Governor Rockefeller's much criticized new drug legislation (geared to stiff mandatory minimum sentences) are a few examples. Some neoconservatives may support one or another of these measures; but, probably, the greater danger is that neoconservatism may encourage less blatant, yet nonetheless dangerous forms of backlash—by contributing to the muddled thinking and emotional uproar about crime that persistently confounds efforts to frame sound crime policies.

Compartmentalizing Crime.   Despite an enormous body of evidence, which long ago should have disabused us of such notions, we seem to cling tenaciously to the belief that crime is some kind of extraordinary phenomenon outside the ordinary workings of society.[7] We find it difficult to discard the idea that there is a distinctive category of persons—"criminals"—that is responsible for all our crime problems. These criminals are enemies *of* society, and crime is something done *to* society. Even fairly sophisticated commentators can fall prey to this deception through which the "causes" of crime appear to be located outside the bounds of the existing social order. This tendency can in part be attributed to our failure to appreciate the basically political nature of all crime. Crime is simply behavior that violates the criminal law, and therefore an analysis of crime can never ignore the sociopolitical context within which decisions concerning the substance and administration of such law are made. Indeed, as Richard Quinney has properly emphasized, the public policies embodied in the criminal law are created "because segments with power differentials are in conflict with one another. Public policy itself is a manifestation of an interest structure in politically organized society."[8] In the United States there is an old and widespread inclination to look upon white-collar offenders as not being "real" criminals, which both reflects and reinforces our neglect of this problem. It remains to be seen whether the evidence of extensive governmental law violation, emanating from Watergate, will alter public perceptions about the nature of crime.

Underlying the compartmentalization of crime is the belief that criminals are basically different from other people, and that this difference "explains" criminal behavior. If some version of this outlook may often be attractive to the neoconservative, liberal reformers, too, have displayed similar compartmentalizing tendencies through an uncritical acceptance of the most popular modern version of the "basic-differentness" theme —i.e., the belief that most criminals are (psychologically) sick individuals. It is undoubtedly true that some criminal offenders have serious emotional problems, and that some instances of violent behavior may be partly attributable to genetic factors. But almost everything we know about the nature of criminal offenses—the social contexts in which they occur and the contingencies of administering criminal justice (which help to determine what individuals are to be officially processed as "offenders"), as well as the legal (and hence variable) nature of the definitions of crime—all this makes clear that no more than a small amount of all crime is attributable to such "causes."

Even as they recognized the social sources of criminality, liberals have all too frequently couched their analyses (e.g., the Moynihan Report) in such a way that the focus remained more on the deviating individual than on the structural sources of deviation. Thus many reformist statements on crime have displayed the tendency William Ryan so aptly described as "blaming the victim":

> The stigma that marks the victim and accounts for his victimization is an acquired stigma, a stigma of social, rather than genetic, origin. But the stigma, the defect, the fatal difference—though derived in the past from environmental forces—is still located *within* the victim, inside his skin. With such an elegant formulation, the humanitarian can

have it both ways. He can, all at the same time, concentrate his charitable interest on the defects of the victim, condemn the vague social and environmental stresses that produced the defect (some time ago), and ignore the continuing effect of victimizing social forces (right now).[9]

This tendency, along with the high prestige of psychiatry in modern American society, helps to explain why liberals have so readily accepted the treatment ideology substituting supposed "rehabilitation" for punishment. Despite euphemisms and good intentions, we know that the rehabilitative approach is having little impact. As a study group of the American Friends Service Committee states, "The legacy of a century of reform effort is an increasingly repressive penal system and overcrowded courts dispensing assembly-line justice."[10] Unfortunately, this very bankruptcy of liberalism's policies of rehabilitation can be exploited by those who would urge a new repression. But again, one must emphasize that this failure in no way demonstrates that crime cannot be reduced through social planning; the relevant policies have simply never been implemented. As the Friends' Report quite rightly insists, "the construction of a just system of criminal justice in an unjust society is a contradiction in terms."[11]

Until the fallacy of compartmentalizing crime is abandoned, the misguided belief in the need of *special* crime policies (i.e., separate and disconnected from general and social change) will prevail. These policies will tend to take the form of stopgap control measures, which may provide some superficial regulation of crime but cannot be expected to have a significant long-term impact. Liberals must counter these tendencies by calling attention to the social and political nature of crime, by emphasizing that our crime problems represent the price we pay for certain decisions we have made and for social arrangements we maintain. Otherwise, they will unwittingly encourage a variety of ominous developments—including, at least, the following.

Technological Despotism.   Given their fondness for the notion of a "post-industrial society," neoconservatives may be expected to favor efforts to combat crime through technology and managerial skill. Although conservatism often implies skepticism toward the social sciences (in this instance, for example, a belittling of social research as a tool for understanding the causes of crime), conservatives are also likely to anticipate substantial success in controlling crime by the use of scientific devices and organizational know-how. The application of "systems analysis"—with its characteristic flow charts and associated techniques—seems to hold for them a particularly great appeal. Without question, some benefits may accrue from work of this sort. More rational organization of police departments and disposition of police resources, relief of court congestion, and greater consistency in sentencing,[12] are but a few of the modifications that may be facilitated by "operations research." But, most likely, this approach will represent no more than a systematization, a tidying-up of our surface responses to crime phenomena, a technical operation that will display little concern for either basic social causes or broad policy goals.

Much of the work of the New York City Rand Institute —which has researched, among other things, police recruitment and disposition patterns—seems to imply this kind of superficial managerialism. An example is its recently publicized statistical report of New York crime rates, arranged by precinct and giving precinct data regarding racial composition, income level, and age groupings. According to a news account, the head of the Institute (a physicist) said the Institute "hoped to use the study to predict where crimes were most likely to occur before they were committed, and thus enable the police to redeploy men to prevent more crime than they now do."[13] This well-intentioned effort may have some short-term preventive impact; but at the same time the implications of the study give rise to concern. Systematization in line with these findings could mean that the snowballing vicious-circle mechanisms—through which, in certain areas, perceived (or anticipated) crime leads to police "crackdowns" that in turn inevitably produce high crime statistics—will simply continue with greater "efficiency" than before.

Although such efforts to rationalize the administration of criminal justice represent the technocratic innovation neoconservatives are most likely to embrace in this area, their general stance on crime could also encourage (or at least fail to discourage) some other, more clearly harmful attempts to control crime through technology. Following the Watergate revelations, one no longer runs the risk of being labeled paranoid for calling attention to the widespread use—and dangers—of electronic surveillance. Apart from "national security" investigations (the implications of which are chilling enough), most officially sanctioned wiretapping and bugging occur in efforts to administer the largely unworkable laws against such borderline offenses as drug use and gambling. According to the American Civil Liberties Union, the cost of such nonsecurity tapping in the years 1969-71 was nearly $8 million. Since they are unlikely to challenge the overreach of the criminal law (see below), conservatives may indirectly promote such largely ineffective and potentially dangerous surveillance. The New York Police Department's recent decision to establish videotape scanning (and recording) in the Times Square area indicates the extent to which these practices may invade the privacy of all citizens. While such techniques (like the use of TV in apartment house lobbies and elevators) may presumably serve as a short-term deterrent to some street crime, or at least facilitate police operations, the notion of Americans continuously being "on camera" as they pursue their daily lives is a frightening one.

A similar insensitivity to privacy issues is apparent in proposals for the "electronic rehabilitation" of criminal offenders, an idea that has created some interest in government circles. According to one advocate who favors dealing with offenders in the community rather than in institutions, this might be accomplished through "the development, in prototype form, of small personally worn transmitters that permit the continual monitoring of the geographical location of parolees."[14]

For those who view offenders as basically different from "the rest of us," the notion persists that we can significantly reduce criminality by doing something about specific individuals. If liberals have tended to adopt psychiatric or social work versions of the treatment ideology, conservatives (whose emphasis on personal responsibility usually makes them wary of psychiatry) may be expected to turn in other directions. One possibility is long-term confinement or quarantine—simply identify and isolate the troublemakers. Another option is to turn to technology for a "break-through" in diagnosis and treatment. Hence the appeal of genetic crime theories, and also perhaps of behavior-modification techniques (operant conditioning, aversive suppression, etc.). Although the latter are based on a variety of psychological theories, they also seem to incorporate a physical or physiological dimension.

The attempt to deal with criminality through such techniques becomes especially ominous when extended to include potential as well as actual offenders (in much the same way that preventive detention represents an even more objectionable version of imprisonment). As a rule, the fallacious belief that special kinds of people commit crime is accompanied by the equally mistaken notion that such people can be identified—before they engage in any actual law-violating or even (some would contend) early in childhood. Despite the fact that years of psychological and sociological research on predicting delinquency and crime have produced inconclusive and unimpressive results, the effort to spot and "treat" troublemakers persists. A particularly dismaying practice is the now pervasive administration of behavior-modifying drugs to school children. According to the former staff director of the Special Subcommittee on Invasion of Privacy of the U.S. House of Representatives, "200,000 children in the United States are now being given amphetamine and stimulant therapy, with probably another 100,000 receiving tranquilizers and antidepressants."[15] Although such measures —disporportionately employed with ghetto children—are only partly aimed at curbing delinquency, they illustrate the dangerous potentialities of individual-oriented technocratic thinking about crime problems. Liberals as well as conservatives have accepted too readily such repressive "therapy."

Vigilantism: Official and Unofficial.   During the past year, in a number of widely publicized incidents, plainclothes narcotics enforcers broke into private homes, destroying personal property and terrorizing individuals who were completely innocent of involvement in drug offenses. While not justifying illegal acts, a spokesman for the federal Drug Abuse Law Enforcement office was reported to have said, "Drug people are the very vermin of humanity . . . occasionally we must adopt their dress and tactics." Many of the protests against these raids short-sightedly emphasized that the people involved were not "criminals." More significantly, these incidents illustrated the extremes that can be justified by the "war against crime" mentality, as well as the almost inevitable recourse to police-state tactics when law enforcement attempts to curb (largely) private transactions that do not generate complaining victims.

Tom Wicker notes:

> The war on crime has been justified and praised, from the White House on down, just as was the war on Communism. So if constitutional shortcuts, massive applications of force, and frequent lies and deceptions were required merely to gain "peace with honor" in the one war, anything less is not likely to be considered hard-nosed enough for the other.[16]

The same kind of war mentality underlies recent requests by New York policemen that they be more heavily armed (and the apparently already widespread practice of carrying extra, unauthorized weapons). Occasionally an especially deplorable incident—such as the killing of a ten-year-old black boy by a white officer in Queens in April 1973—will focus concern on the use and abuse of police weaponry. Yet we are so inured to the omnipresence of guns that public furor rapidly dies down, and the shooting goes on much as before. According to an Associated Press survey, in one recent week some 350 people in the United States were shot to death—an increase of 70 percent over the findings in a similar survey four years earlier.[17] Effective general gun control (which could also permit limiting the use of guns by law enforcers) is one of the few public policy measures directly aimed at controlling crime that could really have a beneficial impact. Yet liberal inertia has combined with the "self-protection" ideology of many conservatives to impede this reform.

The concept of a no-holds-barred battle against criminal "enemies" encourages private citizens as well as law enforcers to take the law into their own hands. While public concern and mutual assistance are certainly to be preferred to the refusal-to-help pattern typified by the well-known Kitty Genovese case, it should be pointed out that the recent efforts have gone well beyond mere assistance or "citizens' arrests." In several instances suspects were badly beaten; at least one was hospitalized in serious condition. Given the easy availability of guns, and the tendency of neighborhood vigilante groups to form along racial and ethnic lines, the encouragement of "citizen anticrime" activity involves decided risks. Here again we see the limitations and danger of adopting an after-the-fact control emphasis, rather than concentrating on reducing the conditions that give rise to crime in the first place.

Overcriminalization. No-knock raids, wiretapping, and other objectionable police techniques are in part attributable to the kinds of legislation the police are expected to enforce. Notwithstanding the disastrous experience of Prohibition, and the wise strictures of numerous legal philosophers regarding the limits of effective legal action, Americans remain addicted to proscription through criminal law. Political deviation, juvenile mischief, and private sexual behavior continue to be subjected to legislative ban, despite the very clear evidence that it would be much more realistic to view the criminal law as a last-ditch limited-purpose mechanism for social control. Particularly unworkable have been the laws against "crimes without victims"—attempts to proscribe the willing exchange of goods or services, even where such exchanges are widely practiced and strongly in demand.[18] Such laws—those aimed against drug use, gambling, abortion, homosexuality, and prostitution for example—are almost totally unenforceable.

Recent discussions of the concept of the victimless crime have failed to clarify this concept's basic meaning. While there may be legitimate debate regarding the existence or nonexistence (according to some supposedly disinterested criteria) of victimization in one or another of these situations, the overriding difficulty is that the individuals involved in the "offenses" are *willing* participants. Since they do not see themselves as "victims," they do not come forward to initiate police enforcement. In the absence of citizen-complainants, evidence of the "crimes" is extremely hard to come by, and police invariably are driven to such tactics as long-term surveillance, use of informers and decoys, and surprise "raids."

Quite apart from the fact that these tactics are legally and ethically questionable, they are undoubtedly doomed to failure. No matter how vigorously such efforts are pursued, if the demand for the proscribed goods or services is great enough, a way will be found to get them. But worse: these laws may produce more harm than good. In addition to fostering highly undesirable enforcement techniques and providing an economic base for illicit trafficking, they unnecessarily label many decent citizens as "criminals," encourage corruption (police and private shakedowns of homosexuals, protection payoffs by illegal suppliers), and promote secondary crime (theft or prostitution by drug addicts to support their habits).

The case for limiting the scope of the criminal law received special impetus from the 1957 report of the Wolfenden Committee in Great Britain. Charged with reviewing statutes on homosexuality and prostitution, this committee asserted that

> Unless a deliberate attempt is to be made by society, acting through the agency of the law, to equate the sphere of crime with that of sin, there must remain a realm of private morality and immorality which is, in brief and crude terms, not the law's business. To say this is not to condone or encourage private immorality.[19]

One of the major issues in the debate ignited by this report is to determine where the burden of argument and proof should lie in imposing criminal sanctions. While the Committee and its supporters have argued that recourse to the criminal law should always require compelling justification, critics like Lord Patrick Devlin—who has insisted that sometimes the function of the criminal law is "simply to enforce a moral principle and nothing else"—maintain that the burden of argument lies with those who would overturn long-standing legislation. Recently in the United States, the former line of argument seems to be winning out. Numerous commission reports and other statements have recommended "decriminalization" of these consensual behaviors; the legalization of abortion in many of the states is perhaps the most impressive evidence.

As the basically political nature of such issues becomes clear, one can expect that a characteristic stance toward them will

crystallize among conservatives. Although particular neoconservatives may vary in their reactions to any of these "social
problems," the general tendency will probably be to express
grave concern about, if not direct opposition to, decriminalization. The rather abstract moralism that implies this outcome is
illustrated in a recent defense of antipornography legislation by
Walter Berns. Arguing that "laws cannot remain indifferent to
the manner in which men amuse themselves, or to the kinds of
amusement offered them," Berns contends (rather strangely it
would seem) that censorship protects political democracy because it "inhibits self-indulgence and supports the idea of propriety and impropriety."[20] Even leaving aside the dangers of
thought control and tyranny latent in this position, surely one
must insist that to concern oneself greatly with pornography is to
be diverted from the issue of real crimes in the American society.

A similar paternalistic stance is displayed by James Q. Wilson
and his associates in an analysis of the heroin problem:

> . . . society has an obligation to enhance the "well-being" of
> each of its citizens even with respect to those aspects of their
> lives that do not directly impinge on other people's lives. In
> this conception of the public good, all citizens of a society are
> bound to be affected—indirectly but perhaps profoundly
> and permanently—if a significant number are permitted to
> go to hell in their own way. A society is therefore unworthy
> if it permits, or is indifferent to, any activity that renders its
> members inhuman or deprives them of their essential (or
> "natural") capacities to judge, choose, and act. If heroin use
> is such an activity, then its use should be proscribed.
> Whether that proscription is enforced by mere punishment
> or by obligatory therapy is a separate question.[21]

As so often in these arguments, the moral issue is oversimplified when one insists that some behavior "should be proscribed" or should not be "permitted"—regardless of whether or
not, realistically, it can be effectively banned. In order to develop
a policy position consistent with their basic premise, these conservative authors make the highly questionable claim that crime
would not decrease substantially if heroin became freely availa-

ble (notwithstanding estimates that up to two-thirds of all property crimes are committed by addicts); they exaggerate the failings of the British drug policies (which have never given rise to any sizable addict-crime, despite some apparent increase in the number of addicts); and they argue, in the face of years of unsuccessful punitiveness, that perhaps a law-enforcement approach to the problem has never really been tried. By this they mean that the focus on smugglers and pushers is misdirected. Enforcement efforts directed at the user might have some real impact. While it is quite correct that the user is the one "indispensable element," the analysis—in a way quite characteristic of all approaches geared to piecemeal control—completely ignores that no amount of enforcement will eliminate users, in the absence of changes in the social structures and values that drive American youth to drugs in the first place. Elsewhere in their article, Wilson and his co-analysts make a good many sensible comments about various drug proposals; but their abstract paternalism and veneration of legal authority prevent them from fully discarding a reliance on the criminal law that by now should be largely discredited.

Distorted Priorities.   There is no single coherent neoconservative approach to crime. Nevertheless, there is a clear overall tendency to embrace theoretical formulations and assert policy preferences that are neither empirically well-founded nor morally sound—in short, to badly distort our priorities in this area. The compartmentalization that has so heavily dominated our thinking about crime is reinforced by conservative emphasis on "individual responsibility," the repudiation of radical socioeconomic change, and the refusal to see the state of the law itself as a major "cause" of some of our crime problems. Ambivalent about the role of science, conservatives nonetheless are likely to embrace technological gimmickry that could well lead us along the path to a police state. And by their willingness to approve law-enforcement "solutions" of deep-seated social problems, this may contribute to the decline rather than the "conserving" of our basic liberties.

The rational, humane, and democratic response to crime has not changed much over the years. Specific problems may alter the details of this response somewhat, but the essential elements remain: measures designed to promote an equitable social order, respect for and promotion of legality, protection of basic human freedoms. Conventional or familiar as it may sound, a concerted effort to shape a decent society will do more to curb criminality then any amount of special "crime policy." By obscuring this central point, the new conservatism does us all a disservice.

Hanna Fenichel Pitkin

The Roots of Conservatism:

Michael Oakeshott and the Denial of Politics*

The seemingly uncontrollable movement of American policy toward domestic repression and imperial warfare makes it of the utmost urgency that we understand what is involved in our "new conservatism." The most perceptive understanding may come not from a hurried look at the phenomenon itself, but through distance, theory, and an examination of roots. For conservatism is not just one phenomenon but many; and much can be learned about our current domestic variant by examining the tradition in political theory on which it sometimes draws. This essay, then, is concerned with the thought of Michael Oakeshott, with occasional glances backward toward Edmund Burke and sideways toward Hannah Arendt. Though he is not well known in America, Oakeshott, a professor emeritus of political science at the London School of Economics, is one of the few great living spokesmen of the conservative tradition; he has been called "the most profound and original political thinker than England has produced in the twentieth century."[1] We shall find that

243

Oakeshott understands much that is missed or denied by the new conservatism in America, indeed, that he might even want to disown it. But in the end the two conservatisms share some fundamental weaknesses.

I

In his later writings, the best of which are collected in *Rationalism in Politics,* Oakeshott articulates a conception of human society that might best be labeled "ecological." [2] He is profoundly aware of the complexity of institutions, customs, ways of life, the extent to which a society is a living whole. Each of us normally perceives only a small and personal part of that whole, but in fact the conditions of our lives, and even our very selves, are the products of culture and history; and what we do has social reverberations that will set the conditions of life for future generations. This elaborate structure is constantly in the process of change, largely as the result of individuals' private choices and activities; it never stays fixed. In general these piecemeal, relatively natural changes are easily absorbed by the system and do no serious harm. But though Oakeshott rejects an "organic" view of society, he shares the organicist's anxiety about planned, large-scale social change. [3] Whenever we deliberately introduce some new policy or institution, we, as it were, upset the ecological balance of the system in ways we cannot control or foresee. "The total change is always more extensive than the change desired," and there is always danger that the harmful by-products may outweigh the intended benefit. [4]

Whether or not one shares the resulting conservative implications for politics, one can find much of value in Oakeshott's vision of what a society is, what a civilization is. For Oakeshott understands that each of us is a product of his society, of history; we become the particular persons we do become by internalizing the language, cultural norms, habits of behavior in the midst of which we are born. Society and individual are not really opposites, but two ways of looking at the same set of phenomena. This means, further, that neither our society nor our civilization is a contractual arrangement which we can renegotiate whenever we find it profitable to do so. We can, of course, make changes, but those changes will be part of the continuity; and we ourselves, carriers of the society, will continue through those changes. Oakeshott sees also the extent to which the patterns and regularities in a culture remain piecemeal and unarticulated, how they are learned from concrete, paradigmatic instances, perpetuated in some instances, changed in other instances.

Yet not all societies are equally continuous and coherent, not all ecosystems in natural balance. Oakeshott can teach us much about what Simone Weil called the "need for roots," about what we have lost in losing traditional society: stability, security, meaning, a sense of self and purpose. He sees the damage done to people—living and suffering human beings—when their lives become fragmented and chaotic, when there is no history and no fixed home, when all possessions are plastic and "disposable," when all agencies are impersonal and faceless, when all sense of continuity is lost so that people become, in Burke's memorable phrase, "little better than flies of a summer."[5] Though Oakeshott may not have the cure for our modern condition, he diagnoses it well; and at least he does not add insult to our injury by claiming that society has always looked and must always look like this. He has a living vision of what community means, of what community was—not a uniform totality in which the individual disappears, but a home within which he can develop, whose norms are less his restraints than the means of his freedom.

Out of this profound vision of the nature of what Marx called human "species life," there evolves the central theme running through almost all of Oakeshott's later writings, a theme that he uses like a great searchlight, turning it to illuminate first one and then another realm of human activity. The details of the argument—and, in particular, its resolution—vary from case to case; but its basic structure is always the juxtaposition of two contrasting approaches to the activity in question.[6] One of these two approaches is always some version of what in politics Oakeshott calls "Rationalism"; I shall use that term for it throughout, though he sometimes gives it different names in other fields. It is always opposed to another, contrasting approach, more difficult to designate, centering on the traditional, the incremental, the inarticulate. In politics, Oakeshott calls it "conservatism," or "the pursuit of intimations." In the end he is always critical of the former alternative, sometimes rejecting it, sometimes modifying, as the subject matter at issue varies; but the entire sequence of his shorter writings seems to be a series of forays against the persistent problem of Rationalism.

In general, Oakeshott means by Rationalism the attempt to reject the authority of all tradition, custom, prejudice, habit, or inherited convention; the desire to call everything into question, rethink it for oneself *de novo*, rebuild on a new and more secure foundation constructed exclusively from one's own direct experience and "reason." Oakeshott traces the origins of this impulse in the modern world to Descartes and Bacon, stressing their simultaneous hostility to the authority of the past, and craving for a new certainty that resulted in the centrality of method in their thought. The Rationalist seeks the certain and orderly, the logically neat and simple, the abstract, the quantitative, the technical, the efficient, the unamibiguous, what can be made explicit and laid out systematically. Rationalism is contrasted with an orientation that appreciates the value of things as they are, inherited from the past, and that respectfully recognizes their complexity and interdependence, the richness of concrete reality. This orientation values tradition, prescription, continuity; it stresses the intricacies of human practice that defy formulation in explicit rules: knowhow, habit, the slow evolution of a civilization, community rather than organization, character rather than technique.

Although Oakeshott is always in one or another way critical of Rationalism, this does not mean that he is hostile to reason or to rationality.[7] Rationalism is no more equivalent to rationality than scientism to science or moralism to morality.[8] Indeed, one of the realms with respect to which Oakeshott traces out the dichotomy between Rationalism and its opposite is reason itself: there is a Rationalistic understanding of reason, and another based on coherence in a tradition. According to the Rationalistic view, being rational means pursuing, in an efficient and logical way, a goal which has been selfconsciously and "independently premeditated," which has not been accepted passively from any traditional source.[9] In this sense, rational conduct "is behaviour *deliberately* directed to the achievement of a *formulated* purpose and is governed solely by that purpose." The alternative approach sees rationality as differently defined in each realm of human activity and thus as a matter of internal coherence within each realm. Being rational in science, for instance, will be quite different from being rational in moral conduct. In each case, rationality depends on fidelity to the traditions of the particular kind of human enterprise involved. It means "acting in such a way that the coherence of the idiom of activity to which the conduct belongs is preserved and possibly enhanced."[10]

Oakeshott finds the same sort of duality in many other fields. Thus science may be regarded either Rationalistically, as a body of achieved knowledge made explicit in systematic theories and hypotheses; or else, as the ongoing, largely unarticulated activity of scientists, rooted in what Polanyi calls "personal knowledge."[11] More generally, all of knowledge may be dichotomized into a Rationalistic sort that Oakeshott calls "technical," formulable in precise rules and seeming to promise certainty; and a different sort that he calls "practical," and "know-how," the knowledge of experience rather than reflection, that exists "only in use."[12] There are also two contrasting "forms," as Oakeshott calls them, "of the moral life": one explicit and didactic, requiring deliberation of systematic ideals, and another based on character and habit, arising directly out of a tradition of behavior.[13] These conflicting approaches to rationality, knowledge, science, and morality correspond also to two conceptions of education. Rationalistic knowledge, whether of science, moral principles, law, or cooking, can be imparted directly and explicitly by *telling* it to the student; but the various kinds of know-how and habitual practice cannot really be taught or learned, "but only imparted and acquired." Such knowledge "exists only in practice, and the only way to acquire it is by apprenticeship to a master . . . by continuous contact with one who is perpetually practicing it."[14]

In politics the Rationalist's distrust of all inherited traditional arrangements seeks expression in action. The political Rationalist wants to restructure society in fundamental ways to make it more uniform, efficient, logical. He sees only chaos in the tradition, and feels that "this is no way for rational human beings to be spending their lives."[15] So he construes political life as the opportunity for "imposing upon" the citizenry his vision of order, "a vision of human activity co-ordinated and set going in a single direction . . . a public and compulsory manner of living."[16] His guide is not history or any tradition of past thought or practice, but what Oakeshott calls "ideology," an abstract principle or set of principles purporting to be independently premeditated.

A political conservative, by contrast, is disposed to preserve inherited institutions. He is willing to reform or adjust them where that is necessary in order to keep them stable, but his manner of reform is always piecemeal and gradual, in ways consistent with the tradition. He prefers existing practice to the abstract imported idea. His politics will be conducted cautiously and minimally, refusing to have anything to do "with innovations designed to meet merely hypothetical situations"; it will proceed by "slow, small changes" only.[17] He sees the task of politics as being to enhance the coherence in a nation's inherited culture and institutions by developing what is implicit in them but "does not fully appear" as yet.[18] Oakeshott's example is, interestingly enough, the extension of the vote to women. The Rationalist might advocate women's suffrage in terms of natural rights or some other abstract principle, but for the conservative "the only cogent reason" was "that in all or most other important respects" women had already been enfranchised. There was thus "an incoherence in the arrangements of the society which pressed convincingly for remedy."[19] In short, the conservative does not oppose all change; he presses for slow change in accord with prevailing patterns and trends.

II

As a number of commentators have noted, an ambiguity runs through Oakeshott's treatment of this central theme of dichotomization: it seems that he cannot decide whether the Rationalism he opposes is impossible, so that we in fact cannot act Rationalistically in politics, morals, education; or merely undesirable, so that there is a real danger that we might do so.[20]

From the time when Oakeshott begins to be concerned with

Rationalism (or its equivalent by other names), he is also convinced that there is something fundamentally wrong with it. He engages it in battle in ways reminiscent both of Hegel's attack on merely abstract formalism that "has lost hold of the living nature of concrete fact," and of Burke's struggle with the "pure metaphysical abstractions" of the French *philosophes*.[21] Basically Oakeshott argues that the ideals the Rationalist claims as "independently premeditated" are in fact derived from and dependent on prior inarticulate activity. Therefore, scientific theories and concepts derive their meaning only from the activity of scientists; our moral ideals are derived from prior moral practice; and our political principles and institutions are the precipitates of earlier traditional activity, evolved without conscious general plan. An abstraction by itself, without the complex concrete practice that underlies it, is meaningless and useless; only the practice tells us how to apply it. In Oakeshott's famous analogy, "a cook is not a man who first has a vision of a pie and then tries to make it; he is a man skilled in cookery, and both his projects and his achievement spring from that skill."[22] We live first and think afterward, and our thought is derivative from what we do.

Thus, the Rationalist's belief in an abstract "technical knowledge" and in goals set without reliance on any inherited tradition is an "illusion"; it is impossible for any "actual engagement" in activity ever to "spring from or be governed by an independently premeditated end."[23] As soon as we try to put the goal or ideal into practice, we are forced to interpret and apply it by means of the traditional skills of the activity. And even the allegedly independent goal itself turns out to derive from the enterprise. "It is impossible even to project a purpose for activity in advance of the activity itself," for the practice is the only available source of problems and questions.[24] Accordingly, Rationalistic morality is "not, by itself, a possible form of morality at all."[25] And abstract political ideology, far from being

> the quasi-divine parent of political activity, . . . turns out to be its earthly stepchild. . . . It is a system of ideas abstracted from the manner in which people have been accustomed to go about the business of attending to the arrangements of

their societies. . . . In short, political activity comes first and a political ideology follows after.[26]

Even the ideology of the French Revolution, the ultimate in Rationalistic abstraction, although certainly the product of reflection, was not the product of reflection in advance of activity, but an extrapolation from traditional English political practice.[27]

Accordingly, politics itself is defined by Oakeshott as "the activity of attending to the general arrangements of a set of people whom chance or choice have brought together," and "who, in respect of their common recognition of a manner of attending to its arrangements, compose a single community."[28] Oakeshott himself explains that he says "attending to" rather than "making" arrangements to emphasize the necessary continuity involved, the fact that at least in the "hereditary cooperative groups" called "states," political activity

is never offered the blank sheet of infinite possibility. In any generation, even the most revolutionary, the arrangements which are enjoyed far exceed those which are recognized to stand in need of attention, and those which are being prepared for enjoyment are few in comparison with those which receive amendment: the new is an insignificant proportion of the whole.[29]

In accord with Oakeshott's definition, then, politics is necessarily "the pursuit, not of a dream, or of a general principle, but of the intimations implicit in a given tradition"; and much of what was introduced in the previous section as characterizing political conservatism is also, or exclusively, treated by him as definitive of all politics.[30] Moreover, he emphasizes that the definition is not intended as hortatory, but "as a description of what political activity actually is."[31] Oakeshott himself raises the question whether his manner of defining politics may not confuse "what is, perhaps, normal" in that realm with "what is necessary," whether it might not ignore "important exceptions" like the Norman Conquest of England or the Russian Revolution.[32] But his answer to the question is negative. Even on such "exceptional" occasions, real Rationalistic politics, real innovation is a logical impossibility; even after a revolution the great bulk of social patterns remains the same. Thus it is an "illusion" to suppose "that politics is ever anything more than the pursuit of intimations," or that there can ever be, in politics, "a destination to be reached or even a detectable strand of progress. The world is the best of all possible worlds, and *everything* in it is a necessary evil.' "[33]

Now one certainly can regard human affairs from such a perspective that genuine change seems impossible; one can stress the continuities in culture and society to the point where "there's nothing new under the sun"; continuities persist through even the most abrupt and traumatic historical crises. Short of divine intervention, everything created or invented by human beings must spring from their minds, and thereby from their past experience. But surely one logical consequence of taking this position about thought and change is that radicalism no longer constitutes any sort of danger. One need not warn against what is impossible. If all ideologies are abbreviations of traditional activity, then it is not clear how any ideology might threaten tradition. If all politics is the pursuit of intimations, then this will be as true of ideological, radical politics as of Burkean conservatism.

Yet this is not, in fact, a position that Oakeshott is content to adopt. He rejects the charge that his view of politics entails any "crude determinism." Human choices are very real; there are better and worse political outcomes, wise and unwise policies. He is profoundly concerned to warn against the dangers of Rationalism, radicalism, and ideology. The main thrust of his writings makes that perfectly clear.

Part of Oakeshott's ambiguity about what's wrong with Rationalism clearly has to do with a corresponding uncertainty about what Rationalism is, and with what sorts of weapons it may best be defeated. We have already noted that his resolution of the basic dichotomy between Rationalism and its opposing view is different in different realms. Sometimes Rationalism is simply rejected outright, and the opposing view is adopted as Oakeshott's own; for example, in higher education vocational training is flatly dismissed as inappropriate to a university.

At other times, Rationalism and its opponent are seen as two abstractions from a single concrete reality that must necessarily always contain both aspects. Then Oakeshott can either treat them as opposite ends of a continuum, advocating moderation and balance between them, as in his discussion of morality. Or else, he can adopt a Hegelian manner of argument, proposing his own teaching as a higher synthesis that rejects but also incorporates both Rationalism and its opponent; this he does, for example, in the essay on "Political Education." But it is in the realm of politics that Oakeshott clearly has the greatest difficulty in finding an appropriate manner of resolution.

It is important to note that there is variation not merely in realms of activity, but also in the way Rationalism is conceived. Sometimes it is treated as theory, an *interpretation* that purports to describe what we actually do; at other times, as a *style* or manner of conduct. As an interpretation of what we do, Rationalism can be decisively defeated if Oakeshott succeeds in showing that it is logically impossible to do what the Rationalist says we do. But as a mere interpretation that cannot become practice, Rationalism constitutes no danger. Who but a theorist cares about an incorrect interpretation?

But as an actual style of conduct in politics, morality, education, Rationalism can be a real danger, its evil consequences evident in the world around us. As a style of conduct, however, it cannot be logically defeated; if criticized, the criticism must be not logical or ontological but practical. The decisive philosophical victory is then no longer available; and Oakeshott must prove the superiority of conservatism in practical (historical and contingent) terms. In part, it seems to me, Oakeshott's ambiguity about what's wrong with Rationalism derives from his unwillingness to abandon the power of the philosophical mode of argument, even—or rather, especially—when he wants to warn us against the practical evils of Rationalism.

The matter is not that simple. For Oakeshott's major concern in his later writings is politics, a realm in which the problems of necessity and choice, interpretation and style, become inextricably intertwined. If philosophy is concerned with questioning the deep necessities of our lives, it must necessarily end in their acceptance, and be retrospective. But the problems of politics are problems of choice and change; the concerns of politics are matters potentially subject to our collective will. Then philosophy must seem irrelevant to politics. Yet it is surely obvious that action will be more likely to succeed where we know accurately what is necessary and what subject to our choice. Specifying this sort of demarcation between "what is to be done," and what is a "providential fact" that sets limits on our possibilities, has always been one of the great tasks undertaken by political theory. Oakeshott, it seems to me, attempts to avoid full acknowledgment of that task by insisting that "philosophy" is different from "doctrine," the task of the former being to "explain" while that of the latter is to "recommend conduct."[34] Yet he well knows that even the most abstract theory can have consequences for action if people believe in it, particularly in politics. Indeed, that is precisely the danger of Rationalism.

It seems to me that what Oakeshott ultimately wants to argue, though he is far from clear about it, is this: Rationalism as an interpretation of what we do is always wrong, because it is logically impossible to do what the Rationalist says we do. Yet people may—and many do—believe in the truth of this false, impossible doctrine, and act on it. The result is not that they act Rationalistically, for this is impossible, but that they act differently from people who believe otherwise, for instance, from those who believe in conservatism. There is thus an identifiable and pernicious style in politics that results from believing in the false doctrine of Rationalism. That is why Oakeshott says that the Rationalist misunderstands what he is doing, "fails to recognize" the "true spring" of his activity.[35] Acting *in accord with* the Rationalistic model is impossible, action *on* it, unfortunately, is not. The problem for understanding Oakeshott's political theory then becomes: what is this style of conduct like and what actual harm does it do?

Oakeshott's answers to this question are multiple and sometimes difficult to interpret. Although continuity and tradition in sociocultural life are inevitable, something extremely valuable can be destroyed by pernicious political action, namely, coherence within the traditions that compose a civilization or society. At any given historical point,

the arrangements which constitute a society capable of political activity, whether they are customs or institutions or laws
or diplomatic decisions, are at once coherent and incoherent; they compose a pattern and at the same time they
intimate a sympathy for what does not fully appear

—as yet; they compose a pattern and at the same time they
contain conflicts and inconsistencies.[36] The task of politics is to
enhance the consistency, pursue what is implicit but not yet
developed in the existing patterns, reduce conflict.[37] The failure
of politics takes the form of increased conflict and fragmentation. A society may pursue many specific goals, but for
Oakeshott it is always "more important for a society to move
together than for it to move either fast or far."[38] Sometimes,
indeed, he suggests that all political goals other than stability are
meaningless: in politics,

men sail a boundless and bottomless sea; there is neither
starting-place nor appointed destination. The enterprise is
to keep afloat on an even keel.[39]

But on a boundless sea there is not merely no "appointed"
destination; there can be no meaningful destination at all. The
only possible value is a stable voyage: don't rock the boat.
But though Oakeshott clearly values stability and coherence
for their own sakes, he also regards them as instrumental toward
achieving some other, perhaps more widely shared political
goals. For only tradition and the slow, gradual accretion of habit
can generate or protect freedom. Real freedom never inheres in
the formality of constitutional provisions or officially proclaimed ideology or institutional structures. Oakeshott agrees
with Burke that the "abstract perfection" of such formal freedom is its "practical defect."[40]

Freedom, like a recipe for game pie, is not a bright idea; it is
not a "human right" to be deduced from some speculative
concept of human nature. . . . The freedom of an Englishman is not something exemplified in the procedure of
habeas corpus, it is, at that point, the availability of that
procedure.[41]

That is why the attempt to export English freedoms to countries that have no related tradition of practice, by introducing the formal structure of some English law or institution, is bound to fail.[42] One of the weaknesses of Rationalism is its foolish "disposition to believe that political machinery can take the place of moral and political education," that one can construct artificial institutions to turn private vices into public virtues and thereby avoid the need to change character.[43] For it is character that determines how institutions will operate, no matter how they are formally constructed.

The reason that only tradition is capable of establishing and protecting freedom is that, secondly, only tradition is an effective restraint on power, and the restraint of power is what freedom is all about. The Englishman's freedom is

> a coherence of mutually supporting liberties, each of which amplifies the whole and none of which stands alone. It springs neither from the separation of church and state, nor from the rule of law, nor from private property, nor from parliamentary government, nor from the writ of *habeas corpus,* nor from the independence of the judiciary, nor from any one of the thousand other devices and arrangements characteristic of our society, but from what each signifies and represents, namely, the absence from our society of overwhelming concentrations of power. This is the most general condition of our freedom.[44]

Clearly, Oakeshott here sees freedom as Hobbes did, as the absence of "external restraints," a *not* being constrained by coercive power. It is achieved by keeping all forms of social power dispersed, the power of government itself at a minimum, just a little bit more than any other "center of power" in the society has.[45] Where "power is dispersed . . . on this account we are free."[46] Again, this cannot be achieved by mere legislation or the imposition of new forms; the only reliable restraint on power is habits of conduct. This is so both because a government that acts arbitrarily will meet far more resistance and therefore needs far more power than one that acts in established patterns; and because only habit can reliably restrain the passions of the rulers themselves, can keep them in their proper role of "neutral umpire" rather than that of one of the players.[47] Oakeshott believes, as Burke said, that tradition is essential to freedom because it is the source of "all the pleasing illusions which make power gentle and obedience liberal." In its absence, in the "groves" of the Rationalist's "academy, at the end of every vista, you see nothing but the gallows."[48]

This is related, in turn, to a further grim consequence of trying to act Rationalistically in politics, seen by both Oakeshott and Burke: the loss of continuity over time, and the resulting reduction of all goals to impulsive appetite. When we try to substitute Rationalistic ideology for habit in politics, Oakeshott says, "the life of a society loses its rhythm and continuity and is resolved into a succession of problems and crises."[49] Each separate successive difficulty is then supposed to be met ad hoc, "by the application of 'reason' uncontaminated by custom, habit, or prejudice."[50] Clearly what he means is that only tradition makes it possible to coordinate people's short-range, conflicting goals into a long-range public good. Reason does have a useful role in relation to a healthy tradition: the role of occasional critic and resolver of inconsistencies. But in Rationalism, "the intellect . . . ceases to be the critic of political habit and becomes a substitute for habit."[51] Or rather, it tries to do so, but it is unable to create. Reason, which has the "power to rescue from superstition, is given the task of generating human behaviour—a task which, in fact, it cannot perform"[52] The requirements of civility and order are so complex that tradition cannot be deliberately created. It can only evolve gradually and inarticulately over generations. As in technical knowledge and vocational training, so in politics: the Rationalist perspective is one of efficient means toward goals which themselves are not examined—the perspective of applied engineering.

The attempt to act Rationalistically, then, succeeds only in destroying coherence—social coherence among individuals, and chronological coherence, the sensed "partnership between present and past."[53] Both psychologically and structurally it becomes impossible to pursue justice or the public good; whoever plans for the long range or invests himself in other than narrowly selfish goals is bound to fail and merely makes a useless sacrifice. It is the vicious circle of a fragmented society that social contract theorists call "the state of nature" and modern sociology calls "amoral familism" or "the culture of poverty."[54] Oakeshott calls it "empirical politics," equating empiricism with "doing what one wants to do" at each particular moment.[55] For in the absence of ties to other people or to the past and future, the only possible goals are private and immediate. The result is "chaos modified by whatever consistency is allowed to creep into caprice."[56]

Oakeshott also calls this political style "the politics of the felt need," for it makes no allowance for needs existing but not yet felt, or not yet articulated, or not yet organized, for the needs of the future or of the powerless, or for goals that transcend need.[57] It makes no allowances, in Aristotelian terms, for going beyond the securing of life and to the pursuit of the good life.[58] Like Burke, Oakeshott believes that in the absence of traditional restraints, human beings are creatures of passion and impulse, and politics becomes a chaos of conflicting wills. And will is not a functional basis for politics. Politics requires a transition from the "assertive" to the "claiming mood," as Joseph Tussman has put it, from "I want" to "I am entitled to."[59] If this transition does not itself resolve conflict, it makes the resolution of conflict possible. But such a transition requires a modicum of trust and stability in the first place; in an excessively fragmented society, where no one can effectively transcend "I want," outcomes will be determined by naked coercive power. That is why Oakeshott would agree with Burke that "neither the few nor the many," neither rulers nor ruled may act politically on the basis of will. Teach people that politics is about satisfying their appetites, and they are bound to teach their rulers to govern coercively and arbitrarily. "In that kind of game, in the end, the people are sure to be the losers."[60]

III

Oakeshott's alternatives to these disasters, his vision of a healthy political life, is attractive in many ways, particularly when he leads us toward it by way of his understanding of continuity in a civilization. We see a happy, peaceful arrangement in which diversified individuals pursue their separate goals in their separate ways, and yet, without having to think or do much about it, they find that their private activity produces harmonious public results. Politics takes place near the surface of this deeply rooted life, making needed minor adjustments as conditions change, by referring to tradition for guidance. There is no real connection required between politics and community; politics is peripheral to the communal, significant life of the society, and is useful only for occasional repairs. Those who govern never need to exercise much power, for the small and partial actions they take are scarcely noticed by the governed; they are the gyroscope that keeps the ship of state on an even keel. The citizens, in turn, are content to be governed, for they have what they need, and feel no reason to question their way of life, the only one they know. There is occasion neither for deviance nor for doubt.

What, then, is wrong with this idyllic picture? Why should anyone but a misanthrope be suspicious of it? The sort of objections usually raised by Oakeshott's critics are: that he fails to realize that within any given society there can be many, sometimes conflicting traditions; that he falsely equates age with goodness, failing to see that some traditions are harmful; that for both these reasons the appeal to tradition provides no reliable guidance for actual political decisions.[61]

But it seems clear to me that Oakeshott does see the things his critics claim he fails to see. Oakeshott is fully aware that all societies contain multiple traditions, and that these are always to some extent in conflict. It is true, as Samuel Coleman points out, that Oakeshott moves ambiguously between using "tradition" to mean the entire cultural inheritance of a society, and using it to mean a particular strand in that inheritance—say, the tradition of the rule of law, or of *habeas corpus*—which may have implications that conflict with those of other particular traditions.[62] But aside from this confusion, Oakeshott is clearly aware that the traditions in our tradition are always "at once coherent and incoherent"; otherwise he could not possibly recommend the enhancing of coherence as the central task of political adjustments in tradition.[63]

Nor does Oakeshott believe that everything old or traditional is *ipso facto* good. He clearly recognizes that Rationalism itself has a history and has now become a tradition: in morality, one by which "we are for the most part dominated"; in politics, a "disease almost as old as the patient himself," the main "inspiration of political activity in Western Europe for the last two hundred years."[64] There is a "positive prejudice" in its favor, "in favor of the yet untried."[65] Oakeshott does not for a moment think that in directing us to tradition for political guidance, he is directing us to ready, unambiguous answers. But, as he points out, no general theoretical principle can provide specific, concrete guidance for particular decisions; the appeal to tradition is in this respect no different from natural law or utilitarianism or social contract doctrine or Marxism. All abstract principles need to be applied in concrete cases. And it is as vain in politics as in any other human activity, to hope for some sort of "mistake-proof manner of deciding what should be done."[66]

What Oakeshott is really saying when he directs us to "tradition" as a basis for political decisions seems to be threefold: First, *do not* introduce principles or institutions alien to the indigenous traditions. Second, strive always to enhance coherence within (among) the existing tradition(s); where the existing patterns conflict, act so as to reduce that conflict. Third, do not hope to find answers in any abstract principle, but immerse yourself in concrete knowledge of your community. Those concrete details *are* the tradition that is to be your guide; the guidance does not come as explicit general principles, but as implications, hints, fragments. Extrapolating a pattern from them is precisely the problem in finding the right political course; that *is* the "pursuit of intimations"; it is an art, not a science.

Nor is it true, then, that Oakeshott fails to see the potential conflict among traditions, or that the weakness of his theory is that it fails to give specific guidance for political action. Yet the critics are right to sense that there is something fundamentally wrong with Oakeshott's traditionalism in relation to political action. Perhaps we can begin to approach the problem by taking a closer look at Oakeshott's proposition that tradition and habit are the most reliable, or perhaps the only reliable security against tyranny and oppression. For it has more than a hint of the tautological about it: habit works well so long as it works well. Rational deliberations, action, innovation, sometimes work well and sometimes fail, as everyone knows. But tradition, as Oake-shott pictures it, never *fails to work;* it only breaks down, or ends. And for Oakeshott, although that is a calamity, it is never the fault of the tradition itself. Tradition breaks down when people stop following it; never because, although they follow it faithfully, it fails to work. The breakdown of inherited habit is most commonly the fault of false doctrine, of Rationalism; and of the causes of Rationalism Oakeshott tells us relatively little.[67] Tradition itself never fails; it is merely abandoned.

But this is not a fully accurate account of Oakeshott's position; he is more astute and subtle than consistent, and sometimes he can see with remarkable clarity the limitations of his own teach-ings. Thus, while he lauds the tenacious adaptability of healthy tradition, he is also able to see—particularly in nonpolitical contexts—its cardinal weakness: the tendency to ossification. In attacking political Rationalism, Oakeshott charges that it suffers from a "rigidity and fixity of character" which leaves it "without the power to correct its own short-comings."[68] All the Rationalist can do if his program fails is to replace it by another; he cannot modify, for everything is explicit and therefore irrevocable.[69] The politics of tradition and habit, by contrast, is "of course, pre-eminently fluid," just as habitual morality is distinguished by its "elasticity and its ability to suffer change without disruption."[70] Yet sometimes Oakeshott can also speak elo-quently of the fatal flaw in tradition, its liability to become rigid and empty of meaning. A moral tradition originating in the powerful spiritual experience of one generation may well be-come pointless formality for the people of a later time; it may "degenerate into superstition."[71] There are difficulties about "translating" the original, charismatic spiritual experience "into a form in which it could be appreciated by those who had never shared the original inspiration"; they are in fact like newcomers in any enterprise who must learn doctrine abstractly, like a foreign language from a grammar.[72]

Oakeshott also recognizes that the preservation of tradition does depend on the objective quality of the inheritance. "If the present is arid, offering little or nothing to be used or enjoyed, then this inclination will be weak or absent."[73] Thus people are not likely to accept their inherited station and its duties indefinitely, if the tradition yields them nothing of real benefit. And traditions are liable to change in this respect, either because of their own internal drift, or because of a failure to adapt to changed social conditions. Oakeshott notes that even traditional institutions are subject to a kind of inertial drift that may totally alter their impact. "Arrangements which in their beginnings promoted a dispersion of power," for instance, "often, in the course of time, themselves become over-mighty or even absolute."[74]

Even more dangerous, however, is the characteristic inability of tradition to cope with crises. Though healthy tradition is more capable of adaptation than is Rationalism, Oakeshott acknowledges that this adaptation only works when change is limited and slow. The conservative must be ever watchful to make continuous small adaptations in his inherited institutions "while the evil is still small."[75] For a sudden or major social crisis may well demand a degree or velocity of adaptation greater than tradition can muster. The change tradition "admits is neither great nor sudden," Oakeshott says; so that its only defense lies in "its resistance to the conditions productive of crisis."[76] Once a major crisis has arisen—as he acknowledges at least in the realm of morality—tradition "has little power of recovery," precisely because it is inarticulate and unselfconscious, lacking "the power to criticize, to reform, and to explain itself."[77] But one must surely suppose that in politics the problem will be, if anything, even greater, for as Oakeshott stresses, politics is the sphere of change *par excellence.*

Tradition cannot defend itself except gradually and piecemeal, or it ceases to be a tradition. It cannot defend itself where it has no supporters, and it will not be supported by those whom it gives "little or nothing to be used or enjoyed." And even those who benefit from it cannot support it well, because they have given the matter no thought, have had no practice in deliberation and action. We will not be surprised, then, if the idyllic conditions of healthy habit that Oakeshott envisages are politically rare.

It is not merely that these idyllic conditions are an ideal of perfection that we may not be able to attain, but toward which we may strive. The problem with Oakeshott's teachings is not that he is an idealistic utopian. Rather, the problem seems to be that for most people in the modern world, the ideal is simply irrelevant. Oakeshott does not teach us how to create a traditional society; indeed, he does not think one can be deliberately created. And the advice to look to tradition and enhance coherence by pursuing intimations is simply meaningless where no worthwhile tradition exists. Of course there is a sense in which there are always traditions, humans being culture-animals. But even Oakeshott recognizes that not every tradition in *that* sense is an idyll worthy of conservation. Oakeshott simply has nothing to say to people without a tradition to preserve.

Consider, for example, a colony of the British Empire, perhaps in Africa or Asia, that is only an artificial administrative unit created without regard for former tribal boundaries. What would Oakeshott advise such a nation? Should it seek independence? And if it attains independence, how should it guide its political conduct? More than one tradition is available here, and very little hope of coherence; the traditions have conflicting implications, and none offers that natural harmony for which Oakeshott strives. Some of the available traditions, perhaps all, may even be hostile to the substantive qualities he cherishes in politics: liberty, the rule of law, free private enterprise. One might imagine Oakeshott advising such a people to cling to the Empire, or to return to their native, tribal traditions. But mostly he would have to give them non-advice: you are in a most unfortunate situation; there is nothing much you can do that will produce beneficial results.

This may, of course, be the truth. Still, it is instructive to look in somewhat greater detail. We have already encountered Oakeshott's view that abstract doctrines and formal institutions cannot successfully be exported to peoples unfamiliar with the tradition of inarticulate practice underlying those abstractions. Such a people is as helpless with its new paper constitution or new institutional system as a layman ignorant of mathematics is with a correct mathematical formula. Accordingly, Oakeshott's maintains that British traditions of liberty and the rule of law cannot be successfully exported to uncivilized tribes in the form of ideology or legal formula; they are bound to be misunderstood. There is, of course, truth in this, but what alternatives does Oakeshott envisage?

The alternative to technical education is apprenticeship; the alternative to a morality of explicit precepts is identification with an authoritative model. Just so with regard to liberty and the Empire: British tradition cannot be exported as ideology, but there is

> an alternative method: the method by which what is exported is the detail and not the abridgment of the tradition and the workmen travel with the tools—the method which made the British Empire. But it is a slow and costly method. And, particularly with men in a hurry, *l'homme à programme* with his abridgment wins every time; his slogans enchant, while the resident magistrate is seen only as a sign of servility.[78]

How does a theorist otherwise so astute and sensitive come wholly to miss the possibility that a colonized people might have good reasons for associating the resident British magistrate with oppression rather than liberty? What is it about Oakeshott's assumptions that renders him in such a context so incredibly blind?

Even Burke, whose vision was so much like Oakeshott's, saw more clearly with respect to empire, even if not clearly enough. And so, concerning British rule in India, Burke was able to see that whether the resident British magistrate can serve as a model of liberty or only as a symbol of oppression depends on his actual conduct and the principles it embodies, not on the political traditions of the country from which he comes.[79] But the problem forced him to argue on the ground of precisely the kind of abstract citation of God's justice independent of any embodying tradition, that he fundamentally opposed in Enlightenment thought. Oakeshott refuses to invoke any such Rationalistic concepts in support of his conservatism; he will not have recourse to natural law or divine purpose or any such "particular beliefs about the universe, about the world in general, or about human conduct in general."[80] If this limits the applicability of his theories to England and countries much like it, Oakeshott is content to accept that. The problems of other societies, he says, are questions that "we need not try to answer: we are concerned with ourselves as we are."[81] (But is an understanding of the realities of the British Empire not part of an accurate British self-knowledge?)

Oakeshott's doctrine obviously has quite similar limitations from the point of view of any oppressed minority in a country that does have a tradition of liberty. Or rather, recalling his example of women's suffrage enacted to complete a pattern already formed in most other respects, the doctrine holds out great hope for those minorities already privileged in most respects but excluded from a particular right. Their remaining claims should soon be fulfilled by the pursuit of what is intimated in the tradition. But no such hope is held out to those who presently lack all status in the society. For slaves, perpetuation of the tradition and enhanced coherence in it can only mean a systematization of their oppression. "Them as got, gits." Oakeshott's is not an attractive teaching for slaves, nor for anyone whom the tradition offers "little or nothing to be used or enjoyed."

The appeal to tradition, then, is useful only to the privileged, both in the sense that one must already be blessed with a healthy tradition in order to make such an appeal, and in the sense that only those already granted privileges by that tradition can expect further privileges from it. But there is a more serious and less obvious disadvantage to the traditionalist view. Even where healthy tradition is available, and even for those who already enjoy its benefits, there is something crucial missing from the picture: namely, genuine politics. And there are those in the tradition of political theory who would argue that this is the worst deprivation of all. But to see this, and how it is so, we shall have to go a more circuitous route.

IV

Oakeshott's conception of politics is profoundly influenced, it seems to me, by his distrust of the "politics of the felt need," his sense that passion, need, will, constitute dangerous threats to civility. And for him, as for Burke, that danger has specific historical embodiment in "uncivilized" social groups seeking admission to the political realm, and particularly in the poor, who carry with them the urgency of physical need. In this regard, Oakeshott's views are remarkably similar to those of Hannah Arendt, and of a whole tradition in political theory on which she draws, from Aristotle through Tocqueville, which fears that politics may well be destroyed through the intrusion of the poor.

Oakeshott links Rationalism directly with the problem of newcomers in politics. With its striving for uniformity and its ideological bent, Rationalism tends to insist on universal suffrage: one man, one vote. It urges the admission into politics of previously excluded strata. And, conversely, it is precisely those new to the political realm who need the Rationalistic style. Precipitated suddenly into the political arena without relevant experience, habit, or tradition, they must find guidance somewhere, and quickly. Rationalism seems to offer what they need, being "the politics of the book," a set of simple rules, an ideological abridgment, an easy "how to do it" course.[82] Thus, says Oakeshott, the new ruler may find in Machiavelli's *Prince* a convenient set of maxims to guide his actions.[83] Similarly, a new nation, having no political traditions, may seek Rationalistic instruction from any available ideologist. Oakeshott's case in point is America, which began with "a specific and express rejection of tradition" and whose politics has been Rationalistic ever since.[84] Besides new rulers and new nations, Rationalism also appeals to strata of society newly emergent into public life. The predominant ideology of newly politicized classes in the last hundred years Oakeshott takes to be Marxism, "the most stupendous of our political Rationalisms..., for it was composed for the instruction of a less politically educated class than any other that has ever come to have the illusion of exercising political power."[85]

It is not that Oakeshott lacks sympathy with the sufferings of the poor; nor does he deny the realities of economic organization in modern society. He acknowledges that "from one point of view, property is a form of power, and an institution of property is a particular way of organizing the exercise of this form of power in a society."[86] Like all power, it limits the freedom, the choices, of those subject to it. A worker is not free, "unless there are many potential employers of his labour," unless he has genuine options; consequently, "wherever a means of production falls under the control of a single power, slavery in some measure follows."[87] Recognizing that the institutions of economic power are creatures of law, "not something that springs up of its own accord,"[88] Oakeshott favors political intervention to suppress "private monopoly in all its forms," and where that is impossible, public operation of the enterprise.[89] Yet in the end he always opts for private property as "the institution of property most favourable to liberty, . . . for it is by this means only that the maximum diffusion of the power that springs from ownership may be achieved."[90] The prime modern danger is Socialist Collectivism, a concentration of power and a threat to freedom far greater than those constituted by any private economic abuse.

Oakeshott sympathizes with the suffering of the poor but fears their intervention in politics. The masses of the poor and uneducated are not fit to participate in political life. Politics, Oakeshott always maintains, is a conversation; but "the major part of mankind has nothing to say; the lives of most men do not revolve around a felt necessity to speak."[91] He does not mean, of course, that the major part of mankind has no needs. On the contrary, most are mere bundles of felt needs unenlarged and unrestrained by any tradition of civility. But the moral life of choice and responsibility "appears only where human behaviour is free from natural necessity," where there are genuine options.[92] The real needs of those who are pressed by necessity but are not fit to converse politically must of course be attended to, but not by their own political activity. As Burke said,

> The most poor, illiterate, and uninformed creatures upon earth are judges of a *practical* oppression. It is a matter of feeling; and as such persons generally have felt most of it, and are not of an overly-lively sensibility, they are the best judges of it. But for *the real cause,* or *the appropriate remedy,* they ought never to be called into council . . . because their reason is weak; because, when once roused, their passions are ungoverned.[93]

Oakeshott accepts the universal adult suffrage that Burke could still oppose, but their views of political participation by the masses are the same.

Such views are, indeed, reminiscent of a tradition of political thought, stemming at least from Aristotle and revived most recently by Arendt, that is concerned to protect the autonomy of politics from the onslaught of excluded social strata. All of the theorists in this tradition see political life as a distinctive form of human organization of special value, the locus of freedom and honor and full human development; but all of them also see it as hitherto restricted in membership, with access reserved to a propertied elite. Aristotle accepted this situation as natural. But with the intrusion of the masses into political action that began with the French Revolution, the problem of modernity became: can political participation and its attendant values of freedom and responsibility be extended to include all the members of a society, or must the intrusion of the masses, with their inappropriate orientations, necessarily destroy genuine political life?

The trouble with the poor, to put the views of Aristotle, Arendt, and Oakeshott in a nutshell, is that they are hungry. This means that they are creatures of appetite, "driven by the needs of their bodies," and therefore not free to make genuine moral and political choices.[94] Traditionally, from its invention in the Greek *polis*, free political life had presupposed the prior mastering of economic necessity; politics had been precisely the realm from which "everything merely necessary or useful" was "strictly excluded," where "no activity that served only the purpose of making a living, of sustaining only the life process, was permitted to enter."[95] Thus Aristotle maintained that a slave was by nature unsuited to be self-governing, and recommended the exclusion of mechanics and artisans from citizenship because of their inappropriate "spirit."[96]

But in the French Revolution, Arendt argues, this multitude of the poor and oppressed, traditionally excluded from the public realm and kept "hidden in darkness and shame," began for the first time "to doubt that poverty is inherent in the human condition," began, that is, to regard their needs as a political issue.[97] They "burst onto the scene" of history for the first time as a political force, introducing into politics the very element of physical appetite, of economic necessity, previously considered antithetical to it. "The public realm—reserved, as far as memory could reach, to those who *were* free, namely carefree of all worries that are connected with life's necessity, with bodily needs," was now to "offer its space and light to this immense majority who are not free because they are driven by daily needs."[98] Arendt thinks that this was what destroyed the French Revolution, made it unable to be a genuine foundation of political liberty for the majority. For the need of the poor "was violent and, as it were, prepolitical"; it drove them, until "freedom had to be surrendered to necessity, to the urgency of the life process itself."[99] Knowing only the endlessness of physical labor and the endless pressure of hunger and physical need, the *animal laborans* demanded food instead of freedom, happiness instead of honor. As a result, even in our modern abundance, we now lack genuine politics and political freedom; under the pressure of the poor, we have achieved plenty but lost liberty.[100]

This is a distressing doctrine, for on the one hand it means that the great values offered by political life are by their nature confined to a wealthy elite, so that the great majority of mankind is condemned to exclusion from self-government and full human development. On the other hand, it is difficult to believe in the great value that theorists like Aristotle, Tocqueville, and Arendt attach to political life, if, by definition, it is impotent to deal with the real needs of most people. One wants to object: no wonder the political debates of those aristocrats were above mere economics and devoted to "higher things"; they helped themselves to what they needed economically outside of politics, by forcibly excluding from the political realm those who needed to raise economic questions. What is so noble about that picture?

But the problem is more complicated. For of course it is not true that the poor, and only the poor, are "driven by economic, physical necessity." Even a moment's thought about historical fact can show us that there is virtually no physical necessity so dire that it totally destroys the human will, the capacity for choice. Even in the concentration camp, some shared their tiny ration of bread. And when the poor burst into the political arena their demands were not, in fact, merely for bread; they demanded dignity and justice for all mankind. As Arendt knows, the early organizations of workers and the poor were the only group "which not only defended its economic interests but fought a full-fledged *political* battle."[101] And as she also knows, it was not the poor themselves who, driven by the iron law of their physical need, demanded of the French Revolution an economic largesse which it could not give. It was in fact the revolutionary governments, "neither of the people nor by the people," who took action in the name of the hungry, out of pity.[102] But pity is not an insurmountable, physical, causal necessity; it is a policy position, chosen as freely or unfreely as any other, and in this case by men who themselves ate regularly.

Neither poverty nor urgent need disqualifies people from free political participation; nor does the introduction of lowly economic issues into the political realm destroy it. Economic issues have always appeared in the political realm—even, or especially, in the Greek *polis*. What is required for free, genuine political life is neither a certain class status nor a certain subject-matter but a certain spirit, and that spirit is not the automatic prerogative of any social group. What Aristotle and Tocqueville, Arendt and Oakeshott really fear and oppose in politics is a short-sightedly utilitarian, narrowly selfish, crassly competitive orientation.[103] And that orientation in fact was not introduced into politics after 1789 by the raging, hungry masses, but by the bourgeoisie.

liberal

It "entered the public realm" in the "disguise of an organization of property-owners" who, instead of claiming access to the traditional values of political participation, sought from it "protection . . . for the accumulation of more wealth."[104] It is not physical hunger but the spiritual hunger of the Protestant Ethic, of the acquisitive self, of status anxiety in the face of an unpredictable market; it is in fact the spirit of a newly developing capitalism that threatens the autonomy of political life and liberty. It is the reduction of politics to a mere means toward other—acquisitive and particularistic—goals that destroys it. As Tocqueville said, "the man who asks of freedom anything other than itself is born to be a slave."[105] But that man, as was perfectly clear to Tocqueville by 1850, was not the starving worker but the shopkeeper, "the middle class, which . . . treated government like a private business, each member thinking of public affairs only in so far as they could be turned to his private profit," until the government "took on the features of a trading company."[106] The result was a total absence of real political life in the supposedly "political" institutions; nothing there but "languor, impotence, immobility and boredom." But outside the official system, in the streets and among the lower classes "an attentive observer could easily see from certain feverish and irregular symptoms that political life was beginning to find expression."[107] What stirred there was a real political life, not because it was free of economic need, but because it combined the demand for bread with the demand for dignity, because it transformed economic need into a question of justice.

The supposed dominion of biological need that makes people unfree and certain questions unsuitable to politics is in reality always largely a question of consciousness. In the French Revolution the previously dominant understanding of what was inevitable was called into question; poverty was made into a political—that is, an actionable—issue. That is part of what it means to say, as we did earlier, that political theory attempts to define the interface between what must be accepted as necessary and what can be altered through active intervention. Consciousness and activity are circular here, and interact. What we perceive as natural and necessary, we will not act to change; but at the same time, our perceptions are shaped by our activity. We feel helpless in proportion as we remain passive. As Arendt herself sees, the "fateful automatism" of physical necessity, of the "biological process," will "assert itself" more forcefully "the less we are doing ourselves, the less active we are."[108] Thus, in the end, as she remarks in a casual parenthesis, "to have a society of laborers, it is of course not necessary that every member actually be a laborer or a worker . . . but only that all members consider what they do primarily as a way to sustain their own lives and those of their families."[109]

It was this realization that the givenness of necessity depends to some extent on consciousness, and consciousness in turn is shaped by our activity, that gave Tocqueville hope. What he saw in America was the possibility that the narrowly selfish acquisitiveness, the fragmentation and competitiveness that characterized the great middle-class economy of the future might—just possibly might—be educated to the political spirit the older aristocracy had known, through active participation in democratic self-government. But the task is difficult, for the only language in which one can appeal to the bourgeois, in which he himself can conceptualize what he experiences in political activity, is the language of utilitarian self-interest. But that way of conceptualizing the world is itself the disease; it can't be the cure. So Tocqueville strives to hold a delicate balance, avoiding the preaching of a civic duty empty of any real, personal meaning, and the pessimistic constitutionalism of, say, a James Madison which attempts to harness narrowly selfish men to an institutional machine that will produce the public good despite their intentions and without changing their character. Aristotle and Arendt faced much the same ambiguities. Aristotle certainly seems to have abandoned hope for the transforming of artisans or slaves into citizens; yet it is he who stresses the educational nature of political participation itself, the extent to which only that activity can fully develop human potential. And Arendt, though she cannot hope as Tocqueville did, since the institutions of political participation that he saw have largely disappeared into a vast bureaucracy, nevertheless does hope, insisting on our capacity even now to change, to choose, to act.

And what of Oakeshott (to return from this excursion into the politics of poverty)? Like other theorists discussed here, Oakeshott fears and opposes the introduction into politics of the spirit appropriate to economic activity and contractual relationships:

> those of producer and consumer, master and servant, principal and assistant—each participant seeks some service or recompense for service, and if it is not forthcoming the relationship lapses or is terminated.[110]

Such relationships and activities contrast with others, like friendship, pursued for their intrinsic value, and in which the other participants are valued for themselves rather than as a means to some other end. But as we shall see, Oakeshott is profoundly ambivalent about how to classify politics in this regard. Though as anxious to protect it against the utilitarian spirit as any of the theorists in this tradition, he does not value it for its own sake, as they do. He would like it to be an end-in-itself like friendship, yet he fears the intrinsic values that they ascribe to active citizenship almost as much as he fears the utilitarian spirit. As a result, his teachings come in the end to resemble the utilitarian-liberal tradition with its minimal, caretaker conception of government, much more than he is aware or would wish.

V

The desire to protect political life against a crassly acquisitive, narrowly selfish utilitarian spirit is only one in a cluster of concerns that Oakeshott shares with Aristotle, Tocqueville, and Arendt (as well as, frequently, with Machiavelli and Burke). Together, these concerns make up much of what is valuable, but usually ignored, in Oakeshott's political theory. They range far beyond a mere stress on tradition as we have discussed it, and they deserve more detailed exploration.

Oakeshott's favorite metaphor for understanding political life is that of conversation. Political education, he says, means learning to participate in a conversation; and politics itself is a conversation, sometimes among past, present, and future, sometimes among governors and governed, or among social groupings.[111] It is not difficult to see why the metaphor attracts him: conversation is a relationship of plurality and mutuality, of self-development. There must be at least two participants, perhaps more; and all of the participants matter to the conversation. In a good conversation, all participate in the gradual revelation of a shared truth, but probably differing from the initial position taken by any of them. It is a matter of "exploring the intimations" of initial positions, laying bare their implications and modifying them cooperatively. Each participant therefore learns about his own views in the process, learns to see himself in the mirror of the conversation.[112] And more is learned in the course of the conversation than any statement of the "conclusion" reached could possibly convey to one who was not present. Indeed, the point is the process, not the conclusion.

Moreover, conversation is a relationship of personal freedom and harmony without coercion, which continues only as the participants persuade each other. One participant may be more persuasive or better informed than others and may prevail for a time, but "none permanently dominates."[113] It is not a question of who will "win," but of mutual participation in a shared development. Oakeshott stresses that a conversation is not an argument: the relations in a conversation "are not those of assertion and denial but . . . of acknowledgment and accommodation," of "oblique recognition."[114]

The metaphor thus illuminates what we already noted in Oakeshott's sociological vision of human community: a profound concern for individual development, for opportunity and personal freedom, together with an appreciation of rootedness and mutual responsibility. He sees that we should not have to choose between individuality and community, that true personal development and true *Gemeinschaft* enhance each other. And this sociological insight has its counterpart in Oakeshott's specifically political doctrine, in his profound awareness that a fundamental plurality and mutuality is essential to politics. Like Aristotle and Arendt, Oakeshott refuses to identify political rule over citizens with mere force, domination, the management of slaves, or the fabrication of objects. He insists that political rule is a relationship, if not among equals—since we know that people are always unequal in power, wealth, ability, character—at least among peers whose views are mutually relevant to their shared enterprise. The metaphor of conversation clearly implies that politics is a matter of persuasion rather than coercion, and that it is not enough for the needs of a subject creature to be cared for, that administrative efficiency is not enough to constitute a political relationship.

The metaphor further shows the extent to which Oakeshott shares the conviction of Aristotle or Arendt that politics always presupposes a prior tradition of basic agreement, a "public forum." Such a forum is not, of course, a physical place—though the *agora* was certainly a constitutive element in Greek political life—but the organization of people in a public, political way.[115] Only where people are already bound by some minimal ties of reciprocity and civility is a political relationship possible at all, as an alternative to domination and naked force. Conversation presupposes a shared language and a shared recognition of something worth talking about, as well as a willingness to *talk* rather than fight.

Oakeshott also shares with the theorists in this tradition a healthy realism and skepticism about what is possible in politics. He teaches us to distrust the pretensions of the "social engineer" who offers allegedly easy solutions to our vexing public problems, claiming with pseudo-authority that they are "scientific" solutions.[116] Oakeshott sees that political issues are precisely those that lack technical solutions of this kind, and that the imposition of a vision of order on a society in the name of "The" correct solution destroys the mutuality essential to political life. There is no final solution or ultimate goal in politics; like human life itself, it is continual, restless activity. Success is "sporadic and uncertain, something which has to be achieved from day to day and is never complete or unqualified."[117] The process of mutual adjustment among human beings is endless. One must be content with partial and limited, which is to say, with *human* achievements. Thus, like Burke, Aristotle, and Arendt, Oakeshott argues for the importance of limits in politics. He is intensely aware that there are real, concrete human lives at stake; and, like Albert Camus, he insists that present suffering must never be lightly justified in the name of some abstract vision of the future.[118]

In sum, Oakeshott joins the other theorists of this tradition in offering a vision of politics that is nonutilitarian; that seeks individuality within *Gemeinschaft;* that stresses mutuality, the need for a public arena, the importance of limits; that is realistically skeptical of easy or technical answers. But at a number of central points in this configuration of doctrine, Oakeshott's views are also strikingly different from those of the other theorists in this tradition; and the character of those differences is crucial.

Take, for example, the shared suspicion of narrowly utilitarian motives in politics, the fear that political life may be destroyed by the intrusion of a merely contractual spirit. And take their correlated skeptical realism, their suspicion of easy or technical "solutions." In all the theorists of this tradition other than Oakeshott these elements are bound together by an understanding of politics as the potential locus of human greatness. What they want to protect against the shopkeeper's or "household" spirit is the possibility of human transcendence, what

Tocqueville called "great politics," Machiavelli "glory," and the Greeks immortality. This possibility was what Aristotle meant in calling man a political animal—a creature that fulfills itself in politics, whose full human development can only take place through participation in *polis* citizenship. Not that every citizen would be a hero and become personally immortal; but only active participation in collective decisions about what the community was to do and be could enlarge the narrow and private self, make human beings fully aware of their capacity to choose and their nonimmediate connections to others.

But Oakeshott, though his metaphor of conversation implies that self-development is an essential ingredient of politics, is not really willing to accept that implication. When he considers universal political participation, he considers it as a duty rather than a right or need or condition of self-development. And even as a duty, he rejects it. For our private activities make just as much of a contribution to the great, underlying stream of our civilization as any explicitly political action; "nothing we do is unconnected with the life of our society, no activity is private in the sense of being without its place or context in the corporate social life."[119] It does not matter that in our private-social activities we are not conscious of their public significance, of alternative choices, of our responsibility for public consequences. It does not matter that "the lives of most men do not revolve around a felt necessity to speak"; this is seen as a fact useful for social stability, not a failure in human development.

Oakeshott is not trying to save politics from petty purposes in order to free it (or us) for great ones; he would prefer to eliminate purpose from politics altogether. All other theorists in this tradition see that in the absence of final or technical solutions, politics always involves risk; that political life requires energy, courage, even heroism. But Oakeshott, although he does at one point mock "those who have lost their nerve," and characterizes his vision of politics as *"nur für die Schwindelfreien,"* never intends more than intellectual courage—the courage to give up "false hopes."[120] He emphatically does not mean that politics should be the locus of courage in action, let alone heroism or the pursuit of glory. Though he will not have politics conducted in a narrowly utilitarian spirit, he does not share the traditional alternative, and will not have it conducted in the heroic spirit either. For him, politics is and healthy politics must be a "secondary activity," of what our newspapers would today call "low profile."[121] Its task is never more than the adjudication of conflicts between private individuals or groups, together with those minor and surface adjustments that need to be made from time to time in the great, underlying tide of the society's habitual life. Oakeshott's vision is one in which people have more valuable things to do with their time than this useful but unattractive "attending to arrangements." They are busy with other enterprises, their myriad private pursuits; and they come to politics only when they happen to "have nothing better to think about," or when they have some concrete, practical grievance that needs attention.[122] Healthy political activity is "repair," the appropriate normal attitude toward politics is one of "indifference"; the appropriate role for government is "not the management of an enterprise," but the coordination "of those engaged in a great diversity of self-chosen enterprises."[123] Its task is not "to make men good or even better."[124] Thus Oakeshott agrees with the utilitarian liberals he otherwise criticizes that government is an "umpire," and freedom means being left to do as one likes in one's privacy. Politics is "a limited activity, a necessary but second-rate affair."[125]

Even Burke, fearful as he was of passion, gave politics more weight and dignity than that. To sense the difference, we need only contrast the connotations of Oakeshott's favorite concept of "conversation" with those of its counterpart in Burke, almost never used by Oakeshott: "deliberation."[126] Deliberation suggests gravity, serious issues, statesmen and judgment, and the intention that at the end of the talking, action will commence. Conversation, by contrast, implies a less directed, less purposeful but perhaps more pleasurable talking, enjoyed for its own sake and for what it will reveal rather than for any agreement in which it may conclude. Oakeshott really does think about politics in terms of conversation rather than deliberation (let alone any more strident activity), in terms of the pleasant, somewhat idle but also valuable, civilized talk of university dons over their afternoon sherry. No wonder he thinks that those with strident demands would have "nothing to say" in such a conversation.

For Oakeshott, what is inappropriate to politics is anything that smacks of passion, zeal, commitment, heroism, or the pursuit of perfection. These do have their value, as he concedes with some reluctance, but only in the private lives of individual persons. The pursuit of perfection is

> both impious and unavoidable in human life. It involves the penalties of impiety (the anger of the gods and social isolation), and its reward is not that of achievement but that of having made the attempt. It is an activity therefore, suitable for individuals, but not for societies.[127]

An individual who strives heroically for the impossible may be willing to pay the penalty, or he may recant and be taken back into an "understanding and forgiving society." But for a political community, the pursuit of ideals has as its penalty "a chaos of conflicting ideals, the disruption of a common life."[128] In politics, therefore, we must be "unadventurous," must never "buckle on armour and seek dragons to slay," and should have no love for "what is dangerous and difficult; . . . no impulse to sail uncharted seas."[129]

Oakeshott's aversion to heroic politics is reflected also in still another striking difference between his views and those of the theorists we have been discussing. We saw that he shares with them a stress on mutuality in politics, a distinction between political rule and domination, and a consequent stress on the need for a political arena—a framework of law or institutions, a tradition of civility—within which politics becomes possible. All of the theorists in this tradition other than Oakeshott are led by such concerns to problems of founding, to questions of how such an arena can be created among men and how, once created, it can be maintained. For Aristotle as for Arendt, the prepolitical and essentially violent act of founding necessarily underlies the life of any *polis*; for Machiavelli, Heaven can offer no greater opportunity for glory than the founding of a new polity or the revivification of one that has decayed into corruption; and for Machiavelli as for Tocqueville, that revivification, the task of maintaining a public forum once it has been founded, depends on conflict and action.

But Oakeshott refuses to think of tradition as *founded* at all; he essentially wants to deny that human beings have the capacity for large-scale or collective creation, for any but artistic creation.[130] In his view, all tradition originates in the unknown recesses of past history, as the unplanned product of countless uncoordinated private choices. And Oakeshott is in the end unable to give any account of how a tradition, once created, might be preserved or protected under attack. He cannot or will not follow a Tocqueville or a Machiavelli here, for he fears too much the destructive potential of the forces their solutions enlist.

VI

Perhaps it is not inappropriate to approach the nature of this deficiency in Oakeshott's theory by way of a psychological analysis, particularly since he is almost as much concerned with education and morality as with government. That there is a psychic component in the conservative's anxiety about the careful preservation of the past is no secret, being revealed most clearly in Burke's unselfconscious (because pre-Freudian) metaphors. Burke always insists that our inherited institutions, the legacy of our fathers, must be regarded as we regard the fathers themselves, in order to give "to our frame of polity the image of a relation in blood," to bind up "the constitution of our country with our dearest domestic ties."[131] These institutions are, as Socrates already pointed out, our true parents, raising and forming us; and like parents, they are mortal.[132] If you challenge them, you endanger your parents; if you care for them tenderly, you are cherishing your parents.

> We have consecrated the state, that no man should approach to look into its defects or corruptions but with due caution; . . . that he should approach to the faults of the state as to the wounds of a father, with pious awe and trembling solicitude. By this wise prejudice we are taught to look with horror on those children of their country who are prompt rashly to hack that aged parent in pieces and put him into the kettle of magicians, in hopes that by their poisonous

weeds and wild incantations they may regenerate the pater-
nal constitution and renovate their father's life.[133]

The real danger is parricide, and the profundity of that danger
is correlated to the depths of men's hidden hatred of authority,
constantly pressing for release within them. That hidden hatred
is so powerful and so dangerous that one must guard against it at
every step. A rebellious thought is as wicked as the deed; it is best
not even to approach and look; thoughts can kill.

All that stands between us and our murderous passion against
those we love and need is the acquired habit of traditional
behavior, of non-thought. Once you begin to question authority,
you undermine the "wise prejudices" and "pleasing illusions"
that sustain civilization.[134] But implicit in such expressions
clearly is the assumption that civilization depends upon illusions,
not on real benefits; that in the absence of a repressive conscience, our love could not restrain the passion of our hate; that
the continuing resolution of conflict and reintegration of
ambivalence cannot be relied upon to prevent disaster.

Oakeshott, of course, does not talk of parricide. Nor is this
only because our post-Freudian sophistication precludes such
naively obvious self-exposure. In an important sense, there are
no fathers in Oakeshott's world, as there still were in Burke's.
For Burke, there was a reliable, wealthy, powerful ruling class, a
"natural aristocracy" suited to govern and take care of the child-
like masses. Oakeshott's thought, by contrast, moves in a world
where fathers have become faceless nonentities; his conservatism is of necessity a doctrine for a democracy in which none is
to be trusted to rule. That is why conversation has replaced
deliberation. But one can hate an absent or faceless or ineffec-
tual father as much as a powerful one—hate him, indeed, partly
for his very ineffectuality. And the resulting fear of being overwhelmed by powerful destructive passions can be just as
compelling.[135]

What Oakeshott does say—and it is interesting and revealing
enough—is that our identity, our very selves depend entirely on
the preservation of continuity with the past. Whether for an
individual or for a community, the new always presents itself as a
threat to selfhood, against which defensive action must be taken.

"Change is a threat to identity," Oakeshott says, "and every change is an emblem of extinction."[136] Thus the conservative is one who is "strongly disposed to preserve his identity." And though Oakeshott recognizes the inevitability of change, that "a man's identity (or that of a community) . . . is not a fortress into which we may retire," but must be expressed in continual activity, still that activity is conceived as defensive, to protect the endangered self "against the hostile forces of change."[137]

The image is as interesting for what it omits as for what it says. It does not even allow the possibility that change might also enhance or develop the self, that change is opportunity, that a self without challenges must either invent some or atrophy. Growth *is* a threat to the old self; Oakeshott is not wrong about that. But it is also a source of the new self, and this aspect he totally neglects. Oakeshott says that conservatism is likely to appear in politics wherever the present inheritance is valued but perceived as threatened. Similarly, conservatism is psychologically likely "wherever a firm identity has been achieved, and wherever identity is felt to be precariously balanced."[138] Yet there seems to be an incongruity between the latter two conditions: a firm identity does not always experience change as a threat but sometimes as an opportunity. Oakeshott's image of selfhood is one in which the ego is relatively weak, and only a severe superego keeps passion in check; it is an image of anxiety and defense, in which every novelty is a danger because a temptation, and the very thought of challenging the authority of the past threatens inner stability. Someone who would be self-conscious must first "be certain of his ability to defend" his principles, "for having been brought into the open, they will henceforth be liable to attack."[139]

Accordingly, when Oakeshott considers primary and secondary education—"school education," as he calls it—his attitude toward the children is much like his political attitude toward the mass of the citizenry. Like the mass of ordinary people, school children do not have "anything significant to say," nor any reliable judgment about what is important to them. Hence what is taught in school "must be capable of being learned without any previous recognition of ignorance," and "at school we are, quite properly, not permitted to follow our own inclinations."[140] Oakeshott has no confidence that there might be something in the child's own innermost needs that drives it toward learning, toward growth, and which might be enlisted in the aid of school education. For Oakeshott, what is natural, the real, inner, passionate self, is always resistant and murderous; authority therefore means restraint.[141]

With respect to higher education, Oakeshott gives us two contrasting models: that of training and that of apprenticeship. The former is much like school education, but narrowly specialized. It produces technicians who can apply but not create, who are good at efficient means but do not question goals. But though apprenticeship is meant to contrast with such training, to produce people capable of creating and criticizing independently, yet there is no place in Oakeshott's world for people with this capacity. There is no place for them, at least, outside art and academia, no place in the realm of actions as distinct from thought.

We might put the matter in terms of Jean Piaget's analysis of the development of judgment in children.[142] The small child, though it does not yet (fully) know the substantive content of the rules, practices, institutions that surround it, regards them as timeless. Similarly, it regards its parents as eternal, omniscient, and omnipotent. As it grows older it learns not only the substantive content of its civilization, but also about how rules and practices are established and can be changed by human beings in historical time, human beings like its parents and itself. From this perspective, maturity has to do with becoming aware of one's own role, one's own responsibility in upholding, transmitting, changing, or replacing inherited institutions and values. Maturity means becoming a "master" rather than either an apprentice or a trained technician.

Although Oakeshott is concerned with a form of higher education that will prepare people to become mature masters in the spheres of culture and intellect; in the realm of action, for instance in politics and morality, he prefers that there be no actual living masters, no mature actors at all.[143] In that realm we are *never* to regard our institutions and practices as the historical product of fallible human beings like ourselves; we are never to see our own responsibility, our own choice in relation to those institutions. We are to remain in a lifelong apprenticeship to past generations. As Burke suggested, we are to regard those institutions as if they *were* our parents, our masters to whom we are apprenticed.

Various critics have charged that such a position is fatal to creativity and progress. Neal Wood, for example, in his excellent article on Oakeshott, insists on the vital necessity that at least "sometimes we emancipate ourselves from the past and confront the present in its own terms."[144] But though the criticism of Oakeshott is valid, Wood's way of putting it fails to get at the reason for Oakeshott's position. For a reference to "emancipation" from the past plays directly into Oakeshott's characterization of the Rationalist as someone who (falsely) perceives the past as an oppressive burden. Wood merely reinforces the dichotomy Oakeshott has assumed between the past as an encumbrance constraining us, and the past to be revered and served like a parent. But it is this dichotomy that must be called into question if we are to understand what is missing from Oakeshott's account.

What is missing, in psychoanalytic terms, is any conception of sublimation as distinct from repression, of ego functions, and therefore of genuinely mature mastery. Oakeshott in effect sees only the repressive superego and rebellious id. And if those are the only alternatives, then indeed both civilization and the very existence of a self depend on rejecting the latter and guarding the former against it. Only, there is then no joy in that choice, no real reason for making it; since, conceived that way, the choice can yield no real gratification, can be only duty and never pleasure. Successful sublimation, however, a psyche organized around a strong ego, defies the kind of dichotomization that Oakeshott assumes. It is neither a matter of "obeying" the past, our parents, the superego, nor of "emancipation" from them, but of *being* an integrated self which contains within it those aspects of the past which it values, and uses them to master and change those aspects of past, present, and its own impulses which it does not value. This does mean control of the id, for the sake of real gratification and a developed, individuated self. It does mean restraint, authority, and the internalization of norms, but not as mere duty owed to some external other—rather, as genuinely desired by the integrated self. It is a terrible mistake—though not uncommon today—to identify the real self with the id; the id is not a viable, individuated, developed person at all. As Oakeshott himself indicates, there is a difference between ourselves and our appetites.[145]

It is not easy to express without paradox the relationship we bear to our parents and our past in a condition of maturity so conceived. For, as both Freud and Nietzsche saw, someone who rejects his past (rejects it, that is, *in the wrong way,* denies and represses it) remains its captive. In that sense Oakeshott is right: there is such a thing as the Rationalist who rejects history and claims to construct all anew in the present, to be as it were father to himself, in order to deny his real father. That is surely part of what Oakeshott means when he calls the conception of a "self-made" man or a "self-made" society "idolatry."[146] Using Wood's words we might say that such a person is so busy continually "emancipating" himself from the past, which he nevertheless cannot shed, that he has no energy to spare for "confronting the present in its own terms."

But someone who has genuinely come to terms with his past, with his parents—who has, as Nietzsche would say, successfully "digested" the past, integrating what is valubale to him into his self—such a person can "forget about" the past in a different sense; having remembered and acknowledged it he can then be really through with it and free of it, though it continues in him.[147] He has stopped being either trainee or apprentice and has become a master, free for action.

Sometimes, in his best moments, Oakeshott seems to see this. Sometimes, indeed, he sounds remarkably like Nietzsche, praising "the unself-conscious" morality of aristocrats that is nothing more than their natural "habit of behaviour in relation to one another," handed on through implicit identification, "in a true moral education."[148] Like Nietzsche, too, but also like Hegel and Marx and Freud, Oakeshott is profoundly concerned to produce in us the recognition of who, in particular, we are; the acceptance of our particular history, our particular community, our particular, concrete, historical circumstances *as* our own. "The proper starting place" is "not in the empyrean, but with ourselves as we have come to be."[149] Thus political education, in particular, requires "knowledge, as profound as we can make it, of our tradition of political behaviour" a knowledge specific and concrete, "municipal, not universal."[150]

Unfortunately, like Hegel but unlike the other great teachers of self-knowledge, Oakeshott insists that we recognize and accept the given as necessary not just with respect to our past, but with respect to the future as well (which is to say, with respect to the conduct of our lives in the present). But as Freud saw, insight is to liberate us for action; as Nietzsche urged, the point in "digesting" the past is to free the will for creating a future; as Marx argued, once we understand the world, the point is to change it. For all of them, acceptance of the self and of past history matters because it is a prerequisite for free and effective action in the present, into the future. For Oakeshott, it is cultivated as a substitute for, an avoidance of such action.

VII

In the end, Oakeshott misses or denies what is distinctive about politics, and this failure accounts for most of what is problematic in his thought. His vision omits the very stuff of political life, problematic but essential: power, interest, collective action, conflict. Oakeshott correctly refuses to equate politics with the efficient administration of things, with the acquisitive utilitarian bargaining of "rational economic man," with the domination of masters imposed upon slaves by naked force. But he does want to assimilate politics to the habitual drift of a society or culture that is full of private, piecemeal activity but passive at the collective level and in which no one takes responsibility for the whole. Such a picture is not inaccurate about certain kinds of human endeavor, about language or about art. It may even be a complete and accurate account of the collective, public life of certain societies—say, a relatively isolated tribal group with a simple technology living under highly stable conditions. But of such a tribe we shall want to say precisely that it lacks politics. Political life has to do with precisely those concerns that are made into issues for public action, that are not permitted to drift or emerge from uncoordinated private conduct. Issues like religion, or prices, or race are not by nature, *a priori*, either political or nonpolitical; they are made or become political in certain times and places. And that means that in those times and places they are lifted out of unplanned drift and placed on the political agenda as conscious, collective concerns. And though Oakeshott is right to insist that political action is always undergirded by a prior, inarticulate political culture, still, that culture only undergirds political action. It is not, itself, politics. Oakeshott's political theory rests in reality on the implicit recommendation that we minimize politics as much as possible—ideally that we eliminate it altogether or conduct it in a nonpolitical way, like culture, language, and art.

Thus Oakeshott is, in the last analysis, one of those political theorists, like Plato, who are so deeply concerned about the dangers of power, interest, conflict, that they develop a theory in which those problems are eliminated rather than solved, a theory essentially unpolitical.[151] It is not, then, that Oakeshott is naively unaware of problems of conflict of power; on the contrary, like Plato, he is so much aware and afraid of them that he cannot conceive of any way in which mere human beings could hope to control them. That is the great advantage seemingly offered by tradition: tradition is the hidden, impersonal and impartial force that will take care of these problems for us, while we remain passive and obedient to it—but not really "obedient" either, because tradition has no interests of its own and exercises no coercive power. Tradition can be active without any of the problems of action; in relation to it, human action disappears.

Of course, we are all part of tradition and express it in our activities. Everything that we do is "communal" in the sense of allowing us to promote the "collective interest" of our society and thus fulfill our "duty" to the public.[152] But politics proper, the conscious, deliberate, and collective pursuit of public goals is to be kept minimal, remedial, limited. It is the province of certain specialists called "government"; except for the duty of voting at elections, most people are not and should not be engaged in politics proper.[153] To be sure, the specialists of government should not be narrow, Rationalistic technicians; the pursuit of intimations is an art and requires a humanistic and concretely historical education. As Crick says, Oakeshott always "prefers the connoisseur to the expert."[154] But those who govern are no Burkean aristocracy either; they wield no real power, and their decisions should have no serious or widespread consequences. They look, indeed, rather like the upper ranks of the British civil service: university educated, cultivated, cautious, eminently suited to administer a civilized conversation.

Since politics proper is the restricted province of specialists, it is clear why Oakeshott is anxious to keep its power to a minimum. Why should "we" give "them" any more power to interfere with "our" lives than we absolutely have to? Freedom is the absence of such interference. What he never even considers as an alternative, is a vision in which "we" might actively and collectively govern ourselves, in which politics might be the concern of an entire, self-consciously engaged community, and freedom might consist in shared self-governing rather than protected privacy.

The alternative would be a conception of politics that accepts the reality of conflict, interest, and power, but undertakes to enlist these problematic elements in a continual reconstruction of community. That would be (as Oakeshott himself would insist) a continuing process without resting place or fixed external goal. The participants bring to the process ever newly conflicting purposes and desires, ever shifting alliances and configurations of power. But that need not make the task impossible; on the contrary, the resulting process of conflict can be used to keep alive an awareness of what is at stake, collectively and for each participant. This is the vision of a healthy political life developed by theorists like Tocqueville and Machiavelli: the continual transformation of private need and partial perspective into an enlarged awareness of the whole.

But this cannot be achieved without the engagement of lived experience, of genuine needs, of passion; it cannot be achieved without risk. Oakeshott rejects that risk as unacceptable because he does not think such forces can be controlled or enlisted. It seems clear to me that this is because ultimately Oakeshott believes, like Burke, that the structures of civilization are "illusions," that if people saw through them to the true realities of need and passion and force, those structures could not survive. That is why Oakeshott fails to see that what a "resident magistrate" *can* symbolize to a colonized people depends on the lived realities of what he does and of the context in which he operates. For Oakeshott, ultimately, symbols are all arbitrary; they come to us out of a tradition that we cannot fathom and should not question. It is foolish of the colonized not to accept the (admitted) illusion that the magistrate is a guardian of their liberty; only that illusion or others equally arbitrary make liberty possible.

What Oakeshott never takes seriously as a possibility is that civilization might not necessarily rest on illusions, but partly on the fulfillment of genuine human needs, so that it would be safe and even desirable to challenge those particular beliefs and institutions that are—in a given historical setting—illusions. It does not seem possible to him that the results of such political freedom might ultimately be stronger than any unexamined inheritance.

Reading Oakeshott in America today is a fascinating and ironic experience. On the one hand, he shares much with our own new conservatives: a fear of conflict and a quest for stability, a preference for minimal politics without participation or passion. On the other hand, he would surely be appalled to see a "conservatism" like ours: devoid of all tradition, contemptuous of the society's history, using its traditions of constitutional liberty only as propaganda slogans while readily sacrificing them in the name of law and order. It might well give Oakeshott pause to see how feeble are the alliances that he always takes for granted: between Rationalism and political radicalism or liberalism, between traditionalism and political conservatism. For our neoconservatives, of course, are Rationalists through and through: idolators of the technological, engineering spirit; antihistorical positivists in education and epistemology; bureaucrats in government, truly engaged in "the politics of empiricism" that sells out the future in return for present private profit or hasty accommodation to the latest civil disturbance.

Oakeshott would be disturbed, but one doubts if he could help us much. He might point out that all this is only to be expected in a nation founded in "a specific and express rejection of tradition." Or he might recall us to the Anglo-American traditions of constitutional liberty and self-government that are, after all, our own. But it seems clear that in our time, "recalling" us to such ideas, or any ideas, is not enough. In the end, traditions exist only in people; we *are* our traditions. And if we are concerned to preserve the tradition of free self-government in America —flawed and feeble as it may be—then we shall have to take the responsibility of putting that tradition into action, in relation to the real necessities of people's lives. In the end, as Oakeshott himself would insist, our problems are not his to solve, but ours.

John H. Goldthorpe

Theories of Industrial Society: On the Recrudescence of Historicism and the Future of Futurology

(A slightly revised version of a paper presented at the Seventh World Congress of Sociology at Varna, Bulgaria, September, 1970. I am grateful to Steven Lukes, Ernest Gellner, Andrew Shonfield, Jean Floud, and Michael Young for their comments on the original paper, although I have not been able to take account of them all. J. H. G.)

I

A quarter of a century has now elapsed since Karl Popper published his celebrated critique of historicism.[1] Looking back, this essay can be seen as an important intellectual watershed. Popper regarded himself—and rightly—as engaged in a great battle of ideas, which carried far-reaching sociopolitical implica-

289

tions. His opponents—notably Marxists—would doubtless have defined the situation in a similar way. However, within a few years of the appearance of Popper's essay the battle had begun to wane. Among the large majority of Western, or at least "Anglo-Western," philosophers, historians, and social scientists, the basic antihistoricist position represented by Popper became in effect accepted, even if sometimes with bad grace and no little caviling.[2] And even those individuals or groups who might be supposed still in principle to dissent showed no great eagerness to engage with Popperians on this particular issue. Now it is, thus, widely assumed that, within the mainstream of Western social thought, historicism is discredited and dead.

However, so far at least as the demise of historicism is concerned, such an assumption is open to question. In this paper, I wish initially to show that, during the last ten to fifteen years, there has in fact emerged *within "orthodox" Western social science* an important new strain of thinking of a historicist, or of what might be termed "crypto-historicist" character.[3] By crypto-historicist thinking, I mean that which, on analysis, can be shown to rest upon historicist assumptions or claims, even though historicist arguments may not be openly advanced or may be actually disavowed. This recrudescence of historicism, it would seem, has been rarely recognized in its full significance; yet it is a phenomenon that calls for serious critical attention. In particular, I shall seek, in the latter part of the paper, to examine its relationship with, and possible implications for, the now rapidly growing field of "future studies."[4] In its new forms as in its older ones, historicist thinking can readily have consequences that go far beyond scientific and scholarly debate; and awareness of this potential would seem no less desirable now than hitherto.

It has been objected to Popper's attack on historicism that he has brought together under this label a number of different tendencies in social thought, which have no necessary connection with each other and may not even show any great propensity to be empirically associated. Such a charge could in some degree be substantiated. However, it must at the same time be acknowledged that Popper makes it clear enough what he takes as being the core of *all* historicist positions. Before attempting his comprehensive characterization of historicism he states plainly: "It will be enough if I say here that I mean by 'historicism' an approach to the social sciences which assumes that *historical prediction* is their principal aim, and which assumes that this aim is attainable by discovering the 'rhythms' or the 'patterns' the 'laws' or the 'trends' that underlie the evolution of history."[5] This formula would seem to require elaboration, in the light of the fuller discussion that follows it, in only two important respects. First, the predictions that historicists advance are to be recognized as ones of a relatively imprecise kind which do not attempt to provide exact and detailed statements about the course of future events.[6] Second, it is to be regarded as an integral part of historicist thinking that the view taken of the necessary lines of future social change becomes the basis for critical evaluations of the present state of society and for present forms of sociopolitical action: "Only such plans as fit in with the main current of history can be effective. . . . Only such activities are reasonable as fit in with, and help along, the impending changes."[7]

An understanding of "historicism" on the lines of the foregoing may then be adopted for present purposes without, I would hope, there being serious ambiguity.

II

The Poverty of Historicism is written from a distinctive, liberal standpoint. It may be recognized as falling within a well-established tradition of thought which dates back at least to Max Weber: one which proposes a basic affinity between the principles of liberal social philosophy and those of scientific inquiry; which is hostile to any form of "theoretical history" or "holism"; and which, above all, rejects any associated idea of a set of objectively correct and consistent values whose realization constitutes the ultimate goal of human society.[8] However, in the recent past, one of the most notable developments within Western social thought has been the emergence of a new kind of liberalism: one which would appear to diverge from—and offend against—many of the canons of the old, and to do so, to put the matter shortly, by drawing less on the intellectual legacy of Max Weber than on that of Herbert Spencer or indeed on that of Marx himself.[9] It is chiefly in the form of this new "evolutionary" liberalism, I wish to argue, that historicist thinking has been revived.

The origins of this somewhat paradoxical development are undoubtedly complex. Nevertheless, at the intellectual level, a pivotal idea can readily be identified: that of "industrial society." During the early 1950s this idea was advanced, notably by Raymond Aron, with a primarily *critical* intent: to emphasize, as against Marxist doctrine, the important structural and cultural features that all economically advanced societies have in common, regardless of whether the means of production are privately owned or under state control. That is to say, the argument that industrialization has certain "imperatives" was in this instance used to *attack* the notion of a unilinear course of societal evolution following upon changes in the economic infrastructure.[10] However, within a remarkably short period of time, the idea of industrial society had taken on a quite different significance. Extended and elaborated, it became itself the basis of theories designed, it would seem, to *rival* that of the Marxists in both their evolutionary cast and often too in their emphasis on the determining force of technological and economic organization.

One imeetus in this direction was given by the reawakening of interest among non-Marxist economists in the possibility of identifying "stages" of economic growth, linked to each other in some determinate sequence—the work of Rostow having a particular impact.[11] Another major influence was that of American structural-functional sociology, at its apogee in the 1950s. In the hands of American writers, the concept of "imperatives" of industrialization was developed into the far more ambitious one of a pervasive and compelling "logic" of industrial society. Thus, in the theories which were propounded, economic and associated technological advance typically constituted the dynamic element, while the nature of the successive consequences of this advance, and of the prerequisites of its continuance, were seen as defined by the operation of certain universal, functional exigencies.

Given, then, this basic structure, a direct implication for the content of the theories in question was the following: that as world industrialization proceeded and societies became increasingly alike in having modern economies, they should become increasingly alike also in the pattern of their social institutions and social life generally. In this way, there emerged the thesis of the progressive "convergence" of industrial societies on one particular model or type: namely, that possessing the structural and cultural characteristics, which would give the best "degree of fit" with the inherent requirements of industrialism, which, in other words, would most perfectly embody the logic it demanded. If such a model was not at the present time actually represented by any existing society, it nonetheless defined the pattern that the future would follow.

The details of the convergence thesis—that is, the forms of work organization, family and community structure, social stratification, political and governmental institutions, etc., which are proposed as being those of the future—are by now fairly familiar, and need not, I hope, be rehearsed. For present purposes it may suffice to say that what, in sum, is depicted is the *ideal type* of the "managed" and "modernized," "open" and "affluent" capitalist society of the Western world. The doubts and objections that have been raised by critics on this score are many and, in my view, serious;[12] but what I wish to concentrate attention on here, and what has, I believe, been hitherto neglected, is the general nature and aims of the theories in question and, specifically, their historicist features.

The fact that the antihistoricist arguments of the old liberalism have not been brought more sharply to bear on the evolutionism of the new liberalism is a somewhat puzzling one. Exponents of the convergence thesis, it is true, have often disavowed any intention of trying to revert to the unilinear, strongly deterministic and value-laden evolutionism of the nineteenth century; and it may be that these disavowals have simply been accepted at face value. Or again, it is possible that new forms of "theoretical history" have not been sufficiently distinguished from—and indeed have been camouflaged by —attempts merely at establishing "sequential propositions" of a quite empirical kind. A number of sociologists claiming to adopt an "evolutionary" perspective have in fact sought to do no more than advance generalizations of this order—against which, of course, a charge of historicism would be quite inapplicable.[13]

However, the aim of "convergence" theorists is essentially different. No matter how obliquely or coyly it is expressed, it is in effect to make historical predictions, even if of a rather imprecise character, and then to use these as the basis for a critical evaluation of current social situations, activities, movements and aspirations. In short, all the hallmarks of historicism are there.

This claim can best be demonstrated by considering at some length the two most highly developed versions of the new liberal interpretation of industrial society thus far produced: those of Clark Kerr and Talcott Parsons. In the theoretical formulations of these authors are incorporated most of the partial versions of the convergence thesis that have been advanced by various other writers. In addition, fixing attention on these two contributions has the advantage of revealing such differences in viewpoint and emphasis as exist within evolutionary liberalism as a result of differing degrees of influence from the two main sources of inspiration already noted; namely, the Marxian and the Spencerian.

What for present purposes is of chief significance in Kerr's writing on the development of industrial societies is his quite explicit emphasis on a "logic" of industrialism, which operates with increasing rigor as technological and economic advance continue. Kerr is not concerned merely to trace evolutionary trends *post factum* but, further, to account for these trends theoretically in terms of *the limited responses that are possible* to certain functional problems intrinsic to industrial growth. He acknowledges that "in the actual course of history the inherent tendencies of the industrial process are not likely, at least for a very long time, to be fully realized . . ."; also, that "the actual course of events . . . is never likely to create the precise society constructed by deduction." Nonetheless, he maintains, "the pure industrial society" is a meaningful abstraction: all economically advancing societies must respond to its logic, and with progressively increasing strictness.[14]

Kerr states openly that his approach here is directly modeled on that of Marx in seeking to apply deductive methods to long-run economic and social processes (as well as in his stress on technology and economic organization as determinants of social structure and culture). At the same time, he claims that he diverges from Marx not only in envisaging the mode of change within industrial societies as being evolutionary rather than revolutionary, but also in adopting a multilinear rather than a unilinear conception of the course of change.[15] This might seem to suggest that, in looking to the future, Kerr would reject Marx's idea of "one destination" for humanity, and that he would discern possibilities for the development of a variety of types of advanced society. Such an impression is strengthened by Keer's further claim that the comments he makes on the future are offered "neither as a manifesto nor as sure prediction"[16]—thus, apparently, implying that he recognizes considerable indeterminacy. However, in the actual substance of Kerr's interpretation of industrialism, these indications are effectively belied. The diversity within the industrializing process which he emphasises turns out to be, evident in the *relatively early stages*—in Rostovian language—that of "the break with traditionalism," "take-off," and "the drive to maturity."[17] And when the question arises of "the road ahead"—for already advanced, as well as developing, societies—Kerr's views of the logic of industrialism is in fact such as to force him, willy-nilly, away from a multilinear and toward a unilinear perspective: or, to be more precise, to force him to see hitherto clearly different processes of industrialization as becoming progressively similar in their sociocultural correlates. As industrialism advances and becomes increasingly a worldwide phenomenon, then, Kerr argues, the range of viable institutional structures and of viable systems of value and belief is necessarily reduced. All societies, whatever the path by which they entered the industrial world, will tend to approximate, even if asymptotically, the pure industrial form.[18]

Kerr describes the general character of the society on which evolutionary trends are thus convergent as "pluralistic." That is to say, it is one in which a highly differentiated structure creates a multiplicity of "interests" typically represented by pressure groups and associations and in which, therefore, economic and political power is dispersed and disputed rather than being monopolized by a single class or party. The future society is, moreover, destined to have two other basic features. First, it will be "an organization society"; one in which the individual's set of organizational memberships will crucially pattern his public life, and in which the managers, administrators, and technical experts who run organizations will be the new men of power. Increasingly, the basis of power will be knowledge, rather than economic resources or political office. Second, though, the future society will also be a liberal one. Founded on freedom of association, it will offer, within the limits set by bureaucratic regulation, the greatest possible degree of individual freedom in all other respects. Outside the organizational embrace, the "new bohemianism" will flower; men will enjoy a large measure of "inner freedom" and "private space."[19]

Such a society is, in Kerr's view, that which will respond most exactly to the demands imposed by the logic of industrialism. This argument he is prepared to uphold point by point, and it is essentially on this basis that he regards liberal pluralism as being the sociopolitical system that is destined to succeed. History, as shaped by the logic of industrialism, is on its side. It is true that from time to time Kerr writes also in a seemingly voluntaristic vein—for example: "Chance may elude men, but choice need not; and the choice of men, within fairly broad limits, can shape history. To predict the future with any accuracy, men must choose their future."[20] But in fact for Kerr choice, at this level at least, is merely epiphenomenal. For it is *part of* the logic of industrialism that the choice of the majority—of what Kerr calls the "inner-society"—*should be in favor of* liberal pluralism. In the actual experience of industrialism, he argues, men accumulate knowledge about what are the "realistic alternatives." As part of the evolutionary process, unworkable "utopian" possibilities are eliminated and only the feasible ones survive. This is because "an industrialised society is such a complicated mechanism with such interdependence of its parts that keeping it going without major disruption becomes an overriding concern." The result then is that "industrial man is seldom faced with real ideological alternatives within his society."[21] In other words, even if he does seek to choose his own future, he can do little other than opt for the "way ahead" that is historically correct—or be doomed, as a representative of an "outer-element" of society, to disillusionment and failure.[22]

To bring in choice the way in which Kerr does is not to avoid historical determinism but, if anything, to make it more complete. And what is chiefly significant is that nothing Kerr has to say about choice prevents him from discussing other sociopolitical systems, which might be thought alternatives to liberal pluralism, entirely in terms of their doubtful survival value (if they are ones that presently exist) or of the impossibility of realizing them (if they are ones projected for the future). Not only are all questions of moral desirability eschewed but, further, any serious consideration of the extent to which a social regime may "succeed" simply through political will and force. Moreover, even within the functionalist frame of reference that Kerr adopts, there is little argument at an empirical level about why—under precisely what conditions and by what processes —particular systems must fail or prove incapable of being instituted or, on the other hand, could conceivably prove viable. The key propositions advanced tend to be of a different type. For example socialism is said to be now "historically exhausted"; having played its part in the early evolution of industrialism, its prescriptions are now irrelevant to the facts of industrial society in its modern phase. Or again, while syndicalism "may find its historic destiny in partial solutions," it cannot, it is held, succeed in full; essentially conservative and instinctive, it can survive, if at all, only in muted form "as against the outside forces in society and the pressures of change." Or finally, Communism faces the threat of extinction because "the gulf between the *status quo* and the new evolutionary movement is now the greatest in communist-run societies"—because, that is, the Party leaderships still seek to concentrate power in their own hands, despite the inevitable trend toward the restructuring of the real bases of power on a pluralistic pattern.[23] It is, I would suggest, in contentions of this kind that the historicist character of Kerr's thinking is most clearly revealed, and his disclaimers are shown to be merely perfunctory.

The interpretation of industrial society offered by Talcott Parsons differs from that of Kerr chiefly in being part of a quite comprehensive approach to the problem of social evolution, and one which is "pronaturalistic" in an overt—indeed, aggressive—manner.[24] Parsons attributes the development of his own, relatively recent, interest in an evolutionary perspective to advances in biology which, he claims, "have generated altogether new conceptions of the fundamental continuity between general organic evolution and socio-cultural evolution."[25] Thus, the Spencerian enterprise of creating a *general* evolutionary theory can now in fact be revived, and with less necessity than even Spencer recognized to treat evolutionary processes in the organic and sociocultural spheres as separate and distinct.

For Parsons, the key phenomenon in both aspects of evolution alike is that of *adaptation:* the capacity of a living system to "cope with" its environment not only by adjusting to it but, further, by establishing some degree of control over it. It is, moreover, adaptation that provides a basic criterion of evolutionary advance. Those systems—organisms or societies—which display the greatest generalized adaptive capacity can be regarded as those which have progressed furthest along the evolutionary path or scale. Parsons is clear that "to be an evolutionist, one must define a general trend in evolution"; thus, the evolutionary sociologist "cannot be a radical cultural relativist who regards the Arunta of Australia and such modern societies as the Soviet Union as equally authentic "cultures," to be judged as equals in *all basic* respects."[26]

However, merely postulating an evolutionary scale, related to adaptive capacity, does not in itself enable systems to be hierarchically arranged. What is also necessary is some set of stage marks, by reference to which the place of any given system on the scale can actually be determined. In this connection, Parsons introduces the notion of "evolutionary universals." An evolutionary universal is defined as an organizational complex "which so increases the long-run adaptive capacity of living systems in a given class that only systems that develop the complex can attain certain higher levels of adaptive capacity."[27] In the organic sphere, Parsoss suggests *vision* as a good illustration. Thus, since organizational features of the kind in question have such evolutionary importance, it is likely that, rather then emerging only once, they will be "hit on" by various systems operating under different conditions. Moreover, in sociocultural evolution, in contrast with organic evolution, their development can be, and regularly has been, extended through processes of *diffusion,* in addition to those of independent innovation. In

Parsons' view, it is then possible to order human societies in terms of the evolutionary universals which they have thus far embodied in their structural and cultural patterns. As special cases, one must note those societies which have in fact failed to maintain a continuous advance through the stages that the evolutionary universals define. These are either societies that have already been historically eliminated "by the socio-cultural version of the negative aspect of natural selection" or ones —such as the societies studied by anthropologists—which have established themselves in "niches" that have enabled them to survive for long periods in a primitive state.[28]

Arguments on these lines in themselves point to the fact that Parsons' ultimate objective is that of producing "theoretical history"—despite the modest remarks that he has usually attached to his writings on social evolution thus far. Like Kerr, one observes, he is not content merely to establish trends of social development empirically, nor yet to account systematically for the pattern simply of *past* occurrences in the manner of *histoire raisonnée*. Rather, it would seem, he is in search of an understanding of the "evolutionary movement" as a whole, and one that will enable him to gain a grasp on the future.[29] When one turns to Parsons' observations that are specifically concerned with the course of further development in societies already relatively advanced, such an interpretation of his goal is amply confirmed.

For instance, one pair of evolutionary universals that Parsons sees as necessary developments for societies on the threshold of industrialism and "modernity" are bureaucratic administration and the "money and market" complex.[30] The model of bureaucracy that Parsons presents is an unmodified Weberian one, and, he writes, "The basis on which I classify bureaucracy as an evolutionary universal is very simple. As Weber said, it is the most effective large-scale administrative organization that man has invented, and there is no direct substitute for it."[31] In other words, bureaucracy, in this particular—nineteenth-century —form, is represented as an unconditional imperative of evolutionary progress, destined to be adopted by all societies modernizing now or at some later time. Similarly, money and markets are seen as an evolutionary universal because they provide the most efficient means of economic exchange and utilization of resources. Parsons notes that "Modern socialist societies may appear to be exceptional here because, up to a point, they achieve high productivity with a relatively minimal reliance on monetary and market mechanisms, substituting bureaucracy for them." He also recognizes "the strong tendency for developing societies to adopt a "socialistic' pattern." Nevertheless, he still maintains that the superior adaptive advantages of the money and market complex are not to be denied. At least in the long run, serious "negative consequences" must stem from such "socialistic" deviations; and these will then, presumably, lead to the societies in question being at some point or other brought back on to the correct evolutionary course.[32]

In much the same way as Kerr, then, Parsons sees the range of possible social structural and cultural variation narrowing down as the higher levels of evolutionary advance are attained—as successive evolutionary universals are superimposed upon each other. Furthermore, he also shares Kerr's view that among the advanced societies of the present day it is those of the Communist world which are most "out of line" in their developmental pattern—because insufficiently pluralized—and which are therefore those scheduled to experience the most radical changes in the period ahead. This presumption is made quite overt when Parsons proposes as the final and "highest" evolutionary universal in his schema that of "the democratic association with elective leadership and fully enfranchised membership.[33]

Just as bureaucracy and money and markets are for Parsons the most effective organizational forms in regard to basic administrative and economic functions, so is democracy—on the Western model—the structural and cultural complex with the greatest adaptive value in the political sphere. In advanced societies, Parsons argues, political effectiveness requires that power be exercized both on a large scale and flexibly. This in turn means that in such societies power must depend overwhelmingly upon *consensus*, and "no institutional form basically different from the democratic association" is able not only to give general legitimacy to political power but, further, to *"mediate consensus in its exercise* by particular persons and groups and in the formation of particular binding policy decisions."[34] Having made this assertion, Parsons is in fact quite frank about the implications that it carries: "I realize," he writes, "that to take this position I must maintain that communist totalitarian organization will probably not fully match 'democracy' in political and integrative capacity in the long run"; and, he goes on, "I do indeed predict that it will prove to be unstable. . . ." In other words, Parsons again presents a situation in which "negative consequences," and thus evolutionary check or indeed regression, are inevitable, until such time as deviant organizational features are appropriately adjusted; that is, in the case in question, until changes occur "in the general direction of electoral democracy and a plural party system."[35] In the evolutionary perspective that Parsons adopts, the same set of criteria which require that the society of the Arunta be adjudged inferior to that of the Soviet Union require in turn that Soviet society be placed on a lower level than that of the United States.[36]

From the foregoing, it may be observed that for Parsons' analysis, as for Kerr's, the industrially developed societies of the Communist world pose a quite crucial issue, and one that tends to give rise to historical prediction as a logical extension of the analysis and as a necessary means of preserving its integrity. Furthermore, before leaving this consideration of evolutionary liberalism, one may note that the matter of the future of Communist society also affords perhaps the clearest indication that Kerr and Parsons cannot be regarded as idiosyncratic in their general outlook. Among American, and other, social scientists with liberal political commitments, predictions concerning the ultimate incompatibility of industrialism and "monistic" regimes have been almost commonplace in the recent past. While from the Soviet side claims of the inevitable triumph of world Communism have been made with declining frequency and conviction, in the West a new "high tide of prophecy" has risen, foretelling the collapse of systems of the Soviet type and claiming to lay bare the historic links between this outcome and the march of technological and economic progress. The nature of these links has in fact been only broadly indicated and has not, even then, been a matter of entire agreement.[37] Nonetheless, there can be no doubting the widespread appeal of the view that political modernity can be equated with the development of democracy on the Western model and that the persistence of, or any tendency toward other forms of political organization represent retardation or distortion of the evolutionary process.[38]

III

Enough, I hope, has now been said to show that theories of industrial society, of the kind represented by the work of Kerr and Parsons, embody significant, if sometimes covert, historicist elements. The inspiration of such theories lies in nineteenth-century attempts to comprehend the totality of the historical, or social evolutionary, process. However, it is at the same time important to note that in one respect at least these theories are characteristically of the present day: that is, in what could be called their *technocratic* emphasis. This is revealed in two different, though closely related, ways. First, it is evident that in so far as the new theories of industrial society seek to identify a particular group or stratum as the key social agency of the future development of industrialism, it is invariably the scientists, technologists, and managers who are picked out. It is they who are seen as destined to bring the new or the "post" industrial society into being. Second, when exponents of the theories in question come to treat the crucial issue of the functional exigencies of advancing industrialism (whether in terms of an inherent "logic" or "adaptive capacity," or whatever) it is clear that the main criterion for the survival value of any institutional arrangement is in fact that of its technical rationality—from the point of view of combining material progress with social order and stability. For, as we have seen, the central problem for the future of any modern industrial society (assuming that it is not seriously out of evolutionary line) is defined simply as that of—to quote Kerr—"Keeping it going without major disruption."[39] In other words, the ultimate goal of industrial societies is taken as given: to maintain economic advance on the basis of a dynamic science and technology, while adjusting the existing social system *ad hoc*, as the requirements and consequences of this advance unfold, and sufficiently to contain social dissensus and conflict to a manageable level. "Industrial society," Kerr writes, "must be

administered; and the administrators become increasingly benevolent and increasingly skilled. They learn to respond where
response is required; to anticipate the inevitable." But "the new
realism is essentially conservative. The *status quo* is changed only
gradually. 'Balance' must be maintained."[40]

There is thus one important and inescapable implication of a
political character: namely, that the stuff of politics, both
theoretical and practical, is effectively reduced to questions of an
instrumental kind—to questions, that is, of a kind that may be
appropriately determined by the "technocracy" without their
discussion in public or even their full communication to the
public. The crucial questions are defined as ones that require
special expertise for their proper comprehension. Questions of
a quite different order which concern the *ends* of political
action—the nature of the good society, the good life, etc.—tend
in this perspective to be given only a minor residual role or
indeed to more or less disappear: for within advanced industrial
society "real ideological alternatives" cannot exist.[41] It follows in
turn, then, that participation in the democratic process must, for
the mass of the population, necessarily be of a decidedly restricted and indirect kind. It becomes in effect limited to joining
in organized groups which can seek, via their own officials and
experts, to influence key decision-makers; and to periodic voting on alternative sets of national political "leaders," who will
tend increasingly to bid for electoral support on the grounds of
their superior technical or "managerial" competence.[42]

It can, therefore, scarcely be questioned that the new technocratic historicism is little less politically committed than were the
historicist doctrines of the nineteenth century. The most significant difference is that while the latter aimed for the most part
to provide legitimation for "extremist" positions, whether of a
laissez-faire or revolutionary character, the politics of technocratic historicism are those of the center—of "moderation,"
"gradualism," and "piecemeal social reform": ironically, very
much the politics advocated by Popper, and those who followed
him, as an extension of their critique of historicism in its earlier,
more dramatic forms.[43]

However, the force of these critiques still remains and they can
be turned with equally decisive effect against the new historicism

as against the old. To set out the full range of relevant arguments would be excessive, but three points would seem worth making with respect both to the previous discussion of evolutionary liberalism and to the remarks which will directly follow on the matter of "future studies."

First, such notions as that of a "structure of history" or of an "evolutionary movement," as utilized by Kerr, Parsons, and others, must be regarded as highly dubious ones on methodological grounds alone. If these notions are intended to imply that the course of history is shaped by certain invariant regularities or "principles" which it is possible to comprehend in the form of a scientific theory, then, as Popper has cogently argued,[44] a basic misunderstanding of the nature of science is revealed. The objectives of scientific inquiry may properly be *either* theoretical *or* historical—but not both simultaneously. The history of man and of human society—a unique and total process—cannot, as such, be the subject of a scientific theory, since the concern of any such a theory is with *recurrent relationships* between *particular aspects* of phenomena which are analytically distinguished. In other words, no scientific means exists of arriving at an understanding of historical development "as a whole," such that its unfolding to date may be systematically explained and its future course predicted[45]: in science, predictions are conditional statements. Thus, if ideas of structure or of evolutionary movement in history are not to be dismissed as quite inappropriate, they must be construed far more modestly; that is, as pointing simply to the fact that, within the historical record, "stages," "patterns," "trends," or other regularities are *empirically* identifiable. In this case, no great objection can be raised—but it has then to be clearly recognized that the formulae in question are no longer ones which can even pretend to offer some special insight into what the future holds. There is no compelling reason why sequences of events discerned in the past, purely as a matter of fact, should be projected into the future; and establishing such sequences offers no grounds whatsoever for daunting claims that "history" or "evolution" require or favor the success of any particular institutions, ideas, movements, etc. What, at best, may be offered are simply speculations, which are in some rather indeterminate way historically and sociologically "based," but which cannot claim to be "knowledge" or to possess any moral or political cogency.

Second, exponents of evolutionary liberalism are also vulnerable to the charge, forcefully directed against earlier evolutionary sociologists, that they provide no explicit analysis of *why*—via what causal mechanisms—historical events have followed the course that is observed in the past, and will follow that which is anticipated for the future. For example, when Kerr refers to the "logic" of industrialism or Parsons to "adaptation," in order to account for a particular aspect of social change, neither manages to explain why the social actors through whose agency the change occurs *should* act in such ways, and with such outcomes, that the functional exigencies in question are in fact met. We are, for instance, left usually uninformed about how, if at all, these exigencies come to be represented in the actors' own definitions of the situation; or about the extent to which, and by whom, "solutions" are purposively sought. In other words, we are given no clear indication of the nature of the *connection* between the immediate historical world, in which individuals and groups pursue their interests, uphold their beliefs, exercise their power, etc., and the emergence of the theoretically intelligible regularities that are postulated.[46] What, it would seem, we are invited to suppose is that the structure of social action, and the values and motives involved in this, are in fact largely epiphenomenal to the functioning of social systems in the course of their evolution. Thus, given that through a theory of social evolution we can hope to comprehend this latter process directly, we need not, as macrosociologists, pay much heed to, as it were, its detailed working-out in innumerable particular instances. However, the obvious comment here is that at least until the *idea* of a theory of social evolution has been rehabilitated, as against arguments of the kind already noted, such a position is not one that can command any great intellectual respect.

Third, it may be objected against the new historicism, no less than against the old, that it entails a striking failure, or deliberate restriction, of the imagination. One manifestation of this is in its ethnocentrism. It has often been remarked how the great social theorists of the nineteenth century tended to regard their own societies as being in the van of the historical movement which they discerned—if not, indeed, as standing on the threshold of the millennium. In quite similar fashion, as we have already observed, liberal "convergence" theorists of the present day envisage the "pure form" of industrial society, on which the process of convergence is focused, as in fact the ideal-type of Western, democratic capitalism. The possibility of the emergence of a range of different types of an advanced or postindustrial society, with highly variable structural and cultural forms, is not seriously contemplated. Furthermore, there follows from this position not only a tendency to view present-day society with a blandness and optimism that, to others, is often staggering, but also the tendency previously noted to seek to dismiss aspirations and programs that stem from different perspectives solely on the grounds that they are incompatible with the way in which history or social evolution is destined to go. That is to say, on the basis of a historicist position which is not defended (or even perhaps acknowledged), the attempt is often made to rule out of court ideals and ideas which could point to genuine sociological and historical alternatives, and which, if more widely propagated and recognized, could significantly extend the range of effective sociopolitical choice.

IV

The evolutionary conceptions of history characteristic of the nineteenth century may be seen as representing one phase, one modality, in the long record of man's attempts to gain some grasp on his own future. In the course of the twentieth century, confidence in such an approach waned as a result both of its lack of predictive success and of the increasingly cogent attacks that were launched on its underlying rationale. What we may regard as the modern phase in future studies began, in fact, in important part as a direct reaction against historicist methodology.

For example, Ossip Flechtheim, arguing already in the late 1940s for the development of "futurology" as a form of applied, empirical social science, was centrally concerned to set the aims and methods of futurology in opposition to those of the writers who produced the theodicies, philosophies of history, and evolutionary schemata of the past.[47] Bertrand de Jouvenel, in presenting the first collection of *"futuribles"*—or "studies in conjecture"—prepared by his associates, has stressed that these authors do not pretend to any *knowledge* of the future, that they reject the assumption that the future is already "given," and that they believe that "what shall be depends upon our choices."[48] Daniel Bell, in his introduction to Kahn and Wiener's massive compilation, *The Year 2000,* distinguishes sharply between modern future studies and earlier, "more apocalyptic modes of thought," and emphasizes that what is now the objective is not to predict the future "as if this were some far-flung rug of time unrolled to some distant point" but rather to sketch "alternative futures" which can inform choice and indicate the likely "costs and consequences" of different desires.[49] In effect, what is being affirmed in all these cases, and in other similar ones that one could cite, is acceptance of a certain set of tenets that are diametrically antihistoricist in character: namely, that theoretical history is impossible; that scientific predictions are different in kind from so-called historic predictions—which are better described as prophecy; that all propositions about the "historic" future should be highly conditional; and that whether or not future "probabilities" or "possibilities" are realized depends crucially upon human action.

In the growing volume of current work that actually essays some form of conjecture about the future, it would be hard to find examples of any of the above tenets being openly rejected or blatantly contravened. At the level of overt argument, historicist positions are as little upheld in the study of the future as in the study of the past. Nevertheless, what I wish to suggest, in what is to follow, is that in covert, subtle but important ways historicist influences often do continue to work upon future studies; and that this is so if for no other reason than that the antihistoricist position, even if accepted intellectually, has not yet become completely "internalized," and has not yet managed to condition totally the stance that is adopted toward the future. In particular, I wish to argue that the influence of the technocratic historicism, manifest in the theories of industrial society previously reviewed, is a discernible and deleterious one on present-day future research, especially that carried on in the United States or guided by American models.

The first observation that is relevant to my argument is that in current future studies there is a clear concentration on *technological and economic forecasting.*[50] There are indeed a number of good reasons why this should be so. Techniques in this area are relatively well-developed; the chances of success, at least with shorter-term forecasts, are relatively high; and there are obvious commercial, policy-making, and other practical pay-offs. However, what is of concern is not that such forecasting is extensively carried on but rather the predominance which it tends to assume over the field as a whole, and not only in terms of the share of available resources that it commands.

Technological and economic changes can both be taken as involving what de Jouvenel has called "processes" in contradistinction to "action": that is, successions of events which, while resulting from human actions, do not necessarily represent the particular outcome that was consciously sought by any one actor. Processes may therefore be described and discussed "as though they fell within the provinces of the physical sciences"—they may be regarded as having their own dynamic which is in important degree independent of human choice and intention.[51] Thus, in this case, forecasting via the analysis and extrapolation of trends—together with attempts to anticipate discontinuities[52]—may be regarded as an appropriate futurological procedure. However, the disturbing tendency is for forecasting on this pattern to become accepted as *the standard* method of future studies, and then further, through the not unfamiliar sequence of preferred methods determining problems, for such studies to become still more generally committed to a concern with processes. Correspondingly, what should be the balancing concern—with the way in which *social actions can impinge upon processes* to speed, check, divert them, etc.—is neglected: attempts at forecasting what the future *will* be, become quite preponderant over attempts at envisaging what the future *could* be.[53] Where such an imbalance exists, talk of "alternative futures" and of enlarging the range of choice is empty; and, more seriously, the way is left open for what de Jouvenel calls the "predisposition towards unique predictions"—that is, a historicist predisposition—to reassert itself.[54]

Moreover, the emphasis on technological and economic forecasting has substantive as well as methodological significance. In those cases where attempts *have* been made to go beyond forecasting of this kind and to consider the future of social structural and cultural forms, the position has still been usually taken that the examination of likely technological and economic trends is the best starting point for these more ambitious conjectures. Insofar as such trends are in fact more "predictable" than most others, such an approach would seem a reasonable one. But what would appear to happen is that what starts as simply a strategy of inquiry often turns implicitly into a sociological theory or indeed into a theory of history. That is to say, built into the analyses that are offered, there comes to be the assumption that processes of technological and economic change are the key dynamic—or alternatively constraining—forces within modern societies; and further, perhaps, that they are the crucial "independent variables" determining the evolution of sociocultural systems. In this way, then, the influence of the theories of industrialism earlier examined becomes most clearly manifest, even while adherence to such theories, or to any historicist position, may be denied.

As one indication of this, one might note the number of similarities that exist between say, the major features of the future industrial society as delineated by Kerr and either Daniel Bell's model of the "post-industrial" society or the "basic long-term multifold trend" of societal change that Kahn and Wiener see as rooted in the history of the West and as "likely to continue"—and to become "increasingly universal"—at least for the remainder of the present century.[55] To be sure, neither Bell nor Kahn and Wiener are prepared to underwrite the convergence argument in all its claims: they stress the possibility of important variations on the themes that they project. And indeed if the similarities in question were all that were involved, one might readily accept that their adoption of "macro-historical" or evolutionary perspectives is, as sometimes pleaded, no more than a heuristic device.[56] However, running through the major programs of American future studies, in which Bell and Kahn have played leading roles, one can trace at least three further tendencies in which affinities with "technocratic historicism" are revealed.

(i) Despite the emphasis usually placed in prolegomena to these studies on widening the range of choice, the part given to the expression of values and to changes in values in conceivably determining the course of social development tends in fact to be often minimized. For example, while major weight is attached to technological and economic advance as being, as it were, the pace-setter of social change, the potential importance of shifts in values which are in some degree independent of this advance appears to be generally neglected. Most notably an assumption of a large proportion of the attempted conjectures is that the level of commitment to economic *growth*—and to the application of science and technology to this end—which prevails in present-day societies will continue into the future more or less unchanged. But this assumption, of course, itself entails a conjecture, and one for which alternatives seem to have been little considered even though there are some that are fairly apparent. For instance, it could be envisaged that at some future point in some societies, economic growth might be subordinated as a policy objective to such other economic goals as a more equal distribution of real income or the improvement of resource allocation in the interests of better environmental conditions, better public amenities, etc. Social forecasters may perhaps wish to set only a low degree of "subjective probability" on these alternatives. Nonetheless, as a number of economists are now insisting, they do represent possibilities which *could* be realized, given the political will to do so.[57] And, as such possibilities, they ought surely to be of central interest within any program of work in which a concern for revealing the full range of effective choice is genuine.[58] One might indeed add that if a fairly radical change in the publicly recognized goals of economic life *were* to occur, then a change would presumably occur also in the "functional exigencies" of industrial society and thus in the pattern of constraints and possibilities that its logic imposes.[59] That such an eventuality has not been seriously explored strongly suggests a propensity to think of such a logic as being in some way *immanent*—part, that is, of a total evolutionary process in which values, choices, and human actions are all absorbed.[60]

(ii)   While the ultimate objective of the future studies in question is usually represented as being that of envisaging alternative possible futures, another interpretation of their purpose is sometimes given which is significantly different and which, moreover, appears in practice to predominate: that is, to envisage the *social problems* that may be associated with technological and economic change, and to consider the kinds of social arrangements that will be most adequate to dealing with them.[61] In this latter conception, futurology is obviously given a more restricted, less adventurous role. In fact, one commentator has gone so far as to suggest that "much of the futurist literature, when it touches on specifically sociological issues—as distinct from technological change—is really not much more than a rhetorical stance for discussing *present* social problems."[62] To the extent, then, that future studies are oriented toward in effect the "managing" of social change—and it would be difficult to deny that this *is* a considerable extent—their major importance would seem to be for Kerr's increasingly benevolent, skilled, and responsive administrators whose task it is to keep modern industrial societies free from major disruption; or to shift to Parsonian terminology, their main function might be said to be that of increasing "adaptive capacity." What is to be adapted *to* is the basic trend of technological and economic development which is taken virtually as given—but which one may attempt to forecast; and what has to be adapted—though always in piecemeal fashion and while avoiding disruption—is the existing social order at any particular time.[63] It has, of course, been more than once pointed out that the language of "social problems," while seemingly commonsensical and down-to-earth, involves some large, and from an antihistoricist standpoint, often highly questionable assumptions: for example, that one can conceive of some ultimate state of normalcy or social "health" on which general moral consensus or objective agreement is possible, and by reference to which "problems" can be identified; or that some "correct" course for social development can be determined which can indicate how problems may be avoided or the direction in which adaptation should be sought. However, in the case in point, it would seem that such assumptions are accepted, or at least not strenuously examined, chiefly in order that a technocratic stance can be maintained. If a situation can be defined as a social problem, then the question that tends automatically to follow is that of what can be done to remedy or alleviate it; that is, a question of means, of techniques. One may thus hope to avoid such more basic, sociopolitical questions as: What exactly is a problem to whom? Whose interests and values are at stake?

Through whose action (or inaction) does the "problem" arise? In other words, the language of social problems can be used to discuss what are often in fact situations of *social conflict* in such a way as to politically "de-fuse" them—minimizing the apparent relevance of partisan differences or rival ideologies, while maximizing that of nonideological, pragmatic, technico-administrative "solution." Politics then becomes reduced to little more than haggling over the respective merits of those "solutions" which the experts deem feasible.[64] Such a strategy may have its own political justification—as, say, a means of furthering national unity rather than exacerbating divisions. But, as incorporated into future studies, it is hard to reconcile with a concern to explore and set out what really are the alternative courses of action and outcomes that might be rationally pursued within a "problematic" situation by the diverse parties involved.

(iii)   In developing the notion of the postindustrial society, both Bell and Kahn have stated that they do not aim to provide a comprehensive model, and that one major gap in their conjectures is in regard to political features, which they accept may be quite variable. At the same time, they acknowledge that the character of any particular postindustrial society will be shaped by political decisions.[65] All this may be taken as welcome recognition of the degree of autonomy which political institutions, ideas, and actions may possess in relation to the societal infrastructure. However, on examining the more detailed analyses that are offered, it is once again evident that some deviation occurs from the quite unobjectionable position initially adopted. For instance, Bell has emphasized that the level of technological complexity in the postindustrial society will mean that one of its defining characteristics will be the centrality of theoretical knowledge as a source of both innovation and policy-making. Thus, he argues, such knowledge and the expertise deriving from it must become an important new basis of social power, comparable with, but significantly independent of, both property and political office. Correspondingly, new men of power, rising through educational and intellectual institutions, will come to challenge the position of formerly dominant groups: "The post-industrial society, necessarily, becomes a meritocracy."[66] What this must mean, then, is that Bell does after all virtually accept a central, though much disputed, contention of evolutionary liberalism: that the adaptive exigencies set by the changing infrastructure of advancing industrialism preclude the continuing dominance of a single class or party and make inevitable a pluralistic political order in which the advantage will, if anything, lie with the "technical intelligentsia." In short, with the coming of the postindustrial society, capitalism and totalitarianism alike are historically transcended. Again, one may also find, notably in the work of Kahn and Wiener, the same tendency as is displayed by Kerr and Parsons to characterize certain movements of sociopolitical thought and action, or certain types of regimes, as being in some way historically "deviant." For example, Kahn and Wiener lump together fascism and communism—and, prospectively, student radicalism—as movements which are guided by "aberrant" ideologies and which draw their strength from mass alienation, this being in turn interpreted as a serious "pathological" feature of material progress.[67] Once more, therefore, the point may be made that judgments of this kind necessarily imply some claim to knowledge of what is "correct" or "normal"—in this case, presumably, as regards the pattern of political development which *is* in line with the general evolutionary course of industrial society.

V

If the foregoing remarks are not inapposite, and in some major part of present-day future studies historicist influences do still persist, underpinning a technocratic political strategy, this must threaten real danger for the future of futurology itself. Jouvenel has remarked that the strong prejudices against future studies which in any case exist are strengthened "every time, which is too often, that a conjecture is disguised as a prophecy"[68] and, he might have added, "every time too that a prophecy is disguised as a conjecture." Already claims are to be heard that future studies are merely an instrument whereby powerful groups, states, or nations seek to impose their own image of the future, to create self-fulfilling predictions in their own interests, and to undermine the hopes and confidence of those attracted to different visions of what the world might be.[69] What, then, might one postulate as *desiderata* for future studies if such claims are not to be regarded as quite conceivably justifiable ones?

To begin with, in guarding against the importation, whether conscious or otherwise, of historicist assumptions and perspectives, the most effective means would be to establish, in principle and practice, that future studies are *not* to be equated with, or organized around, social forecasting. A forecast, however cautiously or tentatively advanced, is a statement to the effect that something is likely to come about. While its value need not be entirely dependent upon its being proven accurate, the primary objective of a forecast is foresight. In forecasting, the presupposition is thus necessarily present that there are phenomena of a foreseeable kind—trends, sequences, cycles, and other aspects of what have been generally termed "processes." There is, of course, nothing to object to in this presupposition itself. But, whether through general psychological or more specific political pressures, it appears always to carry with it the danger that trends and the like become thought of as more than empirical regularities, and that forecasting takes on the character of historical prediction. As a corrective to this propensity, it would therefore seem essential that in the conduct of future studies there is automatically counterposed against the idea of process that of action; and against the activity of social forecasting, that of conjecturing and of what might be termed "social designing."

More concretely, one would suggest the principle that any social forecast that is put forward should be accompanied by an analysis of various conceivable ways in which the phenomenon in question might be "exogenously" affected—and not only by other cross-cutting processes but also by purposive, organized interventions, guided by different models of what the future *could* be like. Each of the possibilities identified could then, of course, be associated with an alternative forecast to that initially advanced; and one could go yet further and make "forecasts" in turn of the likelihood of each of these alternatives actually being realized.[70] However, in this phase of the futurological enterprise, foresight should no longer be seen as the main objective, and indeed to continue to speak of forecasting is of doubtful wisdom. It should rather be recognized that once attention has shifted from processes to actions, the aim is no longer to assess degrees of probability—however understood—but to investigate ranges of possibility. The concern is not with what may be foreseen but with what may be imagined.

This, it should be made clear, is by no means to propose that, in going beyond forecasting, futurologists should give themselves over merely to utopian fantasies. While it is important that no restriction whatsoever should be placed upon the making of conjectures, it is equally important that all conjectures, the seemingly prosaic as well as the seemingly utopian, should be subjected to the most critical appraisal possible in the light of relevant social scientific, and other, knowledge—the chief purpose of this being not to determine whether or not particular conjectures are likely to "come true," but rather their respective conditions and consequences and whether or not incompatibilities exist between them. In this way, therefore, constraints— impossibilities—would certainly come to be recognized, and likewise the need to consider what these imply for the pursuit of any desired end: hence the notion of social designing. But the point to be emphasized is that the impossibilities in question here would not be *historical* ones but rather ones derived from sociological, psychological, or economic analyses.[71] In *these* terms should be discussed such issues as the future of "syndicalism" or of socialism or of monistic regimes (as well as less comprehensive questions) and not in terms of historic destiny or evolutionary movements or, for that matter, of adaptation, deviation, aberrancy, pathology, etc.

In social forecasting, the exercise begins with existing knowledge and proceeds to statements about the future via essentially inductive methods.[72] In social designing, the starting point is with conjectures, and theory and data then serve as the means whereby the implications and viability of conjectures are critically examined. Thus, while in the former case existing knowledge functions in effect to limit the range of what is envisaged for the future, in the latter, the principle that the future is open, even though all things are not possible, is, as it were, built into the activity.[73]

If, then, by rejecting a purely "forecasting" approach and by the development of a counteremphasis on social design, future studies did effectively rid themselves of covert historicist elements of the kind previously illustrated, this would in itself do much to eliminate the possibility of technocratic bias. For the

social designing approach is one clearly inimical to the technocratic acceptance of the *status quo* as given except where "problems" are seen as calling for remedial action; and equally to the
tendency to play down basic ideological or political issues or to
present them as ones to be determined largely by expertise. To
the extent that alternative futures really are spelled out (not just
alternative forecasts or alternative "solutions"), to that extent too
there is revealed the true range of sociopolitical choice, the
degree of existing social conflict, and the possibilities for future
action. It may further be added that the approach in question
entails no presumption in favor of piecemeal social policies. The
viability of designs for the future based on piecemeal methods is
to be as critically considered as that of designs of a more sweeping character. For the question must always be raised of whether
a projected change in the *status quo* can be effected piecemeal, or
only as part of some wider transformation. Examples of the
ineffectiveness of piecemeal social engineering are not, after all,
very hard to find.[74]

Finally, it may also be remarked that changes in the character
of future studies in the direction suggested would tend to bring
about desirable changes too in the audience for futurological
discussion. In so far as a social forecasting perspective is predominant, and especially where linked with a concern with an-
ticipating the "problematic" consequences of technological and
economic trends, then the main users of future research are very
likely to be administrators, managers, and the "technocracy" in
general rather than the politically motivated leaders and activists
of parties, pressure groups, and social movements. With, however, a greater emphasis on social designing, the specifically
political relevance of future studies might be expected to become more widely appreciated—whether as a means of selecting
new objectives or of devising more effective strategies for the
achievement of old ones. Through such a development, the
practitioners of future studies could become less liable to the
suspicion that they function merely as the "servants of power,"
and could assume, and be seen to assume, a more independent
role: that of providing "critically annotated" designs for the
social future intended to serve as a basis for public debate and to
show the diversity of goals that political action might rationally
pursue.

The Contributors

DAVID K. COHEN teaches education and social policy at the Harvard Graduate School of Education and is executive director of the Center for Educational Policy Research and cochairman of the Harvard Center for Law and Education. He is the coauthor (with Christopher Jencks *et al.*) of *Inequality: A Reassessment of the Effects of Family and Schooling in America* (1972).

JOSEPH EPSTEIN, a visiting lecturer in the Department of English at Northwestern University, is the author of *Divorced in America* (1974). His articles, essays, and reviews have appeared in many magazines.

JOHN H. GOLDTHORPE teaches sociology at Nuffield College, Oxford, England. He is coauthor (with David Lockwood, Frank Bechhofer, and Jennifer Platt) of the three-volume series *The Affluent Worker: Industrial Attitudes and Behavior* (1968), *The Affluent Worker: Political Attitudes and Behavior* (1968), and *The Affluent Worker in the Class Structure* (1969).

MICHAEL HARRINGTON, author of *The Other America* (1962), *Socialism* (1972), *Fragments of the Century* (1974), and other books, is national chairman of the Democratic Socialist Organizing Committee. He teaches political science at Queens College, the City University of New York.

MURRAY HAUSKNECHT, author of *Joiners: A Study of Volun-*

tary Associations in the United States (1962) and coauthor (with Jewel Bellush) of *Urban Renewal: People, Politics, and Planning* (1967), teaches sociology at the Herbert H. Lehman College, the City University of New York.

MARK KELMAN, a student in the law school at Harvard University, is the author of a novel, *What Followed Was Pure Lesley* (1973). He has served as a consultant at the Fund for the City of New York, where the work on this article was done.

ROBERT LEKACHMAN, who teaches economics at the Herbert H. Lehman College, the City University of New York, is the author of *The Age of Keynes* (1966), *The Permanent Problem of Boom and Bust* (1973), and other works.

HANNA FENICHEL PITKIN, whose special field is political theory, teaches political science at the University of California, Berkeley. She is the author of *The Concept of Representation* (1967) and *Wittgenstein and Justice* (1972).

BERNARD ROSENBERG teaches sociology at the City College of New York. Among his books are *The Province of Sociology* (1972), *Dictionary for the Disenchanted* (1973), and a work in progress entitled *The Contemporary American Jew.*

EDWIN M. SCHUR, author of *Crimes Without Victims* (1956), *Our Criminal Society* (1969), and *Radical Nonintervention* (1973), teaches sociology at New York University.

DAVID SPITZ teaches political philosophy at Hunter College and at the Graduate Center, the City University of New York. He is the author of *Patterns of Anti-Democratic Thought* (1949 and 1965), *Democracy and the Challenge of Power* (1958), and *The Liberal Idea of Freedom* (1964).

GUS TYLER is assistant president of the International Ladies' Garment Workers' Union. Among his books are *The Labor Revolution* (1967), *The Political Imperative: The Corporate Character of Unions* (1968), and *Labor in the Metropolis* (1972).

MICHAEL WALZER teaches political theory in the Government Department at Harvard University. He is the author of *Revolution of the Saints* (1965), *Obligations* (1970), *Political Action: A Practical Guide to Movement Politics* (1971), and *Regicide and Revolution* (1974).

DENNIS H. WRONG teaches sociology at New York University. He is editor of *Contemporary Sociology: A Journal of Reviews* and author of *Population And Society* (1961 and 1967) and *Max Weber* (1970).

The Editors

LEWIS A. COSER teaches sociology at the State University of New York at Stony Brook. He is the author of *The Functions of Social Conflict* (1956), *Men of Ideas* (1965); *Masters of Sociological Thought* (1971), and other books.

IRVING HOWE teaches English at the City University of New York. His most recent books are *The Decline of the New* and *The Critical Point*. He is at work on a history of Jewish immigration: *World of Our Fathers*.

Notes

JOSEPH EPSTEIN

[1] Thankless because largely unappreciated, where not actually depreciated, by intellectuals. The lowest motives were attributed to Podhoretz for steering *Commentary* along the editorial course he chose. He was the sheerest opportunist, it was said. A righward path was the only turf left open to him by the *New York Review of Books*. The American Jewish Committee, publisher of *Commentary,* had laid down the law to him. So the rumors ran, with few people apparently willing to believe that Podhoretz was simply acting out of conviction. The fact is, *Commentary*'s was very clearly a minority position within the intellectual community during the '60s, and that its editor took it up and pursued it without relief or ambiguity demonstrated courage and intellectual stamina.

[2] The tactical duplicity implied by such a phrase is intended. Until the past five years or so, conservative sentiments among American intellectuals who wished to be taken seriously were best kept hidden. The only home for such thoughts was the *National Review,* the Siberia of intellectual journalism.

MICHAEL HARRINGTON

[1] If I were to get into biography, I would make an analogy between the neoconservatives, who are disappointed liberals, and the mystics and religionists who fled in disenchantment from the New Left. The sixties satisfied no one.

[2] Why does Moynihan contradict himself? The answer is, I suspect, biographical and therefore beyond the bounds of this essay. But let me simply note that Moynihan, the assistant secretary of labor for policy

research under Kennedy and Johnson, knew that the "service strategy" was pathetically funded, while Moynihan, the counselor to President Nixon, felt that he could win over the President to the Family Assistance Plan (which was a real accomplishment) by attacking the "service strategy" in more traditional, Nixonian terms.

[3]Bell refers to "equality of result" as a socialist ethic. Since the most famous discussion of the equality issue in the history of socialist thought—Marx's brief but profound comments on the Gotha Program of the German Social Democracy—is an *attack* on the notion that equality of result is a socialist ideal, this is a surprising assertion from one as well-versed as Bell in the literature. The socialist aim, at least in its serious formulations, has never been the impossible goal of guaranteeing everyone the right to win in a competitive rat race; it has been to abolish the rat race altogether. The formula, "From each according to his ability, to each according to his need," insists upon, and even glories in, human differences—inequalities, if you will—once they no longer rationalize a system of invidious competition. Socialists want to move toward equality, in order then to transcend it.

ROSENBERG AND HOWE

[1]Milton Himmelfarb, *The Jews of Modernity* (New York: Basic Books, 1973).

[2]Add to this complication still another: it is precisely the Jewish visibility in the professions, academic life, and the communications industry that makes a good many Jews nervous. There is a feeling that such people are vulnerable to social and cultural attack, because of gentile resentment of Jewish "control" of cultural life and from insurgent blacks trying to replace Jewish teachers by undermining the merit principle, etc. The possibilities here are explosive.

[3]A small, not at all world-shaking example. In early 1973 Frank Fitzsimmons, head of the Teamsters Union, was given a banquet for having raised $26 million for Israel. We are not the ones to sneeze at $26 million. As a rule, we'd say—well, if they want to give that unsavory character a banquet for raising $26 million, what the hell—it's only a banquet. But at this *particular* moment, at least some Jews, including the present authors, have another interest. We are supporters of Cesar Chavez's Farm Workers Union, and that union is threatened with destruction by a brutal raid from Fitzsimmons' Teamsters Union. We don't want, insofar as California is concerned, to honor Fitzsimmons in any way; we recognize, insofar as Israel is concerned, that there may be a need for this ritual ceremony. So?

DENNIS H. WRONG

[1] For a useful recent critique, see Giovanni Sartori, "From the Sociology of Politics to Political Sociology," in Seymour Martin Lipset, ed., *Politics and the Social Sciences* (New York: Oxford University Press, 1969), pp. 77-80.

[2] *Ideology and Utopia* (New York: Harcourt, Brace, 1946), p. 207. See also Mannheim, *Essays on Sociology and Social Psychology* (New York: Oxford University Press, 1953), pp. 98-101.

[3] *The Politics of Disorder* (New York: Basic Books, 1971), pp. 3-61. Lowi mentions the civil rights movement of the early '60s as an example of such a social movement outside of the established parties and interest organizations (p. 60). See also Lowi's earlier book, *The End of Liberalism* (New York: W. W. Norton, 1969).

[4] *Paths to the Present* (New York: Macmillan, 1949), pp. 77-92.

[5] *Social Change and History* (New York: Oxford University Press, 1969), pp. 240-262.

[6] *Ibid.*, pp. 284-304.

[7] *In Retrospect: The History of a Historian* (New York: Harcourt, Brace & World, 1963), p. 108.

[8] *Ibid.*, pp. 190-191.

[9] O. Utis, "Generalissimo Stalin and the Art of Government," *Foreign Affairs,* 30 (January 1952): 197-214. The author writes: "This—the 'artificial dialectic'—is Generalissimo Stalin's most original invention, his major contribution to the art of government...." p. 210. ("O. Utis," which means "nobody" in classical Greek, was a pseudonym here adopted by Isaiah Berlin.)

[10] *The Prince,* chap. VI. See pp. 21-22 in the Modern Library Edition (New York: Random House, 1940).

[11] *Ibid.*, p. 22.

[12] *The Century of Total War* (Garden City, N.Y.: Doubleday, 1954), pp. 241-261. I am much indebted to Aron's brilliant discussion.

[13] *Autobiography* (London: Longmans, Green, 1908), p. 168.

[14] *Reflections on the Causes of Human Misery* (Boston: Beacon Press, 1972), pp. 156-168.

MICHAEL WALZER

[1] "About Equality," *Commentary,* November 1972.

[2] *Early Writings,* trans. T. B. Bottomore (London: Watts, 1963), p. 191.

[3] I am also greatly indebted to Bernard Williams, in whose essay "The

Idea of Equality" (first published in Laslett and Runciman, *Philosophy, Politics and Society,* second series [Oxford: Blackwell, 1962]) a similar argument is worked out. The example of medical care, to which I recur, is suggested by him. The Pascal quote is from J. M. Cohen's translation of *The Pensées* (London and Baltimore: Penguin Classics, 1961), no. 244.

[4]*Early Writings,* pp. 193-94.

[5]"On Meritocracy and Equality," *Public Interest,* Fall 1972.

[6]The only writer he mentions is John Rawls, whose *Theory of Justice* Kristol seems entirely to misunderstand. For Rawls explicitly accords priority to the "liberty principle" over those other maxims that point toward greater equality.

DAVID SPITZ

[1]Sometimes, oddly enough, as in France and England, strong and ambitious kings granted some political power to the common people in order to limit the power of the aristocracy. Such kings, Tocqueville sardonically observed, "assisted democracy by their talents, others by their vices."

[2]Giovanni Sartori, *Democratic Theory* (New York: Frederick A. Praeger, 1965), paperback ed., p. 327.

[3]Cf. John Rees, *Equality* (London: Macmillan, 1972), paperback ed., chap. 1.

[4]Thomas Hobbes, *Leviathan* (1651 ed.), Part I, chap. 13.

[5]Jean-Jacques Rousseau, *The Social Contract,* trans. Cole (Everyman's ed., 1913), Book II, chap. 11, p. 45.

[6]Aristotle, *Politics,* trans. Barker (New York: Oxford University Press, 1946), Book V, chap. 2, p. 207.

[7]For Mill's doctrine, see his essays *On Liberty* (1859), *Utilitarianism* (1861), and *Representative Government* (1861).

[8]Albert Hofstadter, "The Career Open to Personality: The Meaning of Equality of Opportunity for an Ethics for Our Time," in *Aspects of Human Equality,* ed. Lyman Bryson *et al.* (New York: Harper & Brothers, 1956), pp. 123, 136.

[9]Dorothy D. Lee, "Equality of Opportunity as a Cultural Value," in *ibid.,* pp. 259, 261, 268.

[10]This may explain why certain "socialist" and allegedly egalitarian countries, such as Czechoslovakia, seek to rationalize *their* differences and systems of hierarchy as constitutive of "socialist stratification," as distinct from capitalist, bureaucratic, technocratic, and other "de-

based" forms of stratification. See Ernest Gellner, "The Pluralist Antilevelers of Prague," *Dissent*, Summer 1972, pp. 471-82. It may also explain the curious argument of Professor John H. Schaar, who after denouncing hierarchy and the equal opportunity principle concludes by affirming that "of course there must be hierarchy" and that "the equal opportunity principle is certainly not without value." See his "Equality of Opportunity, and Beyond," in *Equality*, ed. J. R. Pennock and J. W. Chapman (New York: Atherton Press, 1967), chap. 13.

[11] I forgo for reasons of space a range of further problems that should at least be indicated here: whether equality entails a right to equal property or an equal right to property; whether equality before the law requires a public defender no less adequately staffed and funded than a public prosecutor; whether, as the transformation of Eliza Doolittle from a flower girl into a duchess suggests, it is in fact true that persons who are treated alike tend to become alike; and whether equality within a single realm of social life (say the political), or within an aspect of that realm (say the suffrage), can meaningfully coexist with inequalities in other realms (the family, the school, the church, the army, the corporation).

[12] "Equality as an Ideal," in *Justice and Social Policy*, ed. F. A. Olafson (Englewood Cliffs, N.J.: Prentice-Hall, 1961), p. 150.

[13] I am especially indebted here to Rees, *op. cit.*, pp. 134-38.

[14] Cf. John Rawls, *A Theory of Justice* (Cambridge, Mass.: Harvard University Press, 1971), and Brian Barry, *Political Argument* (London: Routledge & Kegan Paul, 1965), especially chaps. 6-7.

[15] Cf. John P. Plamenatz, "Equality of Opportunity," in *Aspects of Human Equality, op. cit.*, chap. 4.

[16] Daniel Bell, "On Meritocracy and Equality," *Public Interest*, Fall 1972, pp. 29-68; Irving Kristol, "About Equality," *Commentary*, November 1972, pp. 41-47.

MARK KELMAN

[1] All SMSA data exclude Southern SMSAs, which are universally far more inegalitarian, so I am always comparing Northern SMSAs to one another.

ROBERT LEKACHMAN

[1] *Setting National Priorities: The 1973 Budget*, by Charles L. Schultze,

Edward R. Fried, Alice M. Rivlin, and Nancy H. Teeters (Washington, D.C.: Brookings).

[2]See "Is Growth Obsolete?" in *Fiftieth Anniversary Colloquium*, National Bureau of Economic Research (New York: Columbia University Press 1972).

[3]During the first Nixon administration, the major auto companies entered into a consent decree with a sympathetic Antitrust Division of the Department of Justice which featured a promise to stop colluding to halt the design of better antipollution devices.

[4]Galbraithians, a professional minority, insist that advertising effectively manipulates and distorts the actual preferences of buyers.

[5]*New York Times Magazine,* April 8, 1973, pp. 33 ff.

MURRAY HAUSKNECHT

[1]Edward Banfield, *The Unheavenly City* (Boston: Little, Brown, 1970). All quotations except if otherwise noted are from this book.

[2]*Political Influence* (Glencoe: Free Press, 1961), p. 66.

[3]*The Urban Villagers* (New York: Free Press, 1962), p. 24.

[4]*Ibid.,* p. 249.

[5]See Herbert J. Gans, *People and Plans* (New York: Basic Books, 1968), Chapter 22. This criticism was developed in reference to the culture of poverty theory, but it is applicable to Banfield. The objections raised by Gans and others are known to Banfield (he cites the relevant literature) but he makes no attempt to deal with them.

[6]Charles A. Valentine, *Culture and Poverty* (Chicago: University of Chicago Press, 1968), p. 120.

[7]Joel F. Handler and Ellen Jane Hollingsworth, *The "Deserving Poor": A Study of Welfare Administration* (Chicago: Markham, 1971), p. 143; pp. 60f.

[8]Banfield's note, page 276, reads: "Jerome K. Myers and B. H. Roberts, *Family and Class Dynamics in Mental Illness* (New York: Wiley, 1959), p. 174. See also [A. B.] Hollingshead and [Frederick C.] Redlich, *Social Class and Mental Illness* [New York: Wiley, 1958], p. 175, and S. Minuchin et al., *Families of the Slum* (New York: Basic Books, 1968), p. 34."

[9]For a review and analysis see S. M. Miller et al., "Poverty and Self-Indulgence: A Critique of the Non-Deferred Gratification Pattern," in Louis A. Ferman et al., eds., *Poverty in America* (Ann Arbor: University of Michigan Press, 1965), pp. 285-302. Banfield cites this paper, but does not respond to the theoretical and empirical points it raises.

[10] For a summary statement—based on Miller et al., *op. cit.*—of the conditions that would have to be fulfilled in order to get valid data testing Banfield's proposition see S. M. Miller and Ronnie Steinberg Ratner, "The American Resignation: The New Assault on Equality," *Social Policy,* May-June 1972, p. 8.

[11] Louis Schneider and Sverre Lysgaard, "The Deferred Gratification Pattern: A Preliminary Study," *American Sociological Review,* April 1953, p. 143.

[12] U.S. Bureau of the Census, *Pocket Data Book, USA 1971* (Washington, D.C.: Government Printing Office, 1971), p. 313

[13] Lee Rainwater, *Behind Ghetto Walls* (Chicago: Aldine, 1970), p. 383.

[14] Leo Strauss, *Natural Right and History* (Chicago: University of Chicago Press, 1953), pp. 132 f.

DAVID K. COHEN

[1] *The IQ Argument* (Freeport, N.Y.: Library Press, 1971).

[2] It could be argued that the research I have summarized understates the influence of social and economic class, because dropouts were not included in the computations; but when they were included, the results barely changed. It could be argued that the role of intelligence is understated because a single test score can't summarize intelligence; yet when scores in four different tests were included instead of just one, nothing much changed either. And while there are plenty of other difficulties with the studies summarized here, none of them seems important enough to change the general pattern of results I have presented.

[3] Occupational status is a term derived from studies of the prestige in which Americans hold different sorts of jobs. Generally, they think that professional and managerial jobs are very prestigious and that common labor is not. Indices of occupational prestige are very highly correlated with general indices of social and economic status.

EDWIN M. SCHUR

[1] Edward C. Banfield, *The Unheavenly City* (Boston: Little, Brown, 1970), p. 163.

[2] *Ibid.,* pp. 183, 184.

[3] *Ibid.,* p. 170.

[4] See Nat Hentoff, "Growing up Mugged," *New York Times Magazine,* January 28, 1973, and correspondence in subsequent issues.

[5]President's Commission on Law Enforcement and Administration of Justice, *The Challenge of Crime in a Free Society* (Washington: U.S. Government Printing Office, 1967), p. 1.

[6]Frank F. Furstenberg, Jr., "Public Reaction to Crime in the Streets," *American Scholar,* Autumn 1971, p. 606.

[7]See Edwin M. Schur, *Our Criminal Society: The Social and Legal Sources of Crime in America* (Englewood Cliffs: Prentice-Hall, 1969).

[8]Richard Quinney, *The Social Reality of Crime* (Boston: Little, Brown, 1970), p. 39.

[9]William Ryan, *Blaming the Victim* (New York: Random House, Vintage Books, 1972), p. 7.

[10]American Friends Service Committee, *Struggle for Justice: A Report on Crime and Punishment in America* (New York: Hill & Wang, 1971), p. 9.

[11]*Ibid.,* p. 16.

[12]With respect to sentencing policy—a matter on which liberals and neoconservatives may largely agree—see James Q. Wilson, "If Every Criminal Knew He Would Be Punished if Caught," *New York Times Magazine,* January 28, 1973.

[13]David Burnham, "Crime Rates in Precincts: Census Data Studied," *New York Times,* July 30, 1973, p. 1.

[14]Ralph K. Schwitzgebel, *Development and Legal Regulation of Coercive Behavior Modification Techniques with Offenders* (Center for Studies of Crime and Delinquency, National Institute of Mental Health; Washington: U.S. Government Printing office, 1971), p. 17.

[15]Charles Witter, "Drugging and Schooling," *Trans-action,* July-August 1971, p. 31; see also Nat Hentoff, "Drug-Pushing in the Schools: The Professionals," *Village Voice,* May 25 and June 1, 1972.

[16]Tom Wicker, "Gooks, Slopes, and Vermin," *New York Times,* May 4, 1973, p. 37.

[17]*New York Times,* March 30, 1973.

[18]Edwin M. Schur, *Crimes Without Victims* (Englewood Cliffs: Prentice-Hall, 1965); Herbert L. Packer, *The Limits of the Criminal Sanction* (Stanford: Stanford University Press, 1968).

[19]Committee on Homosexual Offences and Prostitution, *Report* (Home Office, Cmnd. 247; London: Her Majesty's Stationery Office, 1957), p. 24.

[20]Walter Berns, "Pornography vs. Democracy: The Case for Censorship," *Public Interest,* Winter 1971, pp. 10, 23.

[21]James Q. Wilson, Mark H. Moore, and I. David Wheat, Jr., "The Problem of Heroin," *Public Interest,* Fall 1972, p. 5.

HANNA FENICHEL PITKIN

*This essay is part of a larger work written during free time made available to me by a grant from the John Simon Guggenheim Memorial Foundation, for which I am most grateful. Many of the best ideas in it came to me from Sara Shumer or Tracy Strong; what I owe to them exceeds anything I could acknowledge here.

[1] J. W. Grove, "Preface," to W. H. Greenleaf, *Oakeshott's Philosophical Politics* (London: Longmans, Green, 1966).

Michael Oakeshott was born on December 11, 1901. He attended St. George's School, Harpenden, and then Gonville and Caius College at Cambridge where he read history, graduating in 1923. He became a fellow of the College two years later and was for many years a university lecturer in history. After serving in the army 1940-45, he returned to Cambridge. He was at Nuffield College, Oxford, in 1949-50, and went to the London School of Economics as University Professor of Political Science in 1951.

[2] Michael Oakeshott, *Rationalism in Politics* (New York: Basic Books, 1962). An earlier work on epistemology, *Experience and Its Modes* (Cambridge: Cambridge University Press, 1933), cannot be discussed within the confines of this essay.

[3] Oakeshott, *Rationalism,* p. 183.

[4] *Ibid.,* p. 172.

[5] Edmund Burke, *Reflections on the Revolution in France,* Thomas H. D. Mahoney, ed. (Indianapolis and New York: Bobbs-Merrill, 1955), p. 108. Here and elsewhere I find strong parallels between Oakeshott and Burke. To be sure, Oakeshott sometimes disparages Burke; and as critics have pointed out, there are some crucial differences between them, particularly Oakeshott's determination to make his case without metaphysical concepts such as divine purpose or natural law. But he also cites Burke approvingly, and the parallels as well as the differences between the two conservatisms are instructive. See Oakeshott, *Rationalism,* pp. 183, 23; Michael Oakeshott, "Contemporary British Politics," *Cambridge Journal,* 1 (May 1948): 474-490, at 475; Neal Wood, "A Guide to the Classics: the Skepticism of Professor Oakeshott," *Journal of Politics,* 21 (November 1959): 647-662, at 647; Greenleaf, *op. cit.,* pp. 3, 83.

[6] Because of the differences in resolution of the problem in different realms, which will be discussed further below, Bernard Crick is wrong to suppose that "it matters little which we examine in detail." Bernard Crick, "The World of Michael Oakeshott," *Encounter,* 20 (June 1963): 65-74, at 68.

[7]Oakeshott is sometimes misunderstood in this regard, as he anticipated he might be: "Concept of a Philosophical Jurisprudence," *Politica,* 3 (September 1938): 203-222, and (December 1938): 345-360, at 349.

[8]Michael Oakeshott, "Scientific Politics," *Cambridge Journal,* 1 (March 1948): 347-358, at 348, 349, 354.

[9]Oakeshott, *Rationalism,* p. 83.

[10]*Ibid.,* p. 102.

[11]*Ibid.,* p. 215. Oakeshott acknowledges his debt to Michael Polanyi more than once; *ibid.,* p. 8n; and Michael Oakeshott, "Science and Society," *Cambridge Journal,* 1 (August 1948): 689-697, at 692n.

[12]Oakeshott, *Rationalism,* pp. 8-10; for the conception of "know-how," compare Gilbert Ryle, *The Concept of Mind* (New York: Barnes & Noble, 1949), chap. 2.

[13]Oakeshott, *Rationalism,* pp. 61 ff.

[14]*Ibid.,* p. 11. This treatment of education is also paralleled by Oakeshott's more specific views on the nature of a university, but there is no room to discuss them here.

[15]*Ibid.,* p. 186.

[16]*Ibid.*

[17]*Ibid.* pp. 190, 49.

[18]*Ibid.,* pp. 124, 125. As we shall see in the next section, this is also Oakeshott's definition of politics.

[19]*Ibid.,* p. 124.

[20]For example, J. G. Blumler, "Politics, Poetry, and Practice," *Political Studies,* 12 (October 1964): 353-361, at 357; Crick, *op. cit.,* p. 68; Colin Falck, "Romanticism in Politics," *New Left Review,* 18 (January-February 1963): 60-71, at 64; John C. Rees, "Professor Oakeshott on Political Education," *Mind,* 62 (January 1953): 68-74, at 70; J. W. N. Watkins, "Political Tradition and Political Theory," *Philosophical Quarterly,* 2 (October 1952): 323-337, at 334 ff. A full discussion of the nature and significance of this ambiguity in philosophical terms unfortunately is not possible within the confines of this essay.

[21]G. W. F. Hegel, *The Phenomenology of Mind,* J. B. Baillie, trans. (New York: Harper & Row, 1967), p. 110; Edmund Burke, "Appeal from the New to the Old Whigs," in Peter J. Stanlis, ed., *Edmund Burke: Selected Writings and Speeches* (Garden City: Doubleday, 1963), p. 522.

[22]Oakeshott, *Rationalism,* p. 91.

[23]*Ibid.,* pp. 12, 99.

[24]*Ibid.,* p. 99; cf. pp. 100, 108; Oakeshott, "Concept of a Philosophical Jurisprudence," p. 691; Michael Oakeshott, "The Idea of a University," *Listener,* 47 (March 9, 1950): 424-426, at 424.

[25]Oakeshott, *Rationalism*, p. 75.

[26]*Ibid.*, pp. 118-119; cf. Michael Oakeshott, "The Customer is Never Wrong," *Listener*, 54 (August 25, 1955): 301-302.

[27]Oakeshott, *Rationalism*, p. 120.

[28]*Ibid.*, pp. 112, 123. Oakeshott also proposes another definition in an unpublished paper: politics is "activity and utterance connected with government and the instruments of government"; Greenleaf, *op. cit.* [see footnote 1], p. 43n.

[29]Oakeshott, *Rationalism*, p. 112.

[30]*Ibid.*, p. 124.

[31]*Ibid.*, p. 133.

[32]*Ibid.*, p. 125.

[33]*Ibid.*, pp. 125, 133.

[34]*Ibid.*, p. 29; cf. pp. 132-133.

[35]*Ibid.*, p. 94; cf. p. 133.

[36]*Ibid.*, p. 124.

[37]*Ibid.*, pp. 125, 133.

[38]*Ibid.*, p. 49.

[39]*Ibid.*, p. 127.

[40]Burke, *Reflections*, p. 68.

[41]Oakeshott, *Rationalism*, p. 121.

[42]*Ibid.*, p. 122; "Customer is Never Wrong," p. 301.

[43]Oakeshott, *Rationalism*, p. 6.

[44]*Ibid.*, p. 40.

[45]*Ibid.*, p. 42.

[46]*Ibid.*, p. 41.

[47]*Ibid.*, pp. 42-43, 187, 193-194.

[48]*Burke, Reflections*, pp. 87, 88.

[49]Oakeshott, *Rationalism*, pp. 22-23.

[50]*Ibid.*, p. 5.

[51]*Ibid.*, p. 22.

[52]*Ibid.*, p. 73.

[53]*Ibid.*, p. 23; here Oakeshott himself cites Burke.

[54]For instance, Edward C. Banfield, *The Moral Basis of a Backward Society* (New York: Free Press, 1958).

[55]Oakeshott, *Rationalism*, p. 116. Note, however, that Oakeshott is here talking not about a particular style of politics but about an interpretation of all political activity. Note also the interesting consequence that the attempt to be Rationalistic results in "empiricism."

[56]*Ibid.*, p. 114.

[57]*Ibid.*, p. 5.

[58]And Aristotle emphatically did *not* mean going beyond a minimally

nutritional diet to two color television sets. Aristotle, *Politics,* Ernest Barker, trans. (New York and London: Oxford University Press, 1958), pp. 5, 118.

[59] Joseph Tussman, *Obligation and the Body Politic* (New York: Oxford University Press, 1960), p. 78.

[60] Burke, "Appeal," in Stanlis, *op. cit.,* p. 536; Oakeshott, "Contemporary British Politics," p. 474.

[61] See for exámple, Crick, *op. cit.,* p. 72; Rees, *op. cit.,* pp. 70-71.

[62] Samuel Coleman, "Is there Reason in Tradition?" in Preston King and B. C. Parekh, eds., *Politics and Experience* (Cambridge: Cambridge University Press, 1968), p. 249. But note how sensitively Oakeshott treats precisely this issue in relation to poetry; "Concept of a Philosophical Jurisprudence," p. 359.

[63] Oakeshott, *Rationalism,* p. 124.

[64] *Ibid.,* pp. 29, 75; "Scientific Politics," p. 350.

[65] Oakeshott, *Rationalism,* p. 174.

[66] *Ibid.,* p. 136.

[67] What he says is that the growth of Rationalism in Europe has been owing primarily to the advent of newcomers into politics—new men, new nations, new classes—a topic we shall discuss below. In addition, some Rationalist philosophers occasionally gave "another turn to the screw." Otherwise, the causes are left obscure. Thus insofar as Oakeshott discusses causes here, the threat to traditionalism came from the outsiders, not from any fault in the tradition. *Ibid.,* pp. 22, 29. Cf. Michael Oakeshott, "The Universities," *Cambridge Journal,* 2 (June 1949): 515-542, at 542.

[68] Oakeshott, *Rationalism,* p. 31.

[69] *Ibid.,* p. 32.

[70] *Ibid.,* p. 64.

[71] *Ibid.,* p. 65.

[72] *Ibid.,* p. 77.

[73] *Ibid.,* p. 169.

[74] *Ibid.,* p. 41.

[75] *Ibid.*

[76] *Ibid.,* pp. 64, 65.

[77] *Ibid.,* pp. 65, 70; cf. p. 73.

[78] *Ibid.,* p. 122.

[79] See the section on Burke's role and views on the impeachment of Warren Hastings, in Stanlis, *op. cit.,* pp. 338-418.

[80] Oakeshott, *Rationalism,* p. 183.

[81] *Ibid.,* p. 195.

[82] *Ibid.,* p. 22.

83*Ibid.*, p. 25. Machiavelli himself knew better, Oakeshott says, and offered the new prince "not only his book, but also, what would make up for the inevitable deficiencies of his book—himself."

84*Ibid.*, p. 26.

85*Ibid.*

86*Ibid.*, p. 45.

87*Ibid.*, p. 46.

88*Ibid.*, p. 47.

89*Ibid.*, pp. 56, 57.

90*Ibid.*, p. 46.

91*Ibid.*, p. 43.

92*Ibid.*, p. 248.

93Burke, "Letter to Sir Hercules Langrishe," in Stanlis, *op. cit.*, p. 257.

94Hannah Arendt, *On Revolution* (New York: Viking, 1965), p. 54.

95Arendt, *The Human Condition* (Garden City: Doubleday, 1958), pp. 25, 29, 34.

96Aristotle, *op. cit.*, pp. 3, 9-18, 35, 107-113, 118-120, 300-303.

97Arendt, *Human Condition*, p. 195; *On Revolution*, p. 54.

98Arendt, *On Revolution*, p. 41.

99*Ibid.*, pp. 86, 54; cf. *Human Condition*, pp. 58, 74.

100Arendt, *Human Condition*, p. 115. Arendt blames Marx for bringing the spirit of "labor" into the political arena where only "action" is appropriate. This may be very similar to what Oakeshott means when he accuses Marxism of bringing to politics an ideology that is an abridgment of nonpolitical activity and hence "inappropriate on account of the irrelevance of the activity from which it has been abstracted." Oakeshott, *Rationalism*, p. 121.

101Arendt, *Human Condition*, p. 195.

102Arendt, *On Revolution*, p. 69; cf. pp. 68-94 *passim*.

103I say "really fear" in order to give them all the benefit of every doubt. For some, like Tocqueville, this is obviously true. Arendt seems more contradictory; sometimes she seems to stress that the point is consciousness, yet the idea of the pressure of causal, physical necessity is central to her argument. One suspects that her animus against Marxist totalitarianism may account for some of the discrepancies.

104Arendt, *Human Condition*, p. 60.

105Alexis de Tocqueville, *The Old Regime and the French Revolution*, Stuart Gilbert, trans. (Garden City: Doubleday, 1955), p. 169.

106Alexis de Tocqueville, *Recollections*, George Lawrence, trans., J. P. Mayer and A. P. Kerr, eds. (Garden City: Doubleday, 1971), p. 6.

107*Ibid.*, p. 13.

108Arendt, *On Revolution*, p. 53.

[109] Arendt, *Human Condition,* p. 42.

[110] Oakeshott, *Rationalism,* p. 243; cf. p. 176.

[111] *Ibid.,* pp. 304, 311, 129, 41, 43; cf pp. 124, 133-136.

[112] As in education one learns to "recognize" oneself in "the mirror of" one's civilization; *ibid.,* p. 304.

[113] *Ibid.,* p. 41.

[114] *Ibid.,* pp. 304, 311.

[115] "Wherever you go, you will be a *polis,*" the Greeks said to the colonists they sent out. Arendt, *Human Condition,* p. 177. The concern for a public forum within which persuasion can replace force is also a central theme in Thucydides.

[116] Oakeshott, *Rationalism,* p. 4.

[117] Oakeshott, "Scientific Politics," p. 347.

[118] Oakeshott, *Rationalism,* p. 49; Albert Camus, *The Rebel,* Anthony Bower, trans. (New York: Random House, 1956).

[119] Michael Oakeshott, "The Claims of Politics," *Scrutiny* 8 (September 1939): 146-151, at 147.

[120] Oakeshott, *Rationalism,* p. 127.

[121] *Ibid.,* pp. 112, 192; cf. "Claims of Politics," p. 148.

[122] *Ibid.,* p. 196.

[123] *Ibid.,* pp. 22, 195, 189.

[124] *Ibid.,* p. 189.

[125] Oakeshott, "Contemporary British Politics," p. 486; cf. p. 489.

[126] Oakeshott does speak of "deliberation" once, in Michael Oakeshott, "Political Laws and Captive Audiences," in *Talking to Eastern Europe,* G. R. Urban, ed. (London: Eyre & Spottiswoode, 1964), pp. 292, 295 (thus actually twice).

[127] Oakeshott, *Rationalism,* p. 59. It is characteristic that Oakeshott identifies heroism with attempting to do the impossible; he gives no attention to intermediate cases such as a heroic attempt to do something difficult and unlikely, that might just succeed. Cf. Michael Oakeshott, *The Social and Political Doctrines of Contemporary Europe* (New York: Macmillan, 1942), p. xii, where "regretting our civilization" is identified as a "fruitless, if heroic, act."

[128] Oakeshott, *Rationalism,* p. 59.

[129] *Ibid.,* pp. 172-173.

[130] An excellent discussion of alternative conceptions of tradition, including traditions with heroic founders, is contained in J. G. A. Pocock, "Time, Institutions and Action: An Essay on Traditions and Their Understanding," in King and Parekh, *op. cit.*

[131] Burke, *Reflections,* p. 38.

[132] Plato, *Crito,* 50.

[133]Burke, *Reflections,* pp. 109-110; cf. Edmund Burke, "Speech on the Representation of the Commons in Parliament," in Stanlis, *op. cit.,* p. 336.

[134]Burke, *Reflections,* p. 87.

[135]It may, however, be a fear of the (earlier) engulfing mother; the psychologists disagree on the matter. See Philip E. Slater, *The Glory of Hera* (Boston: Beacon, 1968) and the psychological references cited therein; as well as the work of Melanie Klein. On changes in authority, see John H. Schaar, "Legitimacy in the Modern State," in *Power and Community,* Philip Green and Sanford Levinson, eds. (New York: Random House, 1970).

[136]Oakeshott, *Rationalism,* p. 170.

[137]*Ibid.,* p. 171.

[138]*Ibid.,* pp. 169, 173.

[139]*Ibid.,* p. 66.

[140]*Ibid.,* p. 306.

[141]But note that Oakeshott disclaims any presupposition of natural human depravity; *ibid.,* pp. 183, 189.

[142]Jean Piaget, *The Moral Judgment of the Child,* Marjorie Gabain, trans. (New York: Collier, 1962).

[143]But note that he explicitly claims that in politics we are adults, not children, *Rationalism,* p. 187.

[144]Wood, *op. cit.,* p. 662.

[145]Oakeshott, *Rationalism,* p. 114; cf. p. 48.

[146]*Ibid.,* p. 35.

[147]See particularly Friedrich Nietzsche, *Ecce Homo,* Walter Kaufmann, trans. (New York: Random House, 1969), pp. 225, 229.

[148]Oakeshott, *Rationalism,* p. 35.

[149]*Ibid.,* p. 184.

[150]*Ibid.,* pp. 128, 129.

[151]Need I say that I am not proposing that Oakeshott resembles Plato in all, or many, respects?

[152]Oakeshott, "Claims of Politics," pp. 146-147.

[153]*Ibid.,* passim. Note also Oakeshott's secondary, unpublished definition, cited in footnote 28.

[154]Crick, *op. cit.,* p. 66.

JOHN H. GOLDTHORPE

[1]The Poverty of Historicism, *Economica,* XI (1944), 86-103, 119, 137; XII (1945): 69-89; subsequently republished in book form (London,

1957). All subsequent references are to this latter, revised version.

[2]Much of this being due to disagreement with other of Popper's arguments—eg., regarding "methodological individualism" or "piecemeal social engineering"—closely, but by no means inseparably, linked to his rejection of historicism.

[3]Clark Kerr *et al., Industrialism and Industrial Man* (Cambridge, Mass.: Harvard U. P., 1960); id., *Marshall, Marx and Modern Times: the multidimensional society* (Cambridge: Cambridge U. P., 1968); Talcott Parsons, *Societies: Evolutionary and Comparative Perspectives* (Englewood Cliffs: Prentice-Hall, 1966); *id.,* Evolutionary Universals in Society, *American Sociological Review,* XXIX (1964): 339-357.

[4]Ossip Flechtheim, "Futurology, the New Science of Probability," repr. in *History and Futurology* (Meisenheim-am-Glan: Anton Hain, 1966); Bertrand de Jouvenel, ed., *L'art de la conjecture,* transl. as *The Art of Conjecture* (London: Weidenfeld and Nicholson, 1967); Herman Kahn *and* Anthony J. Wiener, *The Year 2000: a framework for speculation on the next thirty-three years* (New York: Collier-Macmillan, 1967); Michael Young, ed., *Forecasting and the Social Sciences* (London: Heinemann, 1968); Robert Jungk and Johan Galtung, eds., *Mankind 2000* (Oslo/London: Allen and Unwin, 1969).

[5]*The Poverty of Historicism,* p. 3, emphasis in original.

[6]*Ibid.,* pp. 12-14, 49-52.

[7]*Ibid.,* p. 49.

[8]Cf. Max Weber, Politics as a Vocation, in H. H. Gerth *and* C. Wright Mills, eds., *Essays in Sociology* (New York: Oxford, 1948); and also the papers brought together in E. A. Shils *and* H. A. Finch, eds., *The Methodology of the Social Sciences* (Glencoe: 1949); F. von Hayek, *The Counter-Revolution of Science* (Glencoe: 1952) and *The Constitution of Liberty* (London: 1960); and, post-Popper, Isaiah Berlin, *Four Essays on Liberty* (Oxford: 1969).

[9]It may also be observed that the new liberalism is largely of American inspiration, while the old was essentially European. American social thought, incidentally, offers a much earlier example of an attempt to combine elements from Spencer and Marx; namely that of W. G. Sumner.

[10]Cf. Raymond Aron, *Dix-huit leçons sur la société industrielle* (Paris: 1962); *La lutte des classes* (Paris: 1964). These books originated in lectures given at the Sorbonne and were first published in 1955-56 in *Les Cours de Sorbonne.* It is important to add that Aron was at the same time concerned to emphasize the crucial differences between Eastern and Western industrial societies in their political institutions, and that, unlike later liberal theorists of industrialism, he envisaged no particu-

lar propensity for these differences to diminish. Cf. his *Démocratie et totalitarianisme* (Paris: 1965).

[11]W. W. Rostow, *The Stages of Economic Growth* (Cambridge: 1960). The significant subtitle is "A non-Communist Manifesto."

[12]For a fairly comprehensive discussion by a group of British sociologists, see P. Halmos, ed., *The Development of Industrial Societies* (Keele: 1964).

[13]See, e.g., Robert N. Bellah, "Religious Evolution," *American Sociological Review,* XXIX (1964): 358-374—"What I mean by evolution, then, is nothing metaphysical but the simple empirical generalization that more complex forms develop from less complex forms and that the properties and possibilities of more complex forms differ from those of less complex forms". Cf. also S. N. Eisenstadt, "Social Change, Differentiation and Evolution," *Ibid.,* 375-386. A similarly innocuous objective seems to be usually that of writers who eschew the idea of evolution but emphasize the importance of a "developmental" perspective. Cf. Eric Dunning, "The Concept of Development: two illustrative case studies," *in* Peter I. Rose, ed., *The Study of Society* (New York: 1967). In all such cases, I would argue, the propositions advanced are chiefly of value in *posing sociological problems*—how are the regularities demonstrated to be explained? The propositions themselves are not of a kind that could have theoretical—i.e., explanatory—significance. Cf. the distinction stressed by Gellner, in discussing evolutionary theory, between "the tracing of the Path," through the description of its successive stages, and its explanation, which requires an account of the forces and processes whereby its course was determined: Ernest Gellner, *Thought and Change* (London: 1964), pp. 17-18.

[14]See Kerr, *Industrialism. . . , op. cit.* pp. 33-34, 46.

[15]Kerr, *Industrialism. . . , op. cit.,* pp. 22-23.

[16]*Ibid.,* Introduction, p. 12.

[17]*Ibid.,* chaps. III-V esp.

[18]*Ibid.,* chap. X.

[19]*Ibid.,* chaps. II, X. See also Kerr's most recent statement of his position. *Marshall, Marx and Modern Times, op. cit.,* chaps. VII and X especially. Kerr still maintains that "the realistic alternative as industrialism evolves is some form of pluralism." He recognizes more explicitly than before that a number of different kinds of pluralism are conceivable—including "co-ordinated" pluralism on, say, the Yugoslav pattern or even "syndicalist" pluralism; but in "the coming struggle for power" between proponents of these divergent systems, Kerr adheres to the view that history is on the side of the liberal model. In other words, his position is basically unaltered: the realistic choices are

steadily narrowing down in favor of the "free choice," society.

20*Industrialism. . . , op. cit.,* p. 288.

21*Ibid.,* pp. 282-283. For the notion of the "inner-society," see *Marshall, Marx and Modern Times, op. cit.,* chap. VIII.

22Cf. the remarks made by Berlin on such apparently "soft" determinism to the effect that it is "simply a variant of the general determinist thesis," in *Four Essays on Liberty,* Introduction, pp. XIII *et seq.*

23See *Marshall, Marx and Modern Times,* pp. 60-71, 122-123. As regards syndicalism, it is interesting to note that in *Industrialism and Industrial Man* this was consigned to the dustbin of history, along with communalism and cooperativism, as an ideology which had already "almost completely disappeared from the scene" (p. 282). But in the more recent work, syndicalism is reinstated—without reference to the previous judgment—as "the essential challenge to the *status quo*" (p. 123) and indeed, as indicated, is accorded some limited historic role.

24It may be noted that Parsons is expressly concerned to disassociate his own approach from that of "historicism" in the German, "antinaturalistic" tradition of Hegel and Marx or, later, Dilthey. These writers, Parsons stresses, specifically deny what he would wish to maintain: namely, the possibility and relevance of "generalized *analytical* theory (which systematically treats the interdependence of independently variable factors) in explaining temporally sequential sociocultural phenomena" (*Societies, op. cit.,* p. 115, emphasis in original). However, as Popper has argued, there are important similarities, as well as differences, between the tradition in question and "pronaturalistic" attempts at interpreting history in terms of some version of evolutionism.

25*Ibid.,* p. 109.

26*Ibid.,* pp. 109-110, emphasis in original.

27"Evolutionary Universals", *loc. cit.,* pp. 340-341.

28See *Societies,* p. 110.

29For far more detailed arguments to show the fundamental similarities—and related difficulties—shared by Parsons' evolutionism and that of nineteenth-century writers, see Robert A. Nisbet, *Social Change and History* (New York: 1969), pp. 223-239, 258-267.

30A third is "a generalized universalistic legal system."

31"Evolutionary Universals," p. 349.

32See "Evolutionary Universals," p. 350. In regard to relatively advanced societies, Parsons appears not surprisingly, to drop the alternative ultimate possibilities of "elimination" or "niche" existence, although "regression"—to an unspecified degree—may occur.

33*Ibid.,* p. 353. For Parsons' notion, of "pluralization," see his essay,

"Some Comments on the Sociology of Karl Marx," in *Sociological Theory and Modern Society* (New York: 1967). It may also be noted how, in discussing the development of advanced societies, Parsons again comes close to Kerr in the importance that he attaches to technological and economic exigencies in determining institutional forms—despite the view he has expressed that the broad patterns of social evolution are governed at the highest level by cultural rather than material factors. See *Societies*, pp. 112-114. The explanation would appear to be that Parsons regards the setting of a paramount value on economic productivity as virtually a constant within the "modernizing" process. See, for instance, his essay, "Polarization of the World and International Order," in the collection cited above.

[34]"Evolutionary Universals," pp. 355-356, emphasis in original.

[35]*Ibid.*, p. 356.

[36]Cf. also "Polarization of the World and International Order," p. 486 esp.

[37]For example, true to his *Marxisant* method, Kerr stresses in this respect the role of the new *class* of "non-revolutionary intellectuals"—especially, the scientists, technologists and managers. In contradiction with the official ideology that calls for great centralization of political power, the latter groups increasingly demand a share in decision-making, and the development of the "forces of production" increasingly puts *de facto* power into their hands. For Parsons, on the other hand, the major potential for change is to be found in the functional imperative, within a large-scale and complex society, for the political leadership to entrust the increasingly educated *mass* with some share in political responsibility—this being a condition of both the efficiency and legitimacy of the political system.

[38]For example: Walter W. Rostow claims that Communism is merely "a disease of the transition" (to industrialism) and cannot survive the age of "high mass consumption," *The Stages of Economic Growth*, pp. 162-164. Gabriel Almond takes the "Anglo-American" political system as a paradigm of political modernity, and uses "modern Western" and "Western democratic" as virtually synonymous descriptions of political institutions: "Introduction," *in* Gabriel A. Almond and James S. Coleman, *The Politics of the Developing Areas* (Princeton: 1960). Daniel Lerner defines political modernization as "the transition to a participant society" whose "crowning achievement is constitutional democracy": *The Passing of Traditional Society; Modernizing the Middle East* (New York: 1958), see esp. pp. 51-60, 67-71. An MIT study group openly describes political tendencies that are not Western-oriented as "distortions" or "diversions" in modernization: "The Transitional Pro-

cess," *in* Roy C. Macridis *and* Bernard E. Brown, eds., *Comparative politics: Notes and Readings* (Homewood: 1964), pp. 618-641. And finally, and most frankly of all, S. M. Lipset admits as the "basic premise" of his political sociology that democracy (on the American pattern) "is not only or even primarily a means through which different groups can obtain their ends and seek the good society; it is the good society itself in operation": *Political Man* (New York: 1959), p. 403.

[39]*Industrialism and Industrial Man,* p. 283.

[40]*Ibid.*

[41]For a forceful critique of the functions of American liberal sociology in relation to American policy-making in which the propensity in question is amply documented, see Noam Chomsky, *American Power and the New Mandarins* (New York: Random House, 1969).

[42]Recent liberal versions of democratic political theory appear designed to give direct normative support to such a state of affairs.

[43]See, for example, *The Poverty of Historicism,* chap. III. Popper here calls explicitly for a "technological" approach to sociology and social reform, and urges the practice of "piecemeal social engineering."

[44]*Ibid.,* pp. 76-83, 107-119 esp. One may note also Popper's formal refutation of the possibility of historical prediction presented in *The Logic of Scientific Discovery* (New York: Basic Books, 1959). Popper's general conceptions of the nature of science and of the scientific method have not, of course, gone unchallenged. But they have not, so far as I am aware, been questioned by exponents of the new historicism (or by others) in such a way as to make the enterprise more secure.

[45]Elaborating on Durkheim's proposition that "the stages that humanity successively traverses do not engender one another," Nisbet (*op. cit.*) puts the point as follows: "It is not impossible to find conditions and also causes of change. What is impossible is to fix causality into the linear succession of events and changes with which the historian or social scientist deals" (p. 292).

[46]Cf. the cogent arguments in J. D. Y. Peel, "Spencer and the Neo-Evolutionists," *Sociology,* III (1969): 173-191; also the classic attack on Spencer from the historian's point of view, F. W. Maitland, "The Body Politic," in *Collected Papers,* H. A. L. Fisher, ed. (Cambridge: 1911). As Nisbet observes (*op. cit.*): "The question that has haunted the theory of development from its beginnings in the Western tradition is in fact that of how the external historical record can be made congruent with what purports to be a natural science of society or with those processes that are seen as 'natural' to a social system". (p. 233).

[47]See his essay "Futurology," *loc. cit.*

[48]See B. de Jouvenel, ed., *Futuribles: Studies in Conjecture* (Geneva: 1963), vol. I, pp. IX-XI. All these points, and others relevant to the

philosophy of "*futuribles*," are developed at length in Jouvenel's seminal book, *L'art de la conjecture, op. cit.*

[49]See Kahn *and* Wiener, *The Year 2000, op. cit.* pp. XXVI-XXVIII; also Daniel Bell's contributions to the issue of *Daedalus,* "Toward the Year 2000: Work in Progress," XCVI (1967), n⁰ 3.

[50]See, for example, the content of the actual conjectures that are presented in such recent works (cited above) as Kahn *and* Wiener, *The Year 2000*; Young, *Forecasting and the Social Sciences;* and Jungk *and* Galtung, eds., *Mankind 2000.* The *Futuribles* series must be exempted from this comment.

[51]*The Art of Conjecture,* p. 105. Jouvenel gives as a paradigmatic case of a process of inflation. As regards technological change, cf. the remarks of Bell on serendipity and synergism in "Toward the Year 2000," *loc. cit.*

[52]As, e.g., through "Delphi" techniques. Note, however, that such techniques assume considerable future stability in the general environment through which the process under consideration will run.

[53]Perhaps the most notable example of the one-sidedness in question is provided by the papers prepared for the "Next Thirty Years Committee" of the British Social Science Research Council, as represented in Young, *op. cit.* This volume suggests that the Committee virtually equated future studies with the forecasting of processes—on the basis chiefly of trend analyses—to the exclusion of any possible designs for the future which might be realized through large-scale intervention in processes.

[54]*The Art of Conjecture,* p. 103.

[55]See D. Bell, Notes on the Post-Industrial Society, *The Public Interest* (1967), n⁰ 6, pp. 24-35; n⁰ 7, pp. 102-118; see also D. Bell, Knowledge and Technology, *in* Eleanor Sheldon *and* W. E. Moore, eds., *Indicators of Social Change: concepts and measurements* (New York, Russell Sage Foundation, 1969); Kahn *and* Wiener, *The Year 2000, op. cit.* pp. 6-13, 39-65.

[56]Kahn *and* Wiener, *ibid.,* pp. 26-34.

[57]See in particular the work of E. J. Mishan. In his book, *The Costs of Economic Growth* (New York: Praeger, 1967), p. 39, Mishan launches a powerful attack on what he calls "the no choice myth" in regard to economic policy and on "the technocratic view of things, that envisages the country as some sort of vast powerhouse with every grown man and woman a potential unit of input to be harnessed to a generating system from which flows this vital stuff called industrial output." Cf. also the most recent thinking of J. K. Galbraith as found in the interview reported in *The Observer,* 22, November 1970.

[58]The only value change that is at all extensively considered within

the context of advanced industrialism is the possible decline of the middle-class work- and achievement-oriented ethic—because economically redundant—in favor of greater emphasis on leisure, private enjoyment, etc. But significantly, cf. point (ii) below, the likelihood of such a shift is discussed in conjunction with that of increasing alienation as a potentially serious social problem. See Kahn *and* Wiener, *The Year 2000, op. cit.* pp. 198-202.

[59]Andrew Shonfield, *in* "Thinking about the Future," *Encounter* XXXII (1969), 15-26, has characterized the whole Kahn-Wiener approach as a "highly simplified piece of economic determinism—in a familiar Marxist tradition." In consequence it entirely neglects, *inter alia,* the possibility that changes in values might stem from political developments and imperatives, as well as from the economic order.

[60]Whereas, as, e.g., Peter Berger *and* Thomas Luckmann have cogently argued, in *The Social Construction of Reality* (New York: Doubleday 1967), p. 82: "Logic" does not in fact "reside in . . . institutions and their external functionalities" but only in the meaningful character of human action.

[61]Cf. Bell, "Toward the Year 2000," p. 644; Kahn *and* Wiener, "*The Year 2000,*" pp. 158, 217-220.

[62]Otis Dudley Duncan, "Social Forecasting: the State of the art," *Public Interest* (1969), no. 17, p. 88-118.

[63]See, for instance, F. E. Emery, "Concepts, Methods and Anticipations," *in* Young, *op. cit.*

[64]It is thus on the basis of such a conception of politics that Bell can argue "the post-industrial society will involve *more* politics than ever before," while claiming at the same time that it will "require more societal guidance, more expertise" and, presumably, that ideology will remain at an end. See "Knowledge and Technology," *loc. cit.,* p. 238. The foregoing remarks draw heavily on a paper, as yet unpublished, by my colleague, Dr. James B. Rule, "The Problem with Social Problems."

[65]Cf., for example, Bell, "Knowledge. . . ," *loc. cit.* p. 158; Kahn *and* Wiener, *op. cit.* pp. 21-26.

[66]"Knowledge and Technology," p. 160.

[67]*The Year 2000,* pp. 15-19, 199-202.

[68]*The Art of Conjecture,* p. IX.

[69]See, e.g., Jungk *and* Galtung, *op. cit.,* Postscript. In the American case, Bell, Kahn, and others prominent in the field have recently been under strong attack as exemplifying "counter-revolutionary subordination" and as failing in their responsibility as intellectuals on account of their commitment to the *status quo.* See, especially, Chomsky, *American Power and the New Mandarins, op. cit.*

[70]Jouvenel refers in this connection to "secondary" and "tertiary" forecasting. He notes, however, that by the stage that tertiary forecasts are being attempted—i.e., ones entailing guesses about the effects on trends, etc; of unique moves by probably only a small number of actors—historical predictions are being approximated. Thus: "Any confusion between "tertiary" forecasting and other types must be carefully avoided," *The Art of Conjecture,* p. 55. Given this view, it might have suited Jouvenel's purpose better to have distinguished more sharply between forecasting and conjecturing, and to have treated "tertiary forecasting" as a form of the latter activity.

[71]And, as such, they would of course be conditional, if only because of their historic specificity; and, in the same way as "possibilities," subject to continuous revision.

[72]Deductions from theories may be taken into consideration, but the final forecast—about what will happen in the real world—cannot itself be so deduced unless, of course, some "theory of history" is postulated.

[73]A line of argument somewhat similar to the foregoing has, interestingly enough, been developed by a disciple of Popper, I. C. Jarvie. See "Utopian Thinking and the Architect," *in* Stanford Anderson, ed., *Planning for Diversity and Choice* (Cambridge, Mass.: 1968).

[74]In making much the same point, Jarvie refers, in an American context, to the case of urban development and renewal "Utopian Thinking. . . ," *loc. cit.* pp. 17-18). In the British case, one might think of attempts at reducing economic inequality or class differentials in educational opportunity.